Light, Bright and Damn Near White

Black Leaders Created by the One-Drop Rule

Michelle Gordon Jackson

JACKSONSCRIBE PUBLISHING COMPANY
ATLANTA, GEORGIA

Light, Bright and Damn Near White
© 2013 Michelle Gordon Jackson. All rights reserved.

Published in the United States by JacksonScribe Publishing Company.
www.onedropleaders.com

Printed in the United States of America

ISBN: 978-0-9853512-0-5 (paperback)
Library of Congress Control Number: 2013904262

Book interior by Robin Krauss, www.bookformatters.com
Cover design by Michelle Gordon Jackson

Publisher's Cataloging-In-Publication Data
(Prepared by The Donohue Group, Inc.)

Jackson, Michelle Gordon, 1967-
    Light, bright and damn near white : black leaders created by the one-drop rule / Michelle Gordon Jackson.

    pages : illustrations ;   cm

    Includes bibliographical references and index.
    ISBN: 978-0-9853512-0-5 (paperback)

    1. African Americans--Biography. 2. Racially mixed people--United
States--Biography. 3. African American civil rights workers--Biography.
4. African American leadership--History. 5. Racially mixed people--Race
identity--United States. 6. African Americans--Race identity. 7.
Biography. I. Title.

E185.96 .J33 2014
920/.009296073 B   2013904262

*In loving memory of my father, Dr. Gary Michael Gordon,
a graduate of Morehouse College and a member of
Alpha Phi Alpha Fraternity, Inc. He was the first Black American
to graduate from Emory University School of Dentistry.*

TABLE OF CONTENTS

Adam Clayton Powell IV

FOREWORD

Adam Clayton Powell IV

When I was a student at Howard University—a historically black college—we would sit around campus and look at some of the "white" students with some surprise (as I'm sure some looked at me, thinking I was white). As it turned out, those "white" students we were looking at were actually black. Many of them had brown-skinned siblings from the same mother and father. Any African-American will tell you this is not unusual especially when one parent is white.

The "one-drop rule" appears to be unique to this country. It doesn't matter how white, blond, blue-eyed a person may be, if they have any African ancestry, they are considered black. Since the United States has had one of the worst histories of racism in the world, one can only assume that whites used the one-drop rule to discriminate against people of African ancestry. In the early part of the 20th century, several states—mostly in the South—adopted a one-drop statute, although the one-drop rule has been enforced without legislation since slavery.

Now, it appears that no African-American is 100% black. Just look at most of our brothers and sisters from Africa and then look back at us in this country, and you can clearly see the differences. Just like there are few whites in this country who are 100% white as compared to some whites in other parts of the world.

Today, there are some whites who would like to re-define what it means to be black. Some want to call President Barack Obama bi-racial instead of black and other very light-skinned blacks as whites instead. They want to tell Halle Berry that her daughter is white! In other words, after using it against us for centuries, some whites now want to eliminate the one-drop rule. But for most African-Americans, the one-drop rule is a source of pride! Most people with any trace of African ancestry in their roots are proud to be black no matter how "white" they may look. And besides, imagine how awkward it would be to hear someone say they're white, but they have a black father. That just wouldn't make sense given the history and the culture in this country.

Again, we in the black community are proud of the one-drop rule! Even though a person may have 7/8ths (or 87.5%) of their blood come from whites, he or she is still prouder of that 1/8th (or 12.5%) and will identify as African-American. That's an amazing testament to the rich culture of African-Americans and to the strong bonds of our heritage. Being black is not about the color of your skin . . . it's about the color of your soul.

Emancipated Slaves, 1863. (Source: Courtesy of the Charles L. Blockson Afro-American Collection, Temple University Libraries.)

INTRODUCTION

"The One-Drop Rule and Its Strict Enforcement"

The One-Drop Rule was a determinant racial marker exclusive to the United States by which racial identity was defined, and a person was considered "black" if he or she had any African ancestry.[1] No other country in the world has historically defined race in the same manner. This unique rule has been embraced by black and white Americans alike, both socially and legally.[2] It began in the North and was enforced throughout the South during slavery.

The rule completely supplanted the notion that physical appearance alone determines race. And so, even a trace of "invisible blackness," a drop of African blood, assigned a person to the Negro race. Prior to any state legislation on the matter, this principle was understood and widely embraced. According to Floyd James Davis, author of *Who Is Black?: One Nation's Definition*, "One need not look black in order to be black, following the one-drop rule." Davis says:

> Because blacks are defined according to the one-drop rule, they are a socially constructed category in which there is wide variation in racial traits and therefore not a race group in the scientific sense. However, because that category has a definite status position in society, it has become a self-conscious social group with an ethnic identity . . . It *[The One-Drop Rule]* is embedded in the social structures and cultures of both the Black and the White communities in the United States and strongly resistant to change.[3]

The foundation for the One-Drop Rule, also known as "hypodescent," was laid around 1662, when the state of Virginia, in order to address the designation of mixed-race persons, decided to adopt into law the rule of *partus sequitur ventrem*, which held that the status of any child followed that of his or her mother.[4] The edict read as follows: "Whereas some doubts have arisen whether children got by any Englishman upon a Negro woman should be slave or free, be it therefore enacted and declared by the present grand assembly, that all children born in this country shall be held bond or free only according to the condition of the mother."[5] Universally accepted throughout the southern United States, the partus law sealed the fate of every child whose mother was a slave.

The economic soundness of the One-Drop Rule during the antebellum years is obvious, in that it insured more slave hands to toil the southern plantations. Children produced by unions between slave owners and their female slaves carried the subordinate lot of bondage. In *Red, White and Black: The Peoples of Early America*, Dr. Gary B. Nash describes the politics behind the rule, saying:

> Though skin color came to assume importance through generations of association with slavery, white colonists developed few qualms about intimate contact with black women. But raising the social status of those who labored at the bottom of society and who were defined as abysmally inferior was a matter of serious concern. It was resolved by insuring that the mulatto would not occupy a position midway between white and black. Any black blood classified a person as black . . . By prohibiting racial intermarriage, winking at interracial sex, and defining all mixed offspring as black, white society found the ideal answer to its labor needs.[6]

By the 18th and 19th centuries, miscegenation or race-mixing had become so prevalent that American plantations had on them what some began to term as "white slaves." And yet, there was still no wavering in the application of the One-Drop Rule. European dignitaries, who visited the United States, documented several accounts of this phenomenon. These reports indicate their perplexity regarding this nation's strict enforcement of the rule, as well as the apparent irony it created. Captain John Ferdinand Dalziel Smyth, an

Isaac & Rosa, Slave Children from New Orleans.
PHOTOGRAPHED BY KIMBALL, 477 BROADWAY, N. Y.
Ent'd accord'g to act of Congress in the year 1863, by GEO. H. HANKS, in the Clerk's Office of the U.S for the So. Dist. of N.Y.

Emancipated slave children: Isaac White and Rosina "Rosa" Downs of New Orleans, Louisiana. Slaves found on most plantations ranged in appearance due to miscegenation or "race-mixing." The one-drop rule was strictly enforced regardless of appearance. (*Source: Library of Congress*)

Englishman with the Queen's Rangers toured the American South in the 1770s. He recorded in his 1784 memoir that there were "female slaves who are now become white by their mixture."[7] In 1788, French revolutionary leader Jacques Pierre Brissot reported seeing "a white boy in a Philadelphia school for Negro children."[8] Captain Frederick Marryat, a British naval officer and novelist, traveled throughout the South in 1837. While in Louisville, Kentucky, Marryat says, "I saw a girl, about twelve years old, carrying a child; and, aware that in a slave state the circumstance of white people hiring themselves out to service is almost unknown, I inquired of her if she were a slave. To my astonishment, she replied in the affirmative. She was as fair as snow, and it was impossible to detect any admixture of blood from her appearance."[9]

Fredrika Bremer, a Swedish novelist and feminist activist, visited the United States in 1849. She subsequently wrote about a number of slave children she had witnessed while at a slave auction in Augusta, Georgia. Bremer says, "One young girl of twelve was so white, that I should have supposed her to belong to the white race; her features, too, were also those of the whites. The slave-keeper told us that the day before, another girl, still fairer and handsomer, had been sold for fifteen hundred dollars."[10] Bremer also observed "a pretty little white boy of about seven years of age sitting among some tall Negro girls. The child had light hair, the most lovely light brown eyes, and cheeks as red as roses; he was, nevertheless, the child of a slave mother, and was to be sold as a slave."[11]

Even American northerners, so far removed from the antebellum South, were similarly baffled. Dr. Jesse Torrey wrote in his 1817 book, that while visiting a public house in Fredericktown, Maryland, he observed "a decently dressed white man" in the company of "one who was totally black." He was told by the landlord that both men were Negro slaves. To which he responded, "How can that be possible?" The landlord informed him that the fairer slave was "a descendant, by female ancestry, of an African slave."[12] Other accounts include Reverend John H. Aughey who told of preaching to southern slaves, some of whom had "red hair and blue eyes, a third of whom were just as white" as himself. Dr. Alexander Milton Ross attended a slave auction in New Orleans where, he states, many of the slaves were "much whiter than the white people who were there to buy them."

As historian J.C. Furnas points out, these "near-white" slaves were

Slave children (l-r): Rebecca Huger, Charles "Charley" Taylor, and Rosina "Rosa" Downs. Rebecca Huger, age eleven, was a slave in her own father's house and the special attendant to a white girl a little older than herself. Charley was the son of a mulatto slave and her slave master, Alexander Wethers of Lewis County, Virginia. The boy was taken from his mother at the age of eight and given to a slave trader named Harrison, who then sold him to Mr. Thornhill of New Orleans, Louisiana. Charley's sister was sold to a plantation owner in Texas, and his brother was allowed to stay in Virginia. Rosa was one of five children born to a light-skinned slave. Rosa's sister was fair, and her three brothers were dark-skinned. *(Source: Library of Congress)*

WHITE AND BLACK SLAVES
FROM NEW ORLEANS.
PHOTOGRAPHED BY KIMBALL, 477 BROADWAY, N. Y.
Entered according to act of Congress, in the year 1863, by P.
Bacon, in the Clerk's Office of the United States, for the
Southern District of New York.

Slave children Isaac White and Augusta Broujey stand with Mary Johnson.
(Source: Library of Congress)

often auctioned off at a higher price because of their use as sexual objects.[13] The mulatto slave woman approximated the white ideal of feminine beauty, and yet she was property and had no rights. And though female slaves, regardless of color, were raped, Furnas says, "the mulatto afforded the slave owner the opportunity to rape, with impunity, a woman who was physically white (or near-white), but legally black."[14] Hence, slave children continued to be born whiter and whiter. Reverend Francis Hawley of Connecticut said in 1839, "It is so common for the female slaves to have white children, that little or nothing is ever said about it."[15]

Lighter-skinned blacks were generally house slaves. They were sometimes afforded educations, trades, and other considerations not available to field slaves. Nevertheless, they were still slaves. One former slave who escaped to Canada, Lewis Garrard Clarke, believed that house slaves were worse off in some respects than field slaves. He says in his 1845 narrative, "We were constantly exposed to the whims and passions of every member of the family; from the least to the greatest, their anger was wreaked upon us. Nor was our life an easy one, in the hours of our toil or in the amount of labor performed."[16] Despite some privileges, mulattoes also had to contend with the fact that they were constant reminders of rape and concubinage, which took place throughout the slave institution. This often exposed them to additional punishment at the hands of their mistresses. Mary Boykin Chesnut, the aristocratic wife of South Carolina Senator James Chesnut, wrote in her diary in March of 1861:

> Like the patriarchs of old, our men live all in one house with their wives and their concubines, and the mulattoes one sees in every family exactly resemble the white children— and every lady tells you who is the father of all the mulatto children in everybody's household, but those in her own she seems to think drop from the clouds, or pretends so to think.[17]

As slavery continued, slaves increasingly escaped North via the Underground Railroad, a system run by abolitionists to get runaways to free land. It is estimated that by 1850, over 100,000 slaves had escaped using the Underground Railroad.[18] Walter Hawkins, a former slave who

ROSA.   REBECCA.   AUGUSTA.
EMANCIPATED SLAVE CHILDREN,
From our schoo's in NEW ORLEANS.

Entered according to act of Congress, in the year 1863,
by S. TACKABERRY, in the Clerk's Office of the U.S
for the So District of N. Y.

Phot. by WHITNEY & PARADISE. 585 Broadway, N. Y.

These newly freed children attended the same Negro school in New Orleans, Louisiana. (*Source: Library of Congress*) fled to Canada, wrote in his book, *From Slavery to Bishopric* that slaves talked constantly amongst themselves about escaping. Hawkins says:

> There arose in some an irrepressible desire for freedom which no danger or power could restrain, no hardship deterred, and no bloodhound could alarm. This desire haunted them night and day; they talked about it to each other in confidence; they knew that the system which bound them was as unjust as it was cruel, and that they ought to strive, as a duty to themselves and their children, to escape from it.[19]

The following 19th century advertisements for the capture of runaway slaves affirms the prevalence of white-looking Negroes as far back as slavery. It also speaks to the strict enforcement of the One-Drop Rule. These ads appeared in newspapers across the United States.

> "$100 reward will be given for my man, Edmund Kenny. *He has straight hair, and a complexion so white that it is believed a stranger would suppose there was no African blood in him* . . . was apprehended but escaped under pretense of being a white man."
>
> — Anderson Bowles
> *Dentonville P.O.*, Jan. 6, 1837

> "Ranaway from me, *a Negro woman*, named Fanny. *She is as white as most white women; with straight light hair, and blue eyes, and can pass herself for a white woman.* She is very intelligent; can read and write, and so forge passes for herself. She is very pious, prays a great deal, and was, as supposed, contented and happy. I will give $500 for her delivery to me."
>
> — John Balch
> *Alabama Beacon*, Tuscaloosa, Alabama, June 14, 1845

> "Ranaway from the subscriber, *a very bright boy*, twenty-two

years old, named Wash. He might *pass himself for a white man, as he is very bright, has sandy hair, blue eyes,* and a fine set of teeth."

— George O. Ragland,
The Chattanooga Gazette, Tenn. Oct. 5, 1852

"$10 reward for the apprehension of William Dubberly, a slave belonging to the estate of Sacker Dubberly, deceased. He is about nineteen years old, *quite white, and would not be readily taken for a slave.*"

— John J. Lane
The Newbern Spectator, N.C., March 13, 1837

"Ranaway, *a bright woman*, named Julia, about twenty-five years old. *She is white and very likely may attempt to pass for white . . .* $200 reward, if caught in any Free State and put into any good jail in Kentucky or Tennessee."

— A.W. Johnson
The Republican Banner and *The Nashville Whig*
Tenn., July 14, 1840

"$25 REWARD. Ranaway from the chain-gang in New Orleans, *a Negro boy*, named Stephen; *a very light mulatto, with blue eyes, and brownish hair*; very strongly built and muscular. He is a habitual runaway, and was shot in the ankle, while endeavoring to escape from a Baton Rouge jail."

— A. L. Bingaman, New Orleans

"Ranaway, *a white Negro man*, about thirty-five years old; *has blue eyes, very fair skin, and a yellow woolly head.*"

— Subscriber unknown
From the *New Orleans Picayune*, Sept. 2, 1846

"Detained in jail, Maria; *pretending herself free*; round face, *clear* ger would suppose there was NO African blood in him. He is so very artful, that in his language it is likely he will deceive those who might suspect him. He was with my boy Dick a short time since in Norfolk, and offered him for sale, and was apprehended, but escaped under the PRETENCE of being a WHITE MAN.

ANDERSON BOWLES,

Jan. 6, 1837.   Dentonville P. O.

$100 REWARD.

RANAWAY from James Hughart, Paris, Ky., the Mulatto Boy NORBON, aged about 15 years; a *very bright* mulatto, and would be taken for a WHITE BOY if not *closely* examined; his hair is black and STRAIGHT. Aug. 4, 1836.

ABSCONDED from the subscriber, HER negro man JOHN. He has a VERY LIGHT complexion, *prominent nose*, &c.

Charleston Mercury, 1837.   W. J. SANGLOIS.

$100 REWARD.

RANAWAY from the Subscriber, living in Sumter Co. Ala., a *bright mulatto* man slave named SAM, calls himself SAM PETTIGREW* ... LIGHT SANDY HAIR and *blue eyes*, RUDDY complexion, very stout built, and will weigh about 180 pounds; he is so WHITE as *very easily* to pass for a free white man.... He carries a small memorandum book in his pocket, and will pass *very easily* for a *white man* unless *closely* examined—is a first-rate blacksmith and barber.   EDWIN PECK.

Mobile, April 22, 1837.

V. The fifth point to be proved is that FREE men are often sold into slavery to *pay the expense* of THEIR OWN UNJUST IMPRISONMENT.

SHERIFF'S SALE.

COMMITTED to the Jail of Warren County, by WM. EVERETT, one of the JUSTICES of said county, a Negro MAN who calls himself JOHN J. ROBINSON; says that he is FREE. The OWNER of the said BOY is requested to come forward, prove PROPERTY, pay charges and take him away, or he will be dealt with as the law directs.   WM. EVERETT, Jailer.

And how does the law direct? Read the following:

NOTICE is hereby given, that the above described BOY, who calls himself John J. Robinson, having been confined in the Jail of Warren county as a Runaway for SIX MONTHS—and having been *regularly advertised* during this period,—I shall proceed to SELL said Negro boy at public auction, to the highest bidder for cash, at the door of the Court-house in Vicksburg, on Monday, 1st day of August, 1836, between the hours of 11 o'clock A. M. and 4 o'clock P. M. of said day, in pursuance of the *STATUTE* in such cases made and provided.   E. W. MORRIS, Sheriff.

Vicksburg, July 2, 1836.

* So we might, perhaps, see, "ARCHY, calls himself ARCHY MOORE," advertised by Col. Carter.

white complexion."

— P. Bayhi, Captain of the Watch
From the *New Orleans Bee*, July 4, 1837

"Ranaway, *a light mulatto woman; has long, black, straight hair,* and usually keeps it in good order. She generally dresses neatly, is very intelligent, converses well, and can read print."

— U. McAllister, From the *Southern Standard*
Mississippi, Oct. 16, 1852

"Ranaway, *a bright mulatto man* named Alfred; about eighteen years old; *has blue eyes, light flaxen hair, and skin disposed to freckle.* He will *try to pass as free born."*

— S. G. Stewart, Green County, Alabama [20]

Abolitionists were keen to capitalize on the phenomenon created by the One-Drop Rule and began circulating photographs of white-looking slave children throughout the North. The intent was to build northern sentiment and urge for the immediate eradication of slavery. These anti-slavery crusaders believed that if white northerners could "see the faces of their own children" in the faces of children in bondage, it would incite them to immediate action.[21]

On January 30, 1864, *Harper's Weekly* printed an engraving of a photograph, entitled "Emancipated Slaves, White and Colored," depicting three adults and five children who had been set free by Major General Nathaniel P. Banks and brought North from Louisiana by Colonel George H. Hanks. The group made a series of public appearances as part of a campaign to raise funds for public schools for freed slaves. Kathleen Collins in "Portraits of Slave Children," says the hope was that "these enigmatic portraits of Caucasian-featured children" would galvanize "Northern benefactors to contribute to the future of a race to which these children found themselves arbitrarily confined."[22]

Prior to the war, Abraham Lincoln gave his famous "House Divided" speech in which he stated, "I believe this government cannot endure, permanently half *slave* and half *free* . . . it will become all one thing, or all the other."[23] Historians have cited various reasons as to why the war began, including economic reasons due to the invention of the cotton gin, strife between slave versus free states, and the fight between federal versus state rights. But Lawrence R. Tenzer, author of *The Forgotten Cause of the Civil War: A New Look at the Slavery Issue*, proposes that one of the fundamental causes of the American Civil War had to do with these mulatto slaves that fit into the "one-drop rule" construct. Runaways, like those referenced in the newspaper ads, became an increasing threat to the free white population in the North. Tenzer relays that because of the Fugitive Slave Act of 1850, runaways could be recaptured and sent back into slavery. He says that the chance that some northern whites could be mistaken for these runaways and forced into slavery gradually led to a "psychological undercurrent of an ongoing threat." The potential of being claimed as one of these "white-looking" runaways was on the minds of many white northerners. This contributed to the increased urgency on the part of those in the North to end slavery in the South.[24]

At the conclusion of the American Civil War and the freeing of all slaves, U.S. Census records indicated a substantial number of mulattoes. Reports regarding the appearance of newly freed slaves confirmed this country's long history of miscegenation. Vincent Coyler, superintendent of the Union Army in New Bern, North Carolina said after the battle:

> The light color of many of the refugees is a marked peculiarity of the colored people of Newbern. I have had men and women apply for work who were so white that I could not believe they had a particle of Negro blood in their veins.[25]

Census taken in 1850 (prior to the war), showed that mulattoes represented about 11.2 percent of the free black population. By 1910, that number had increased to 20.9 percent. Both records were based on visible white ancestry, so it was more than likely an undercount.[26] In 1918, the U.S. Census Bureau estimated that at least three-fourths of all Negroes in the United States were racially mixed, and it predicted that "pure blacks" would soon disappear altogether. After the 1920 census, no further attempt was made to count the number of visible mulattoes; not solely because there were so many

LEARNING IS WEALTH.

WILSON, CHARLEY, REBECCA & ROSA.

Slaves from New Orleans

The children are being taught by Wilson Chinn, a branded slave.
(Source: Library of Congress)

of them, but also because so many persons with known African ancestry "appeared white."

The One-Drop Rule in U.S. Legislation

In the history of the United States, there have been nearly 300 appealed cases that determined Americans' racial identity.[27] These cases began early in the 1800s. In 1831, Polly Gray, a white-looking, free mulatto woman from Hamilton County, Ohio was tried for robbery and convicted by an Ohio court based on the testimony of a black witness for the prosecution. Despite Gray's acknowledgement that she had some African ancestry, Gray appealed the conviction to the Supreme Court of Ohio, on the grounds that she was white. Ohio statutes forbade blacks from testifying against whites. Further, Ohio law, at that time, ascribed to the "law of physical appearance" in determining the race of the person. This case readdressed the issue and the Ohio Supreme Court remained firm that physical appearance was the only measure. The judge decided that the difficulty was in where to draw the line, stating that, "We believe a man, of a race nearer white than a mulatto . . . should partake in the privileges of whites. We are of the opinion that a party of such a blood is entitled to the privileges of whites, partly because we are unwilling to extend the disabilities of the statute further than its letter requires, and partly from the difficulty of defining and ascertaining the degree of duskiness which renders a person liable to such disabilities."[28] Nevertheless, the court decided that Ms. Gray "appeared, upon inspection . . . to be a shade of color between the mulatto and white." She was, therefore, found to be, not quite white enough to claim immunity under the statute.[29] *Gray v. Ohio* was an important historical turning-point in the establishment of the One-Drop Rule. It was the last appeals case in the free states in which neither party argued that a drop of African blood rendered a person "black." Henceforth, some form of the One-Drop Rule was applied or cited in cases regarding the color line which sprung up throughout the U.S. Less than a century later, the rule would negate physical appearance, blood fractions, and associations, and stand primarily as this nation's criteria for race designation.

The first time in U.S. history that a lawyer seriously argued the One

-Drop Rule in court, was in May of 1834 in Ohio. The case was *Williams v. School District*. It involved an Ohio couple, who had tried to register their five European-looking children in a racially segregated District 6 public school. Both parents looked white, but the father admitted to having some Negro ancestry, and so the children were denied admission. The couple sued the school board.[30] For the rule to have been argued in court, it had to have been relatively accepted by the general population. We find that it was sometime around the early 1830s, that the One-Drop Rule arose as a staple in United States culture.[31] American literature, including novels, plays, and short stories, as well as the personal journals and diaries of noted Americans began to emerge with themes pertaining to the One-Drop Rule, miscegenation, and crossing the colorline ("passing"). U.S. courts soon began justifying the use of the rule through "judicial notice." Congressmen even argued the theory on the floor of the House. Speaking before the House of Representatives in 1860, Congressman Harrison G.O. Blake of Ohio said:

> You hold a man in slavery, who is born of a slave mother, without reference to the amount of negro blood in his veins . . . A man having so light an admixture of negro blood that you can discover no difference between him and the pure Caucasian – yet such men are held in slavery.[32]

It was in 1880, that an appellate court upheld the rule during a criminal prosecution case in Texas, regarding the marriage of a white woman and a black man. In 1894, an appellate court in Massachusetts indisputably upheld the rule in the case of *Van Houten v. Morse*.[33] The case involved a breach of promise suit. Anna D. Van Houten sued Asa P. Morse after he breached his promise to marry her. Morse's defense was on the basis of the fraudulent concealment of Van Houten's racial lineage. The court's judgment read in part: "In an action for breach of a promise of marriage, there was evidence tending to show that the plaintiff had negro blood in her veins; and that, in making statements to the defendant regarding her parentage, she suppressed that fact. The plaintiff was allowed to introduce in evidence photographs of her parents and sister, and of the latter's children, which she testified were correct likenesses, and had been shown by her to the defendant. *Held*, that no error appeared." Also established at the trial, was the fact that Van Houten's father was a colored barber in Charleston, South Carolina, and her mother was at least one-eighth black. The court, however, found that Van Houten had no obligation to disclose "all of the previous circumstances of her life," but was only required to answer any inquires by her fiancé truthfully. Judgment was, therefore, ruled in favor of Van Houten, and she was rewarded forty-thousand dollars.[34]

The One-Drop Rule had long been accepted and enforced as legal precedent in state appellate courts by the time it was enacted into state law in the United States. In 1910, Tennessee became the first state to legislate the One-Drop Rule as statutory law.[35] The same year, Louisiana adopted the statute, followed by Texas and Arkansas in 1911, Mississippi in 1917, and North Carolina in 1923. In 1910, the state of Virginia, in order to insure racial purity, decided to apply the one-sixteenth rule to persons, believing that lesser amounts of African blood could not easily be detected upon sight. Virginia adopted the One-Drop Rule in 1924, with the passing of the Racial Integrity Act, which stated that "any Negro blood at all" made a person black. This Act also required that a racial description be recorded of each individual at birth, and that race be divided into two distinct categories: white and colored. Alabama and Georgia followed in 1927, and Oklahoma in 1931. Around this time, Florida, Indiana, Kentucky, Maryland, Missouri, Nebraska, North Dakota and Utah decided to retain their old blood fraction statutes *de juris*, but amended these fractions (1/16, 1/32) to be equivalent to the one-drop *de facto*.[36] Any challenges to the rule were met with swift reinforcement.

Miscegenation (Race-Mixing) in the U.S.

Despite the recent emergence of the multiracial movement in America and the urging by some in the movement for there to be a separate category for racially mixed people on the census, miscegenation is nothing new. This nation's long history with miscegenation began with the Slave Trade. Some of the first female slaves to arrive in North America from the Ivory Coast were already pregnant with the children of their white captors. Race-mixing continued throughout the slave institution as a common practice.

F. James Davis says in *Who Is Black?*, "At the beginning of miscegenation between two populations presumed to be racially pure, quadroons appear in the second generation of continuing mixing with whites, and octoroons in the third." A quadroon is one-fourth black, and an octoroon is one-eight black. The understood designation of these persons as "Negroes," can be ascribed to the one-drop rule and its adherence, since generally octoroons appear white.[37] Expounding on the mechanics of genetics, Davis mentions that well-known leaders Booker T. Washington and Frederick Douglass were born to slave mothers and white fathers and, "To whatever extent their mothers were part white, these men were more than half white."[38]

Immediate post-slavery found that centuries of race-mixing had produced a large population of mulattoes who appeared white, and who passed whenever they wanted to. According to statistics, between 1880 and 1925, approximately 12,000 blacks "crossed the color-line" each year in hope of a better life.[39] Many blacks "lost" family members to this circumstance. "Passing" promised a better job and a means for upward mobility. Many blacks lived duel lives. Some worked up North as white for part of the year and lived down South as black the rest of the year. With the oppressive Jim Crow Laws (1876-1965), southern blacks were further alienated and denied equal opportunities for advancement. And so, the motivation to pass grew stronger.

Davis also points out that miscegenation takes place within the black race. The circumstance of "light marrying light" or unions between two light-skinned blacks can produce children who are fairer skinned or "more white in appearance," than the two parents, because of the recessive gene component. Hence, some of the "whitest-looking" blacks are not necessarily "immediately mixed" people (one black and one white parent), as is the case with actress Halle Berry or President Barack Obama, but people like NAACP leader Walter White, actress Fredi Washington, and singer Lena Horne, who were all born of two Negro parents, with an extensive history of admixture in their lineage.

Light, Bright and Damn Near White is an accepted term, used frequently within the cultural rhetoric of the black community to describe Negroes with obvious genetic admixture, or whose racial physiognomies do not conform to stereotypical conceptions of blackness.[40] The term is also used casually to describe "immediately mixed" or bi-racial persons regardless of

THESE CHILDREN

Were turned out of the St. Lawrence Hotel, Chestnut St., Philadelphia, on account of Color.

These children were not allowed to stay in a Philadelphia hotel because of their race. When the owner of the hotel found out that they had been slaves, he demanded they leave his hotel, stating that his establishment was for "whites-only." *(Source: Library of Congress)* their appearance, as well as blacks who have "white blood" in close genetic proximity.

Almost every black American has within their own family line, at least one or more family members who could have "passed for white" or did. This revelation is understandably intriguing to people of other races, who have no direct knowledge of this historical practice. People who belong to other races often assume that people who look white are white. And yet, most black Americans are quite aware that this is not always the case, because these *Light, Bright and Damn Near White* people are in our family-tree and can be seen in old family photos.

Historically, blacks who could have passed, but chose not to, often expressed pride in their ethnic heritage, as well as fears of being ostracized by their own community. Andra Gillespie, assistant professor of political science at Emory University, adds that, "Mixed-race individuals with black heritage may identify more closely with blacks because of a shared history and experience."[41] Writer James Baldwin relayed this in his observance of a 1956 incident, which occurred at the Conference of Negro-African Writers and Artists. The conference was held in Paris and involved John Davis, who was the head of the delegation of writers and artists from the United States. The French chairperson introduced Davis and then asked him why he considered himself a Negro, since he certainly did not look like one. Baldwin wrote, "He is a Negro, of course, from the remarkable legal point of view which obtains in the United States, but more importantly, as he tried to make clear to his interlocutor, he was a Negro by choice and by depth of involvement—by experience, in fact."

Strongly Resistant to Change

The One-Drop Rule still frames the manner in which most Americans perceive race, and it is "strongly resistant to change."[42] A study conducted by Harvard University psychologists in December of 2010 discovered that the one-drop rule persists. In an article documenting their research, the psychologists stated that their work "reflects the cultural entrenchment of America's traditional racial hierarchy." According to their findings, "The centuries-old 'one-drop rule' assigning minority status to mixed-race individuals appears to live on in our modern-day perception and categorization of people like Barack Obama, Tiger Woods, and Halle Berry."[43] The article also points out that, "The legal notion of hypodescent has been upheld as recently as 1985, when a Louisiana court ruled that a woman with a black great-great-great-grandmother could not identify herself as 'white' on her passport."[44]

Black Americans generally employ the one-drop rule as the principal measure in claiming who is "their own."[45] Actress Halle Berry cited the one-drop rule when inquiries were raised about her daughter's race. Berry's daughter is one-fourth black. The actress told *Ebony* magazine, "I feel like she's black. I'm black and I'm her mother and I believe in the one-drop theory."[46] But the best example of this country's continued allegiance to the rule, is in the election of President Barack Obama and the collective reference of him as "The first black President of the United States." He will go down in American history with this distinction, despite the fact that his mother was white.

Light, Bright and Damn Near White Leaders

America's One-Drop Rule incorporated beliefs once used to justify slavery and later used to buttress the castelike Jim Crow system of segregation.[47] Nevertheless, it was this "rule" as well as its strict enforcement which created a dynamic leadership pool of educated *Light, Bright and Damn Near White* revolutionaries. Harvard College Professor Jennifer L. Hochschild states:

> Of the twenty-two Blacks in Congress during and after Reconstruction, all but three were of mixed race. About half had 'marked Caucasian features'– light complexions and straight hair.[48]

Immediate post-slavery or Reconstruction proclaimed a time when the Negro voice could be heard loudly and all the immeasurable suffering, degradation, and dehumanization of slavery could be transformed into Negro empowerment. It was a time to reconcile some of the damage done by bondage and an opportunity to reclaim what had been stripped away centuries prior by the slave trade. Many of the men and women who rose up and took a stand on behalf of the entire Negro race were *Light, Bright and Damn Near White*. American historian Eugene Genovese explains that, "Throughout the history of the slave regime there were planters who openly or surreptitiously accepted responsibility for the paternity of mulattoes, educated them, freed them and when manumission became difficult, made special provisions for their care."[49] Therefore, "the leadership that emerged after the war," said Genovese, "had a disproportionate share of mulattoes" . . . because they were in "a better position to step out front."[50]

The struggle for black equality continued throughout Jim Crow and the Civil Rights era. Emory University professor Andra Gillespie says, "You look at many of the people who have been at the forefront of getting civil rights for African Americans . . . Many of them clearly had white ancestry and often had it very close to them in terms of their genealogical line."[51]

The men and women in this book, many of them fair-skinned, some with blond hair and blue eyes, some born slaves and some born free, were celebrated by the black community as some of its most prominent leaders on the forefront of social change and civil rights reform in America. These *Light, Bright and Damn Near White* leaders emerged as the major powerbrokers of the black race, during Slavery, Reconstruction, Jim Crow and the Civil Rights era. This was not only because they more closely resembled the majority rule to which they appealed for justice, but they were often the most educated among the race, due to the opportunities that had been afforded them. They are an enormous part of Black History— giants in the fight for freedom and equality for all.

Their contributions to United States history cannot be underestimated. Many of them fought for the civil liberties of not only blacks, but women and other minorities, whose inalienable rights had been compromised by customs or restricted by legislation. Hence, they were torch bearers of American democracy—the unsung heroes and heroines of this great nation. The plight of many Americans might be drastically different today, had these leaders not carried forth their missions and stood tall in the face of enormous adversities and injustices. This is history . . . American History and Black American History.

"Many of the nation's black leaders have been of predominantly white ancestry."

– Scholar Floyd James Davis

INVICTUS

Out of the night that covers me,
Black as the Pit from pole to pole,
I thank whatever gods may be
For my unconquerable soul.

In the fell clutch of circumstance
I have not winced nor cried aloud.
Under the bludgeonings of chance
My head is bloody, but unbowed.

Beyond this place of wrath and tears
Looms but the Horror of the shade,
And yet the menace of the years
Finds, and shall find, me unafraid.

It matters not how strait the gate,
How charged with punishments the scroll.
I am the master of my fate:
I am the captain of my soul.

William Ernest Henley (1875)

1

WALTER FRANCIS WHITE
1893 - 1955

*NAACP President, civil rights leader,
anti-lynching crusader*

*"I am a Negro. My skin is white, my eyes are blue, my hair is
blond, the traits of my race are nowhere visible upon me . . .
I am not white. There is nothing within my mind and heart
that tempts me to think I am."*[1]

– Walter White

Walter Francis White served as executive director of the National
Association for the Advancement of Colored People (NAACP) from 1931
until his death in 1955. He was considered the foremost spokesperson for
blacks in America for almost a quarter of a century. It was under White's
leadership that the NAACP became a dominant force in the fight against
racial inequality. The organization won numerous political and judicial
victories and was on the forefront of major governmental changes that
would affect blacks for decades to come. His administration launched
initiatives to end segregation, voter discrimination, and poll taxes. White
was the key player in several desegregation campaigns, including the
landmark case of *Brown v. Board of Education*. It was White's influence that
led to the United States Senate's rejection of President Hoover's Supreme
Court nominee Judge John J. Parker of North Carolina, a known opponent
of Negro suffrage.[2] Some critics of the Walter White era said he wielded
far too much power and the organization was involved in American policy
on too many fronts. But supporters of White and the NAACP knew the
urgency of the civil rights struggle. White's personal motto on racial
matters was "Now is the time."[3]

In 1941, White joined labor leader A. Philip Randolph in persuading

President Franklin Delano Roosevelt to issue an executive order that created the Fair Employment Act, legislation that banned discrimination in defense industries and federal bureaus.[4] It was the first federal action ever taken in the United States to promote equal opportunity in the workplace and prohibit employment discrimination.

White is considered one of the founding fathers of the Harlem Renaissance Movement. He avidly supported the careers of several Renaissance artists, including writers Langston Hughes, Countee Cullen, and Claude McKay, singer Marian Anderson, tenor Roland Hayes, actor Paul Robeson, and others. He vetted manuscripts, introduced writers to top publishers, and brought national attention to stage and concert performers.[5]

He also led a relentless campaign against the degrading images of blacks promulgated throughout Hollywood films. Fighting hard to secure better roles for blacks, he took on Hollywood producers and directors, as well as the actors and actresses who played stereotypical roles. His well-known public feud with Hattie McDaniel, the acclaimed "Mammy" in *Gone with the Wind*, is legendary. Using his power and resources as leader of the NAACP, he was ultimately able to stop the excessive use of Jim Crow caricatures like "Toms," "Bucks," "Coons," "Mammies," and "Tragic Mulattoes" on the big screen. These stereotypes were negatively impacting the perception of blacks in the United States and abroad.[6]

White's most important contributions to civil rights came through his determination to get a federal anti-lynching bill passed, and his selfless efforts (both overtly and covertly) to end the widespread, brutal lynching of Negroes in America. Perhaps no other man in the history of this country contributed more to this cause than Walter Francis White.[7]

> *"We have laws against murder, yet murder continues. But murder, unlike lynching, has always had universal condemnation. One of the achievements of the Anti-lynching Bill would be to put an end to the possibility of unprosecuted, unpunished lynchings. Lynching thereafter would have no possible public sanction. It would be stamped with federal disapproval."*[8]

> – *Walter White*

Walter Francis White was born of two Negro parents, grew up in the colored section of Atlanta, Georgia, attended segregated schools, and sat in the rear of buses. *(Source: Rose Martin-Palmer/Courtesy of the Herndon House Museum)*

Walter Francis White, executive director of the NAACP from 1931 to 1955. *(Source: Photographs and Prints Division, Schomburg Center for Research in Black Culture, The New York Public Library, Astor, Lenox and Tilden Foundations)*

Thomas Shipp and Abram Smith, lynched in Marion, Indiana on August 7, 1930. *(Source: Lawrence H. Beitler)*

Walter White's appearance allowed him to infiltrate and investigate white supremacist groups and racist communities, in an effort to stop the lynching of blacks in America. *(Source: Photographs and Prints Division, Schomburg Center for Research in Black Culture, The New York Public Library, Astor, Lenox and Tilden Foundations)*

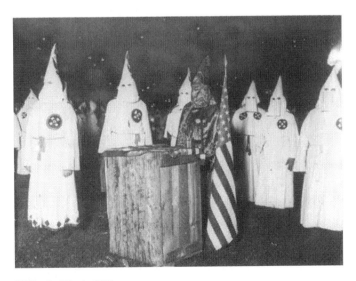

KKK rally, Illinois, 1920.

White was born in Atlanta, Georgia on July 1, 1893, to two light-complexioned Negro parents of mixed ancestry. Both were descendants of slaves. "There were nine light-skinned Negroes in my family," says White in his autobiography, *A Man Called White*.[9] His father, George White, was a mail carrier and a deacon at First Congregational Church. His mother, Madeline Harrison White, was a graduate of Clark Atlanta University and a school teacher. Madeline had been born in LaGrange, Georgia. She was the granddaughter of a slave named Dilsia and William Henry Harrison, who would later become the ninth President of the United States.[10] White was born with blond hair, blue eyes, and pale skin. Most of his siblings could have "passed" for white, a reality that was common during his time. The choice to pass was available to him, affording him an escape from the debasing plight of the American Negro; yet he never considered it. Both his parents were black, and he knew nothing of being white.

Nevertheless, it was White's ability to pass that would prove to be his greatest asset. He used his appearance later in life to secretly infiltrate white-supremacist organizations like the Ku Klux Klan, as well as some of the most racist communities in America.[11] He went undercover as a white man during a time of strict Jim Crow laws and elevated racial divide, to both investigate and expose Negro lynchings throughout the country. Working closely with national newspapers, he brought public attention to these horrific acts and published his findings in the NAACP's magazine *The Crisis*. The possibility of exposure proved too great for many whites, gradually deterring lynching participation altogether.

White was a wanted man for most of his life. He was considered "public enemy number one" to racist organizations. With his on-the-spot investigations of forty-one lynchings and eight race riots across America, White was targeted by the Klan. They were aware that a Negro was passing as white and revealing their agendas; but little did they know it was the prominent leader of the NAACP, Walter White.

> *"It is the startling removal of blackness that upsets people. Looking at me, without knowing who I am, they disassociate me from all the characteristics of the Negro."*[12]
>
> – *Walter White*

Socialized as a "colored boy" in the racist South, his large family resided in the colored section of Atlanta, Georgia. Their two-story, eight-room house sat on Houston Street, a few blocks from the Candler Building, on the edge of a ghetto. White described his father as a Negro man who was "naturally very light," yet "deeply tanned from many years of exposure to sun and wind in his work as a mail carrier. His hair was brown, as were his eyes." Of his Negro mother, White says, she "had almost severely aquiline features, with light blue eyes and the most golden hair that I have ever seen."[13]

Because of their appearance, White and his siblings were often subjected to taunts and sometimes isolation by other black kids at school. Atlanta was under Jim Crow, so White and his siblings attended segregated schools, sat in the rear of buses, and suffered the many humiliations of southern blacks. The family discovered that if they sat in the "white section" of the bus, other blacks who knew them would accuse them of passing; and if they sat in the "colored section," they were generally stared at by white passengers, who thought they were white. To avoid this constant dilemma, the children often walked to their destination or rode in their father's surrey.

> *"I am a Negro. There can be no doubt. I know the night when, in terror and in bitterness of soul, I discovered I was set apart by the pigmentation of my skin (invisible though it was in my case) and the moment at which I decided that I would infinitely rather be what I was than, through taking advantage of the way of escape that was open to me, be one of the race that had forced the decision upon me."[14]*
>
> *– Walter White*

In 1906, on a scorching September day in Atlanta, Georgia, Walter White's life changed forever. He was just thirteen. The city of Atlanta, ominously quiet just hours before, was suddenly engulfed in a race riot of dynamic proportions.[15] The colored section was under siege and homes were being torched at random. An armed white mob of ten thousand men flooded the streets, violently maiming and killing blacks, while making its way through the colored neighborhoods.[16] Some blacks hid, some ran, while others were terrorized and beaten. The White's family home was on the path of organized hatred, as the vicious mob approached.

The riot began shortly after 8 p.m. on Decatur Street, prompted by rumors published in Atlanta newspapers of alleged rapes committed by black men against white women.[17] White, who had accompanied his father on his mail route that day, could hear the roar of the angry mob begin to grow. Suddenly, a lame black man appeared, far off. He was attempting to outrun the mob but to no avail. He was brutally clubbed in the middle of the street and left in a pool of blood. A white undertaker rushed by them in his carriage, his horses' reins held tightly in his hands, as he helped three black men crouched in the rear of his buggy to safety. As the night grew, cries of terror could be heard throughout the city. White and his father hurried down Forsyth Street in their carriage. The huge crowd in the near distance spanned curb to curb. As their horses rounded the corner with relative speed, his slender father found hidden strength to hoist a portly black woman into their carriage and away from danger.[18]

The next morning was Sunday, but blacks stayed home from church. Word of another riot had spread throughout the neighborhood. The warning was that a mob would form again that evening on Peachtree Street and march down Houston street, an area whites called "Darktown," in an effort to "clean out the niggers."[19]

As midnight approached, the violent assembly could be heard again in the distance. A group of black men knocked out the street lights, as families prepared for the worst. White's father instructed his mother and sisters to go to the rear of the house. White's older brother George was away, so only thirteen-year-old White and his father were home to defend the family. They quickly grabbed their rifles and went to the front of the parlor to wait for the lynch mob. As the crowd drew near, a familiar voice emerged. It was their grocer's son yelling, "That's where the nigger mail carrier lives. Let's burn it down. It's too nice for a nigger to live in." At that moment, White's father turned to him and said, "Son, don't shoot until the first man puts his foot on the lawn, and then, don't you miss."[20]

The youngster peered through the window of the parlor, watching the mob move slowly toward his house. Walter White recalls in his autobiography, *A Man Called White*:

> I knew then who I was. I was a Negro, a human being with an invisible pigmentation that marked me a person to be hunted,

hanged, abused, discriminated against, kept in poverty and
ignorance, in order that those whose skin was white would
have readily at hand a proof of their superiority . . . Yet as a boy,
there in the darkness, amid the tightening fright, I knew the
inexplicable thing—that my skin was as white as the skin of those
that were coming at me.[21]

Suddenly, a round of bullets emerged from the basement unit below their house. Friends of White's father had barricaded themselves down below and were firing at the crowd. The shots were enough to dissuade the mob from their impending attack, and they dispersed.

This was a defining moment for Walter White. Traumatized by his brush with death, not only did he awaken to the monstrosity of racism, but also to the realization that he was as white as those who hunted him. This horrifying event remained embedded in his mind for years and was the catalyst that later inspired him to risk his very life, by infiltrating racist communities, towns, and organizations, in an effort to stop the lynching of blacks in America.

Growing up in the South, White was constantly reminded of his place. Just staring at a white woman too long or defending oneself against a racist infraction could subject a black man to unthinkable consequences, even lynching. One day, as a young White was sneaking a drink of water from a forbidden fountain on Courtland Street, a white boy ran up to him, slammed his head into the spigot and screamed, "Niggers drinking from white fountains." White chased the boy through the streets. He was almost to the white section of town, when he picked up a rock and hurled it at the boy, hitting him in the back of the head. The boy staggered, clutching his bleeding head. White's anger turned into instant fear. He had struck a white boy. In shock, he ran home and begged his mother to whip him for what he had done. But before he could explain, the mother of the injured boy was knocking at the door. The white lady told his mother she would have the law on her colored boy. White's mother demanded he explain what had happened. After hearing the full story, she defended him against the angry visitor, stating that it was the accuser's son who had assaulted White first.

The lady backed down and left the house. White thought he was out of the woods, until his mother instructed him to go to the backyard and pick out a switch from the peach tree.[22]

White worked for most of his life. He got his first job at the age of ten, as a cleaning boy in a tailor shop on Peachtree Street. His salary started at 50¢ a week, but with tips he sometimes made as much as $1.50. A few years later, he began working as an office boy but became discouraged with his salary and stopped. After enrolling in Atlanta University, a historically black college, he knew he needed to find a good job to help pay for his tuition. Several of his friends told him that he could make a dollar a day plus tips as a bellhop in Atlanta hotels.

White applied for a job at the Piedmont Hotel, one of the nicest in the city and was hired as a page boy. He had been working for over a week, when he realized that he was unknowingly passing—the job of a page was reserved for white males only. The owner, Mr. Dutton, had assumed White was white, based on his appearance. Horrified by what could happen to him if anyone found out the truth, White sought the advice of his mentor, Fred Toomer, a prominent black executive at Atlanta Life Insurance Company. "Mr. Dutton didn't ask you if you were white or colored. It's a good job, and you're doing it well. All he can do to you is fire you. You are making good money, so go ahead and earn it until you are fired," said Toomer. White decided to stick with it, until Mr. Dutton offered him a promotion. It was then that he confessed. Dutton admitted that he personally had no issue with his race, as he was from the North. But, if his southern customers found out, it could ruin his business.[23] White left and got a job as a bellhop at a neighboring hotel. This new job afforded him the opportunity to observe whites, study them, their mannerisms and ways. It would come in handy later in life.

After graduating from Atlanta University in 1916, White began working for Standard Life Insurance Company and quickly became active in politics of interest to people of color. Early in his civil rights career, he organized a protest against the Atlanta Board of Education. The board had announced it planned to drop the seventh grade for black students, in order to finance the construction of a new high school for whites. In 1917, White became the secretary of the Atlanta Branch of the NAACP and organized a "delegation of Negroes" to demand equal facilities for black school children.[24] "We have got to show these white people that we aren't going to stand being pushed around any longer. As Patrick Henry said, so

Walter White. *(Source: Photographs and Prints Division, Schomburg Center for Research in Black Culture, The New York Public Library, Astor, Lenox and Tilden Foundations)*

Walter White. *(Source: Photographs and Prints Division, Schomburg Center for Research in Black Culture, The New York Public Library, Astor, Lenox and Tilden Foundations)*

must we say, 'Give me liberty or give me death!,'" shouted White at one rally.

His local campaigns captured national attention and the recognition of James Weldon Johnson, director at that time of the national chapter of the NAACP located in New York City. In January of 1918, Johnson offered White a full-time position as assistant secretary, and he accepted. Almost immediately, White became the chief investigator of lynchings. Until then, he had fought publicly to secure equal rights for blacks. But just twelve days after joining the NAACP staff, his covert efforts began when he volunteered to go to Estill Springs, Tennessee to investigate the lynching and subsequent burning of a Negro sharecropper named Jim McIlherron. The murder took place on Lincoln's birthday. Estill Springs was a small settlement situated near a railway, with a strong religious undercurrent. The townspeople were described as "leisurely of manner and slow in comprehension."[25]

> "Most lynchings take place in small towns and rural regions where the natives know practically nothing of what is going on outside their own immediate neighborhoods. Newspapers, books, magazines, theatres, visitors, and other vehicles for the transmission of information and ideas are usually as strange among them as drypoint etchings."[26]
>
> – Walter White

In an effort to gather pertinent information about the incident, White "crossed the color-line," posing as a white reporter interested in giving the South's side of the story. The mission was extremely dangerous, as White could be lynched himself if his cover was blown. Tennessee was deep in the racist South, where outsiders were viewed with suspicion. Upon arrival, he checked into a motel and quickly gained the trust of locals eager to talk about the recent lynching. Never suspecting he was a Negro, the townspeople gave White valuable information about the murder. He received such a welcome that he was even invited to join the local Ku Klux Klan. The sheriff later pinned a badge on him, handed him a loaded gun, and asked White to accompany him on a "hunt for niggers."[27]

His investigation revealed that the victim, Jim McIlherron, was perceived as somewhat wealthy for a Negro in that he owned his own land, which his family farmed. One woman who was interviewed described the family as "big-buggy niggers," meaning that they were too prosperous.[28] They were not liked, considered not humble enough for blacks, and did not take kindly to slights by local whites. McIlherron was also a fighter and was known to carry an automatic. One year prior, he had cut his brother with a knife. When arrested by the county sheriff, he had vowed revenge. It was common knowledge that the sheriff was afraid of him.

The trouble began when McIlherron went into town to purchase fifteen cents' worth of candy. As he walked back down the main street, he passed three white men: Pierce Rogers, Frank Tigert, and Jesse Tigert.[29] It had become customary for local whites to pelt rocks at blacks for fun. This had happened to him previously, and he swore that the next time someone would get hurt. As he strolled by, one young man commented about his candy eating. McIlherron turned around, asked if the man was speaking to him, and a war of words ensued. Threats were hurled, fists were flung, and one man headed for the nearby store. According to a witness, McIlherron apparently thought the situation was going to get violent, so he took out his gun and began shooting. Two of the men were killed and one was seriously injured. McIlherron hurried back to his farmhouse, but the townspeople did not pursue him immediately. They sent for a pack of bloodhounds from a town fifty miles away and a large mob assembled. Some more reasonable locals insisted the mob allow the sheriff to handle the matter, but shouts of "lynch the nigger" soon began.[30]

They headed straight for the farm to retrieve the man, but he had escaped with the help of a resident Methodist minister. McIlherron's plan was to get to the neighboring town of McMinnville where he could catch an outbound train at the Tennessee Central Railroad station. But the minister was only able to transport him part of the way; he would have to travel the rest by foot. The hunt lasted for days. Finally the hounds chased the man down and found him hiding in a barn. Gunfire began between the mob and McIlherron. The standoff endured through the night. After his eye was shot out, he was shot twice in the body, and his ammunition expended, the barn was rushed and McIlherron was captured. The crowd wanted to lynch him there, but the citizens of McMinnville would not allow it. The man was weak from blood loss, but the mob insisted on transporting him by train back to the exact location where he had shot the three men days prior.

> *"The attacks begin first on the most vulnerable group, which in America has always been the Negro. The technique is soon established. The public conscience, accustomed to frequent attacks upon the Negro, becomes calloused and shortly comes to accept the denial of court trials. Thus is established the philosophy of bigotry."* [31]
> – Walter White

As news spread of the capture, men, women, and children gathered to wait for the arrival of McIlherron. Some two thousand people descended on the small town of Estill Springs in anticipation of the impending lynching. They collected excelsior, boxes, iron rods, pokers, and other materials for torture. The train finally arrived around 6:30 p.m. on Tuesday evening, and the crowd was in a frenzy. Too weak to stand, McIlherron was carried to the execution spot. But some women rose up and demanded he not be lynched in the town. He was taken to a patch of woods in front of a church on the outskirts of the community. The crowd was uncontrollable, shouts of revenge grew louder, and the sister of one of the men shot days prior insisted on killing him herself.[32]

McIlherron was chained to a hickory tree and wood saturated with coal oil and other flammable materials were thrown at its base. But the mob was determined to torture the man first. A fire was built some feet away and hot iron rods and pokers were heated to a red-hot pitch and set on the man's body. The awful stench of burning flesh rose into the air, mingled with the lustful cries of the mob, and curses from McIlherron.[33] "We are going to parade him through the main street when we pass through Memphis; then we are going to take him to Arkansas and that will be the end of him," shouted one man. Finally, another man doused McIlherron's trousers and shoes with coal oil, and a fire was lit around him. The flames engulfed the man's body in minutes.

Memphis papers carried headlines earlier that day which read: "May Lynch Three to Six Negroes this Evening" and "Taken though Memphis Today." But law enforcement had offered no protection. The sheriff said,

"Nearly every man, woman, and child in our county wanted the Negro lynched. When public sentiment is that way, there is not much chance left for the officer."[34] When one spectator was asked why the horrific ordeal took place, he responded, "Any time a nigger hits a white man, he's gotta be handled or else all the niggers will get out of hand."[35] White returned to New York and published his findings; he also traveled to Washington, D.C. to tell congressmen the gruesome details, hoping to encourage them to endorse the anti-lynching bill.

It was not long before White went on another undercover assignment. The NAACP official returned to Georgia later that year to investigate the savage lynching of ten men and a pregnant woman near term. White recounts:

> I reached the scene shortly after the butchery, and while excitement yet ran high. It was a prosperous community. Forests of pine trees gave rich rewards in turpentine, tar, and pitch . . . The white inhabitants belonged to the class of Georgia crackers— lanky, slow of movement and of speech, long-necked with small eyes set close together, and skin tanned by the hot sun to a reddish-yellow hue.[36]

White entered a local store and struck up a conversation about the lynching with the owner, allegedly one of the mob leaders. The man appeared cautious at first, but after White expressed that he had never been so fortunate to witness a lynching, the owner sat White down, offered him a soda, and told him all about the incident. "You'll pardon me, Mister, for seeming suspicious, but we have to be careful. In ordinary times, we wouldn't have anything to worry about; but with the war, there's been some talk of the federal government looking into lynchings. It seems there's some sort of law during wartime making it treason to lower the manpower of the country."[37]

White responded with disguised perplexity, "But couldn't the federal government do something, if it wanted to, when a lynching takes place, even if no war is going on at the moment?" The man responded confidently, "Naw. There's no such law, in spite of all the agitation by a lot of fools who don't know the niggers as we do. States' rights won't permit Congress to meddle in lynching in peace time."[38] White again expressed his curiosity about the murders. The owner began laughing as he recalled the lynching of the pregnant woman. "The best show, Mister, I ever did see. You ought to have heard the wench howl when we strung her up," he said. Though sickened, White encouraged the story in an attempt to find out the names of the participants. He soon discovered that some of them were bankers, businessmen, newspaper reporters, and law enforcement officers.

After a few days of asking questions around town, the residents began to get suspicious. When White returned to the general store to speak with the owner again, the man said, "You're a government man, ain't you?" "Yes," said White, hoping the revelation would scare the man to back off. But that tactic proved futile. By nightfall, word had traveled through the town. As White was entering his motel room, a black man approached him. He had been sent to warn White to get on the next train out. But White was determined not to abandon his investigation. "You go back to the ones who sent you," said White, "and tell them this: that I have a damned good automatic, and I know how to use it. If anyone attempts to molest me tonight or any other time, somebody is going to get hurt."

Despite the blatant threat, White stayed for a few more days, collecting evidence against the suspects. He knew rumors that he worked for the Department of Justice were spreading fast, and his every move was being watched. But when he found out that information had surfaced that he was in fact a Negro, he set course to leave immediately. White had acquired enough information and turned over a detailed report of the murders to the governor of Georgia, a proponent of the federal anti-lynching bill.[39]

In 1919, Walter White narrowly escaped being lynched. He was eager to get to the site of a massacre in Elaine, Arkansas, despite extreme personal danger should his identity and race be discovered. This massacre was perhaps the bloodiest racial conflict in this nation's history. White appealed to other NAACP officials, "I am exceedingly anxious to make the investigation personally, and I do so with full realization of the past, and am assuming complete responsibility for any personal consequences which may possibly arise."[40]

It is estimated that five white men and several hundred blacks were murdered. The conflict began on September 30, 1919, after Negroes had organized a protest against the economic exploitation by white landowners, who were openly practicing peonage. Over a hundred Negro farmers, who were members of the Progressive Farmers and Household Union of America, held a meeting at a church in Phillips County, three miles north of Elaine, to discuss the union's objectives. Armed men had been placed outside the church to prevent spying by white opponents. It is not clear who shot first, but a shootout occurred between the black guards and some white men outside the church, resulting in the death of one white man, and the wounding of another. When word of the incident grew, a mob formed. Whites were afraid that blacks were planning an insurrection, and the massacre was said to have been in defense. But White's investigation contested such allegations. He wrote in an article in the *Chicago Daily News* on October 18, 1919, that the insurrection claim was "only a figment of the imagination of Arkansas whites and not based on fact." He added, "White men in Helena told me that more than one hundred Negroes were killed."[41] Within days of the initial incident, two hundred eighty-five blacks had been jailed in Helena, the county seat. Two white members of the Phillips County posse, T. K. Jones and H. F. Smiddy, stated in sworn affidavits that they committed acts of torture at the jail and named other participants.[42] On October 31, 1919, a grand jury charged one hundred twenty-two blacks with crimes ranging from racial disturbance, to night-riding, to murder. The trials began the following week. White attorneys from Helena were appointed by Circuit Judge J. M. Jackson to represent some of the accused. Attorney Jacob Fink, who was appointed to represent one of the accused, admitted that he had not interviewed any of the witnesses, nor had he made any motion for a change of venue, nor did he challenge any prospective jurors, accepting all who were called. On November 5, 1919, the first twelve black men tried were convicted of first-degree murder and sentenced to the electric chair. Eighty more black men were sentenced to prison terms for up to twenty-one years for second-degree murder.[43]

White began his investigation at the Arkansas capital of Little Rock. He interviewed the governor and state officials before heading to Elaine. But shortly into the investigation, word came from Little Rock that White was a Negro. Unaware, he proceeded to the local jail, where he had an appointment with the town sheriff and had interviews set up with some of the jailed men accused of inciting the massacre. As he walked down West Cherry Street toward the jail, a large black man approached requesting

White follow him. Once out of sight from the general public, he urged White not to go to the jail, stating there was hostility against him in the town and great harm would come to him. White headed straight to the train station. He was in such a hurry to leave Elaine, that he did not even purchase a ticket before boarding. The conductor, puzzled by White's urgency, said, "Why, Mister, you're leaving just when the fun is going to start! There's a damned yaller nigger down here passing for white, and the boys are going to have some fun with him." When asked the nature of the fun, the man responded, "When they get through with him, he won't pass for white no more."

In 1921, Walter White found himself in Tulsa, Oklahoma, after one of the worse race riots ever recorded. The lives of fifty white men and approximately three hundred black men, women, and children were lost; over three thousand homes were torched; and thirty-five city blocks of businesses in the prosperous black neighborhood of Greenwood were razed. Property damage totaled in excess of $1.5 million.[44] The destruction took place over a twenty-four hour period, beginning on Memorial Day and lasting until the morning of June 1. White traveled in disguise to Tulsa to survey the damage. His findings were published in *The Nation*.

The circumstances surrounding the riot started a few days prior when a nineteen-year-old black youth named Dick Rowland (a shoe shiner) had delivered a package to the top floor of a downtown Tulsa building. After dropping the package off, the boy pushed the bell for the elevator. The elevator operator that day was a young white woman named Sarah Page, who was not pleased with having to service a Negro. Reluctantly, she opened the gate for him to enter, but before he could get in fully, she pushed the button to descend. To prevent being crushed, the boy quickly threw his weight forward and in the process, stepped on her foot. Page claimed Rowland had attempted to rape her.[45] This occurred at midday, in a crowded building, in an open elevator that was only descending a few floors down. But despite the absurdity of the allegation, the young lady's claim was believed, and the boy was arrested and thrown in jail. The story was published the following afternoon in the *Tulsa Tribune*. By 4 p.m., Police Commissioner J. M. Adkison reported to Sheriff Willard McCullough that there was considerable talk throughout Tulsa of lynching the boy; but no precautions were taken.

That night, a lynch mob assembled to get the young man. Some black townsmen hurried to the jail to offer the sheriff assistance in protecting the boy, but he refused. As the men were leaving, the mob was waiting outside, and a confrontation began. Outnumbered, the men fled back to their neighborhood. But reports of the conflict grew, and by daybreak an angry crowd (in excess of five thousand people) had gathered. Armed with machine guns, rifles, revolvers, and gasoline cans, they headed to the black neighborhood. Blacks were unprepared and ill-equipped. Lives were lost, including an elderly couple slain as they knelt together in prayer.[46]

White arrived within days of riot. He contacted a former New York newspaper reporter in town, who informed him that special deputy sheriffs were being sworn in to protect whites from any Negro retaliation. White headed straight for City Hall and was sworn in as a town deputy. One man turned to White and said, "Now you can go out and shoot any nigger you see, and the law'll be behind you."[47] As he was leaving the courthouse, he saw a man staring at him with some suspicion. White tells of the account:

> I noticed a man, clad in the uniform of a captain in the United States Army, watching me closely. I imagined I saw in his very swarthy face (he was much darker than I, but was classed a white man while I am deemed a Negro) mingled inquiry and hostility. I kept my eye on him without appearing to do so . . . At last, the man seemed certain to know me and started toward me. He drew me aside a deserted corner on the excuse that he had something he wished to ask me, and I noticed that four other men, with whom he had been talking, detached themselves from the crowd and followed us. Without further introduction or apology, my dark-skinned, newly made acquaintance, putting his face close to mine and looking into my eyes with a steely, unfriendly glance, demanded challengingly: "You say that your name is White?" . . . "You say you're a newspaper man?" "Yes," White responded, "would you care to see my credentials?" "No, but I want to tell you something," said the man. "There's an organization in the South that doesn't love niggers. It has branches everywhere. You needn't ask me its name, I can't tell you. But it has come back into existence to fight this damned nigger Advancement Association.

We watch every movement of the officers of this nigger society, and we're out to get them for putting notions of equality into the heads of our niggers down South here."[48]

White surmised that his cover had been blown; and, of course, the organization that the man was speaking of was more than likely the Ku Klux Klan. In front of the five men, White reached into his pocket for a cigarette, taking care to steady his hand as he smoked. Firmly, he asked what this had to do with the fact that he was a reporter who was in Tulsa to cover the recent riot. After a long stare and a flipped response, the man let it go. White, on high alert, found little sleep that night. He wrote a full report of the riot, and the circumstances that led up to it, and published his account in several newspapers. Thereafter, the accused boy was acquitted. White, whose racial identity was noted in the report, received over a hundred death threats from across the country.[49]

On February 15, 1922, White married a black lady named Leah Gladys Powell, whom he described as "the most interesting member of the NAACP staff." Her father had been a performer in the Broadway production *Deep River*. The couple had two children, Walter Carl Darrow and Jane, who would later become an actress. Their beautiful apartment in Sugar Hill was called the "White House of Harlem" and served as a center for cultural and social events.

While White's involvement in Harlem increased, his secret missions to the South became more frequent as well. By the early 1920s, the Klan claimed between two and three million members, and the organization controlled hundreds of elected officials and several state legislatures (not just in the South).[50] Early one Sunday morning, Walter White was awakened by an officer from the New York City Bomb Squad. The morning edition of the *New York World* had a story about a Klan meeting held in the Bronx. The Imperial Wizard of the Klan in Atlanta was the guest speaker and had reminded fellow Klansmen that they had taken an oath to protect the order with their lives. He then informed them that "a Negro named Walter White" had come into possession of Klan secrets, which they must keep at any cost from being made public. Officers had been assigned to protect White's family. The threat prompted both leaders and ordinary citizens in the black community to offer the White family additional security. Their phone rang throughout the day. People also assembled at White's parents' home in Atlanta to stand guard. "No Kluxer will ever put his hand on you and your family," vowed one volunteer.[51]

In 1926, White was commissioned by a New York newspaper to go to a town in Aiken, South Carolina, to investigate the triple lynching of three family members: Bertha, Damon, and Clarence Lowman, who had been falsely accused of murder.[52] Upon arrival, White learned of a local lawyer with significant information about the murders. This man had heard that the lynchings were going to occur and had warned a local judge and prosecutor. But they did nothing. White went to this lawyer for assistance with the investigation, and the man obliged. He provided names of some of the participants, who resided in a nearby cotton mill town. When White asked the attorney if he would escort him to the town to talk to some of the men, the man responded hesitantly, agreeing to go only if they were back by nightfall. White promised. They reached the town and drove to a house perched on a hill. On the lawn stood a man with iron-gray hair and piercing eyes. After introductions, the man invited them in. He told them to have a seat and left the room. Minutes later, White looked up, and there in the doorway stood the man in full clad Ku Klux Klan regalia. He removed his hood, looked sternly at White, and said, "I show you this, so that you will realize I know what I am talking about." White discovered that the man had been a top leader in the Klan. He had joined due to his frustration with corrupt town officials, but he soon learned that the very people the organization was claiming to be against were actually running it. Now, essentially a defector, the man feared for his life. Escorting White to an adjourning room, he showed him an arsenal of weapons and ammunition he had for protection. White says in his autobiography:

> Although everything in me hated everything connected with the
> Ku Klux Klan, I could not help feeling again, as I looked at that
> arsenal in a home, the sense of terror which I had known that
> night in 1906 when my father and I, guns in hand, had knelt in
> the dark at a window of our house in Atlanta, and I felt a bond
> of sympathy between this ex-Kluxer and myself. We both knew
> what it was to be among the hunted.[53]

After expressing his strong beliefs in white supremacy, the man gave an explicit account of the murders, as well as the corruption and cover-up that followed. Town officials were involved. The three accused had been falsely convicted and sentenced to death, while armed Klansmen stood guard in the courtroom. The conviction was appealed to the state's Supreme Court and later overturned. Strong evidence supported the innocence of one of the accused, so the judge ordered his immediate release. But as soon as he was out of jail, he was rearrested on a frivolous charge and thrown back in.[54] That night a mob went to the jail, got the two men and the woman out, took them to an open field, and told them to start running. As they ran for their lives, they were lit up with bullets. Both men died instantly. But the woman was still alive. One man went over to her as she lay on her back, fighting for her life, and shot her several more times. "We had to waste 50 bullets on the wench before one of them stopped her howling," sneered one lyncher.[55]

Evidence taken by White in the affidavits indicated that several law enforcement officials, including the sheriff, his deputies, various jailers, policemen, three relatives of the governor, a member of the state legislature, and several prominent locals were members of the mob and active in the cover-up.[56] White sent his findings to the governor of South Carolina and published details of the murders and the participants in the *New York World*. Several courageous northern and southern newspapers followed suit. Furious about the publicity, the named individuals vowed to get back at White. The sheriff announced that he planned to ask a grand jury to indict the NAACP official for "bribery and passing for white." White even received a letter from a white townsman he had interviewed during the investigation. The puzzled man asked if White was really a Negro. "You did not tell me nor anyone else in my presence that you were white, accept as to your name. I had on amber-colored glasses and did not take the trouble to scrutinize your color, but I really did take you for a white man."[57]

In 1929, James Weldon Johnson retired as the NAACP's executive director. White succeeded him and served as national leader until 1955. He assumed leadership at a time when the organization was struggling to survive. The NAACP had a collapse in its branches, a marked decline in membership, and an exhausted treasury.[58] White focused on strengthening the organization's economic agenda. With this in mind, he assisted in delivering the black vote to Franklin D. Roosevelt in 1932, in exchange for economic assistance for blacks under Roosevelt's New Deal. He allied with the Joint Committee on National Economic Recovery in 1933, an umbrella organization created to ensure black influence and inclusion in New Deal policies.[59] White also became a good friend and confidant of First Lady Eleanor Roosevelt, thereby opening a path to the Oval Office.

White continued his lynching investigations even after becoming the head of the NAACP. On August 7, 1930, three black teenagers (Tom Shipp, Abram "Abe" Smith, and James Cameron) were dragged by a mob of men, women, and children from a Marion, Indiana jail and brutally beaten. Shipp and Smith, the two older teens, were hanged from a tree at the Grant County courthouse square, while thousands watched. The boys had been in jail awaiting trial on the alleged rape of a white woman and murder of a white man.[60] Walter White was brought to Marion in an attempt to prosecute the lynchers. His investigation determined that the state's governor had refused to call out the National Guard. The sheriff, who had been elected with heavy support from the Ku Klux Klan, had conveniently left three doors leading to the jail cell open, and the cell door unlocked. White concluded that the officers were "guilty of gross if not criminal negligence" and believed that Sheriff Jake Campbell, in attendance that evening, was "guilty of gross failure to perform his duty as sheriff" and should be removed from office.[61] Indiana's attorney general, James Ogden, and Walter White took the lead in pressing for a court trial of the two mob leaders and got one, but they were later acquitted by a jury.

The third and youngest teen, James Cameron's life was spared because of the moral protest of an unidentified, white male bystander, who insisted the sixteen-year-old had nothing to do with it and should be released. Cameron dedicated the last decade of his life to telling his story. His book, *A Time of Terror*, recounts the horrific night.[62] White later said the Marion lynching was "among the most horrible and brutal in the whole history of lynching." Some five thousand people, including men, women, and children, were in attendance.[63] The murdered teens showed evidence of ante-mortem maiming and post-mortem mutilation, and their corpses were left hanging as an object lesson for the black community.[64]

In the 1930s, White focused his efforts on securing the passage of a federal anti-lynching bill. Huge political realignments were taking place in both the Democratic Party and Republican Party. "The Negro must be ready, through political independence, to take advantage of these changes and thus better his lot," said White. He recognized the value of an independent political force like the NAACP to represent the needs of black people, but he was also aware of the importance of white support and alliances. "Only by intelligent organization, such as represented by the NAACP," and "only through biracial movements," can "white and colored people" overcome the social and economic forces that exacerbate racial hatred.[65]

In 1934, the anti-lynching bill (also called the "Costigan-Wagner" bill) came before Congress. If passed, it would make lynching a federal crime. There was enormous resistance by filibusterers in the Senate, who declined to consider the bill that year, despite substantial support from the Senate Judiciary Committee, and the state legislatures of California, Colorado, Kansas, Minnesota, New Jersey, Pennsylvania, Indiana, New York, and Illinois. The bill also garnered allegiance from religious organizations, labor unions, civil rights groups, fraternities, and women's organizations throughout the country. White also secured endorsements from the American Civil Liberties Union, the National Council of Jewish Women, and the National Urban League. Several newspapers backed the bill, including the *Richmond News Leader*, the *Chattanooga Times*, and the *Greensboro News & Record*.[66]

On April 16, 1935, the bill was taken up again. Immediately, Senator "Cotton Ed" Smith launched a venomous attack on the bill and a defense of lynching as necessary "to protect the fair womanhood of the South from beasts."[67] In addition to Smith, Hugo Black of Alabama was eager to destroy the legislation. Black charged Senator Costigan (the sponsor) with "simply fronting for the NAACP and resurrecting the specter of Negro domination."[68]

After several more attempts by senators to dislodge the bill from the Senate floor, White sought the urgent assistance of his long-time friend, First Lady Eleanor Roosevelt. White often conferred with Mrs. Roosevelt about issues of interest to black Americans. Eleanor was a civil rights proponent and backed many of the NAACP's agendas. She promptly arranged a meeting between White and her husband, President Franklin D. Roosevelt (FDR). White needed Roosevelt to take a definite stance on the stalled legislation. The conference took place on a warm spring Sunday, on the south portico of the White House. Eleanor and Mrs. Sara Delano Roosevelt (the mother of the president) were present.[69] FDR and White had a friendly debate on the arguments raised by Senate filibusterers. After a few exchanges, Roosevelt turned to White and said, "Somebody's been priming you. Was it my wife?" White smiled but remained silent. The president then asked Eleanor if she had been coaching White. She smiled, which led Roosevelt to turn to his mother, "Well, at least I know you'll be on my side." But his mother also expressed her approval of White's position, which made the president roar with laughter and confess defeat.[70] Nevertheless, White states in his autobiography that it was only "a moral victory." Roosevelt, perhaps fearing political suicide, was unwilling to challenge the southern majority in the Senate and the House. "If I come out for the anti-lynching bill now, they will block every bill I ask Congress to pass, to keep America from collapsing. I just can't take that risk," said the president.[71] The two developed a good relationship, which lasted until FDR's death. White seized any opportunity to talk to him and lobby for the bill.

White sent FDR numerous letters and telegrams in an effort to gain his backing for the legislation. White was not well-liked by the president's staff because of his racial activism. Press Secretary Stephen Early had written a confidential memo to Eleanor Roosevelt's personal secretary Malvina Schneider in an attempt to cut off White's access to the White House.[72] Secretary Marvin McIntyre was another saboteur of White's correspondence to the Oval Office. One time when White had a meeting scheduled with FDR, McIntyre informed White that he had only fifteen minutes to speak with the president.

Roosevelt was known to tell lengthy, amusing stories to avoid discussions on uncomfortable subjects. When White entered the office, he was greeted warmly. But before he had a chance to speak, Roosevelt said, "I've got a perfectly corky story for you, which I have been saving because I know you will enjoy it." White ignored protocol, citing his brief fifteen minutes, and insisted he speak first. Roosevelt was startled but said, "Alright, go ahead. But save me two minutes, because it's a darn good story."[73] White says in his autobiography:

I talked as rapidly as I could, because I was very annoyed at the President's failure to take a more forthright stand against the Southern filibusterers and the steadily increasing wave of lynching. At the end of 13 minutes, I looked at my watch and informed the President that two minutes remained for his story.[74]

In 1935, White hired Charles Hamilton Houston as chief counsel for the NAACP's legal team. Houston had been dean of Howard University's law school. White and Houston led an ardent fight against Jim Crow segregation in public facilities, education, and housing. Houston was also responsible for the NAACP's recruitment of Thurgood Marshall in 1936. As director of the NAACP Legal Defense and Education Fund, Marshall won twenty-nine out of thirty-two cases before the Supreme Court, including the groundbreaking case *Brown v. Board of Education*. Marshall argued more cases before the High Court than anyone else in history.[75] He would later become the first black justice of the United States Supreme Court.

In the late 1930s, White crusaded against the distorted depictions of blacks in film and spearheaded a drive to secure positive roles for black actors and actresses. He considered "the matter of the treatment of the Negro in the motion pictures of such importance that," he said, "it takes rank over some other phases of our [the NAACP's] work."[76] Other black intellectuals shared his views and joined the battle. Well-known black conservative George S. Schuyler captured the sentiment of the black community when he wrote in the *Pittsburgh Courier* that Hollywood needed to get rid of the "grinning darky stereotype, the slew-footed, liver-lipped, swivel-eyed cretins, male and female, who shuffled, jigged, and dropped consonants throughout the films that reached not only America, but the whole world, white and colored."[77]

Some years prior, Clarence Muse, a pioneering black actor, had published a pamphlet called "The Dilemma of the Negro Actor." In it, Muse said, "There are two audiences in America to confront: the white audience with a definite desire for buffoonery and song, and the Negro audience with a desire to see the real elements of Negro life portrayed."[78] Muse had made his career playing stereotypical minstrel roles such as "Toms" and "Coons." Cinematic historian Donald Bogle lambasted the coon caricature as one of the worst racial images of that era:

> Before its death, the coon developed into the most blatantly degrading of all black stereotypes. The pure coons emerged as no-account niggers, those unreliable, crazy, lazy subhuman creatures, good for nothing more than eating watermelons, stealing chickens, shooting crap, or butchering the English language.[79]

White recognized the dilemma posed in Muse's pamphlet, but the incredible harm done to the Negro race by these stereotypes was far too great to negotiate. He asked Archer Winsten of the *New York Post* to send him a list of the black actors and actresses who were most often cast in racially demeaning roles. Oscar award-winning Hattie McDaniel, who starred as Mammy in *Gone with the Wind*, was at the top of the list. White asked another friend to compile a list of movies that were excessively "anti-Negro," which resulted in movies such as *Gone with the Wind*, *The Little Colonel*, and *Maryland*. All three films starred Hattie McDaniel.[80]

In 1938, White had written Hollywood producer David O. Selznick about the NAACP's concern over *Gone with the Wind*, saying, "We have found among white and colored Americans a very definite apprehension as to the effect this picture will have." White suggested that Selznick not abandon the film, but rather that he hire a consultant ("preferably a Negro").[81] Selznick passed White's suggestion to Sidney Howard, a Pulitzer Prize-winning playwright, who was adapting the book for the screen. The Hays Office, which set the moral code for films, believed Selznick would comply; but the producer got cold feet and did not hire a consultant.

Selznick's secretary, Marcella Rabwin, wrote to his New York assistant, Kay Brown. "We're so concerned about White," Rabwin confided, "because he is a very important man and his ill-will could rouse a swarm of bad editorials in Negro journals throughout the country." She described White as "a white man sincerely interested in the Negro cause." But after a meeting with the NAACP leader, Rabwin wrote Brown again: "Mr. White, honey chile . . . is a Negro . . . and promptly told me he was one, during the first five minutes of the interview."[82]

When *Gone with the Wind* was released, black intellectuals were incensed. Columnist Earl Morris of the *Pittsburgh Courier* said the movie would prove worse than the racist film *Birth of a Nation*, and he believed that the black cast were little more than "economic slaves." He described their roles as "racial suicide." He said, "It means about $2,000 for Miss McDaniel in individual advancement [and] nothing in racial advancement."[83] He urged blacks to boycott the film and demanded black actors reject such roles. Hundreds of letters poured into Selznick to shelve McDaniel's projects.

Not long after, White was approached by leaders in the Republican Party for his assistance in securing the black vote for presidential candidate Wendell Willkie. White consented—provided that Willkie agreed to use his influence with Hollywood producers to secure more sophisticated roles for blacks. Willkie had represented Hollywood during a Senate probe of the film industry, and he had made some powerful friends in Tinseltown.[84] White flew to Los Angeles to discuss the issue and was interviewed by the California Eagle. He told the reporter, "Hollywood's treatment of the American Negro has stamped an indelible false impression upon the minds of people in every corner of the globe."

White was given first-class treatment as Willkie's guest. A meeting was held with several major Hollywood producers and filmmakers, such as Twentieth Century Fox's Darryl Zanuck, Motion Picture Academy President Walter Wanger, and others. White came equipped with a personal letter from his friend Eleanor Roosevelt, which read, "I am sincerely interested in this problem [of black stereotyping] and hope that Mr. White will meet with success."[85] This first meeting with Hollywood met with marginal success, but White continued pressing.

After months of being avoided again by studio executives, White was finally able to sit down with major movie producers a second time in July of 1942, to further discuss the matter. White was in Los Angeles for the NAACP's national convention. This Tinseltown meeting included several filmmakers; the head of the Screen Actors Guild, Edward Arnold; director Frank Capra; censor Will Hays; producer Hal Wallis; and director/producer John Stahl. White appealed to the attendees, saying, "Restrictions of Negroes to roles with rolling eyes, chattering teeth, always scared of ghosts, or to portrayals of none-too-bright servants, perpetuates a stereotype that is doing the Negro infinite harm." He called upon filmmakers "to have the courage to shake off [their] fears and taboos and to depict the Negro in films as a normal human being and an integral part of the life of America and the world."[86] The Pittsburgh Courier reported that movie bosses agreed to White's terms, "collectively pledging to improve the black cinematic presence and create characters that reflected the reality of black life."[87] White would later deny that such a meeting ever took place. And yet soon after, much more positive depictions of blacks began to emerge on the big screen.

This change posed difficulties for black acting veterans like Hattie McDaniel, Clarence Muse, Mantan "Google Eyes" Moreland, Nicodemus Stewart, and Lincoln "Stepin Fetchit" Perry, who made their living playing subservient roles. McDaniel and Muse waged a campaign against White and the NAACP, claiming the organization was interfering with their bread and butter. Their roles had been significantly reduced, and they took it personally. McDaniel began to attack the NAACP leader publicly. White appealed to McDaniel to abandon her selfishness and look at the bigger picture, affirming that the fight was greater than her. But she dismissed reason, and the war between White and McDaniel escalated.[88] White was resolute, stating he was "not in the least bothered with the criticisms and attacks of Clarence Muse and others."[89] White was determined to get rid of them all.

The NAACP's fight to dispel Hollywood's negative representations proved far harder on Lincoln Perry (Stepin Fetchit) than Hattie McDaniel or Clarence Muse. Perry was the first black actor to become a millionaire, and he had done so by playing the quintessential Uncle Tom. He was reviled throughout the black press as the epitome of racist caricatures.[90] Eventually, the feud had gotten out of hand. White sought to set up a meeting to diffuse the contention, but he was advised by NAACP officials that because of the strong personalities involved, he should not meet with them through the organization.[91] The conflict soon died down, and White and McDaniel were able to bury the hatchet.

White was also quite active in race relations abroad. He was selected as a delegate to the Second Pan African Congress in 1921. He served the Advisory Council for the government of the Virgin Islands from 1934–1935, advised the United States delegation to the founding conference of the United Nations in 1945, and counseled the 1948 General Assembly session in Paris, France. His work as a foreign correspondent during World War II inspired him to write the book *A Rising Wind* (1945), which explored the widespread discrimination faced by Negro soldiers. This book had a great influence on President Harry S. Truman, who later issued an executive order to desegregate the armed forces. White authored several other influential books, including *The Fire in the Flint* (1924), *Flight* (1926), and *Rope and Faggot: A Biography of Judge Lynch* (1929), which provided a rousing study on the psychology behind lynching. Other writings include his autobiography, *A Man Called White* (1948), and *How Far the Promised Land?* (1955).

Throughout his life, White sought to understand the psyche that drove people to participate in mass mobs. He was concerned with the "normalization of barbarism" in America.[92] In his book *Rope and Faggot* he wrote, "Mobbism has inevitably degenerated to the point where an uncomfortably large percentage of American citizens can read in their newspapers of the slow roasting alive of a human being in Mississippi and turn, promptly and with little thought, to the comic strip and sports page." When asked in an interview about the public hanging of a Negro man in Owensboro, Kentucky in 1946 (an event that an estimated 15,000 people attended), White said:

> The principle victim was not the executed man, but the minds and souls of those who witnessed his death. The psychologists and psychiatrists are right when they tell us that the spirit which prompts thousands to gather at such events is sadistic and abnormal. Indeed, the abnormality already affecting those who went to the spectacle became all the greater after they had witnessed it. Owensboro left a terrible and lasting mark on all who participated in the ghastly spectacle.[93]

White's long-time friendship with First Lady Eleanor Roosevelt proved invaluable, even after her husband's death. This fact became apparent when later in his career, White encountered a public struggle, regarding his personal life. In 1922, White had married a black woman, Leah Gladys Powell. That marriage ended in divorce in 1949, and the same year, he married a white South African woman, Poppy Cannon.[94] This interracial marriage provoked protests, incensed black leaders, and there were calls for White's resignation as leader of the NAACP. Some black people were hurt and felt betrayed, as if he had committed cultural treason. White, a

Walter White said, ". . . the spirit which prompts thousands to gather at such events is sadistic and abnormal." The lynching of Laura Nelson and her son Lawrence Nelson in Okemah, Oklahoma on May 11, 1925. *(Source: George Henry Farnum Collection, Oklahoma Historical Society Research Division)*

The lynching of George Meadows, January 15, 1889, near the Pratt Mines in Jefferson County, Alabama. *(Source: Library of Congress)*

defender of integration, shrugged off the criticism, maintaining that his choice for a spouse was a private matter. But the controversy steadily grew, at which point Eleanor Roosevelt stepped in. She had joined the NAACP's board of directors after her husband's death, and she threatened to resign if White was dismissed.

Later that year, White offered his resignation to the NAACP, citing health reasons. The board urged him to remain and granted him an extended leave of absence. Roy Wilkins was appointed interim president. When White returned to his post, the leadership was under a dyadic system with Wilkins. This system continued for the remainder of White's administration.

Walter Francis White devoted his life to racial reform, as well as to the protection and advancement of the Negro race. He died on March 21, 1955, ten months after the historic *Brown v. Board of Education* decision. His white appearance allowed him to investigate activities no other black man had ever witnessed and survived.[95] He fearlessly met Klansmen and attended their meetings. White investigated forty-one lynchings and eight race riots. He published his findings in national newspapers—thus making it no longer possible for Americans to ignore the murder of blacks by lynching. He not only worked clandestinely, but also openly spearheaded nationwide campaigns for the enactment of a federal anti-lynching law. Though no such law was ever passed, Walter White had changed the climate of public opinion about Negro lynching. His relentless investigations, exposés, impassioned propaganda, and courageous acts were paramount in saving the lives of countless American Negroes. In the year that White died, only three lynchings were recorded; and in the five years prior to his death, none were recorded. Lynching, now a rarity, was soon to disappear from the American landscape.[96] Walter White's dedication to its abolishment had proven successful.

Civil Rights Leaders (left to right): W.E.B. Du Bois, Mary McLeod Bethune, and Walter White.
(Source: Courtesy of the National Park Service, Mary McLeod Bethune Council House National Historic Site, National Archives for Black Women's History)

Congressman Adam Clayton Powell, Jr. speaks at a rally in Atlantic City, New Jersey. *(Source: George Ballis photographer/Courtesy of Matt Herron, Take Stock Photos)*

2

ADAM CLAYTON POWELL, JR.
1908–1972

Congressman, civil rights icon

"Just like little David had those smooth stones and killed big Goliath with them, use what you have right in your hand. That dollar . . . that ten cents. Use your vote. The Negro race has enough power right in our hands to accomplish anything we want to."[1]

– Adam Clayton Powell, Jr.

Adam Clayton Powell, Jr. was the first black congressman from New York. He served twelve terms as Harlem's representative in the House of Representatives from 1945 to 1971. In 1961, Powell assumed the position of chairman of the Committee on Education and Labor, the most powerful position held by a black person in Congress.[2] Legislation introduced by Powell's committee helped shape much of the social policy of the John F. Kennedy and Lyndon B. Johnson administrations.[3] He served as chairman for three terms, during which time his committee approved more than sixty measures authorizing federal programs for education, student loans, school lunches, vocational training, assistance for the deaf, and increases in the minimum wage.

Throughout his life, Powell was a warrior for civil rights. He was often described as having a confrontational approach to racial discrimination, but his style did yield results. His demand for social change through legislation commanded so much attention on Capitol Hill that he became known as "Mr. Civil Rights."[4] To black Americans, he was a hero, the personification of black pride. He never compromised himself, his positions, or what was in the best interest of the race. In 1966, Powell convened the first Black

Power conference in Washington, D.C.[5] Handsome, passionate, and charismatic, he was even liked and respected by his political adversaries. A rebel to congressional protocol, he was not afraid to openly challenge the established authority. Powell was known to debate fervently any racially biased legislation before the House. It was this congressman who paved the way for later generations of black politicians to stand unbowed in the arena of American politics.[6]

> *"The hour for Negroes to move ahead has long since struck. We've got too many Uncle Toms among our leaders. We've got to streamline our race and come to realize that mass action is the most powerful force on earth."*[7]
>
> – Adam Clayton Powell, Jr.

Like other dynamic leaders of the civil rights movement, his political career began in the church. In 1937, he succeeded his father as pastor of Abyssinian Baptist Church in Harlem, New York. Abyssinian had the largest black congregation in the country at that time, with a membership of over fifteen thousand. Some said that Powell held "a community in the palm of his hands."[8] The pulpit became his platform as he fought for jobs and fair housing for people in Harlem. He worked diligently to get jobs back for black doctors, and he forced bus companies to hire black drivers and mechanics. Powell led boycotts against white store owners who refused to employ blacks, with his "Don't Buy Where You Can't Work" campaign.

Early in his career, he organized more than six thousand blacks in a march on city hall in New York City. He gathered rent strikes and picket lines against several companies. In 1939, he assembled a large picket line at the executive offices of New York's World Fair, located at the Empire State building, which resulted in the hiring of more than five hundred black employees. Another huge boycott of the transit authority resulted in two hundred more jobs for blacks. His popularity in Harlem soared; and after earning the endorsement of New York City Mayor Fiorello LaGuardia, the thirty-three-year-old Powell easily won a seat on the New York City council in 1941, becoming the first black person on the council.[9] This position paved the way for his historic career in Washington, D.C.

Adam Clayton Powell, Jr. was born on Thanksgiving Day, November 29,

Adam Clayton Powell, Jr. *(Source: Library of Congress)*

Reverend Adam Clayton Powell, Jr. addresses the
citizens' committee mass meeting, Washington, D.C.
*(Source: Gordon Parks, Office of War Information/
Library of Congress)*

1908, in New Haven, Connecticut. His mother, Mattie Fletcher Schaeffer, was of African and European descent, described as "a gorgeous woman with long, chestnut-brown hair."[10] His father, Reverend Adam Clayton Powell, Sr., was a civil rights activist; he had missed being born a slave by only two weeks. Powell, Sr. graduated from Yale Divinity School and traveled the country lecturing on race relations. He was pastor of Abyssinian Baptist Church, a founder of the National Urban League, and a prominent leader in the NAACP.

Powell, Jr. was pampered by women at a very early age. Both his mother and his older sister, Blanche, were very attentive to him. But there was also Josephine, an older black woman (the family's self-proclaimed servant) who lived in the Powell home. He was quite fond of her.[11] Josephine took great pride in dressing young Powell and donned him in stylish attire whenever they went out. Powell said later that he hated walks through the neighborhood after breakfast, because Josephine would have him dressed in Little Lord Fauntleroy suits, Buster Brown collars, and flowing black ties. She would even fix his pale-yellow hair in curls. He had a gray, Persian lamb coat for the winter, and she often placed a broad-brimmed hat with streamers on his head that resembled (according to Powell) the hats worn by Venetian gondoliers. When renowned journalist Roi Ottley first saw the youngster being led into church by Josephine, he turned to blues pioneer W. C. Handy and said, "My God, is that a boy or a girl?"[12] Ottley recounted that day years later, saying that Powell was "white to all appearances, having blue eyes, an aquiline nose, and light, almost blond hair, yet he became a bold, effective black leader. As a congressman, he was not afraid to attack the white power structure, and he lobbied hard for the passage of anti-discrimination legislation."[13]

Adam Clayton Powell, Jr. was brought up in a middle-class family. He attended Townsend Harris High School, received his bachelor's degree from Colgate University in 1930, and his master's degree from Columbia University in 1932. But acquiring these degrees had not been easy. He had stopped and started college several times, due to his perpetual partying and general lack of determination. Powell, who began his collegiate career at the City College of New York, had failed three courses by the end of the first semester, and he had flunked out completely the following semester.

Powell, age four. *(Source: Courtesy of the Powell Family)*

Powell with his nanny Josephine. *(Source: Courtesy of the Powell Family)*

The congressman's family in West Virginia: The congressman's grandfather, Anthony Powell, is on the left and his uncle, Dee Powell, is on the right, c. 1885. *(Source: Courtesy of the Powell Family)*

Powell with (1-r): Fannie E. Robinson, Powell's wife Isabel Washington Powell, sister-in-law Fredi Washington, and Bill "Bojangles" Robinson. *(Source: Courtesy of The Fredi Washington Papers, Amistad Research Center at Tulane University)*

The handsome and charismatic congressman had Hollywood appeal, c. 1948. *(Source: James J. Kriegsmann)*

"...women have always spoiled me. And I have done everything within my power to assist them."[14]

– Adam Clayton Powell, Jr.

Undeterred, he continued partying. The roaring twenties were ripe for Harlem's nightlife. There were numerous dance halls, speakeasies, and pretty women. Powell, a strikingly handsome young bachelor, had a way with the ladies. Most of the money he made during the day working hard in a kitchen, was spent in the evenings on gambling, alcohol, and women. As the son of a reverend, his lifestyle was at times embarrassing. Powell later claimed to have been rebelling against his father's "holier-than-thou" attitude and his "Calvinism."[15] But his brazen conduct was also ascribed to the masking of a deep pain, his own private despair. Blanche, his beloved older sister, had died suddenly of a ruptured appendix in 1926, after doctors had misdiagnosed her. Powell idolized her. Blanche was ten years his senior, and he called her his "princess." She was very pretty, tall, dressed in the most fashionable flapper dresses, and smelled really good. "Sometimes as she came walking toward me down the street as I sat on the stoop, my heart would jump right into my mouth and hang there and wouldn't beat and I couldn't breathe," says Powell in his autobiography. He was devastated by her passing, saying she was "my real love . . . That was the end . . . of college, of church, and of faith! My sister was dead. And I just didn't give a damn."[16] Grief-stricken, his mental anguish became outwardly apparent as his life began a downward spiral. Powell says:

> This particular death, this shock, this particular moment in my life turned me against everything and everyone without reason or logic. I began to hate, mistrust. God was a myth, the Bible a jungle of lies. The church was a fraud, my father the leading perpetrator, my mother a stupid rubber stamp. The smiling good people of the church were grinning fools . . . All the girls I knew, as many and as fast as possible, were only something to be used as a hopeless catharsis to rid me of Blanche's death . . .[17]

Powell's father intervened, demanding that he stop his destructive behavior and concentrate on his education. His father sent him to Colgate

University, a predominately white university in upstate New York. Powell kept to himself on campus and did not openly identify as black. The white students assumed he was white until his father came to the school to speak out on racial intolerance. Powell returned to his dorm room to find his roommate had pinned a note to his door stating, "I can't live with you anymore because of the way your father defended Negroes today. You must be a Negro!" University officials forced Powell to change dormitories.[18] He pledged Alpha Phi Alpha, a black fraternity, soon after this incident.

During the summer, he worked as a bellhop at the prestigious Equinox House Hotel in Vermont. An elderly Robert Todd Lincoln, the son of President Abraham Lincoln, lived nearby and was a regular at the hotel's dining hall. He would drive up nightly in a dazzling Rolls-Royce, and the black bellhops would race up to his vehicle to help the old man exit. But upon seeing the brown hands of any bellhop who dared to touch his car, Robert Lincoln, a blatant racist, would grab his wooden cane and whack the bellhop across the knuckles.[19] Because of Lincoln's conduct, the manager of the hotel asked Powell to intervene in exchange for a raise. Powell, who was described as "white enough to pass," said of this experience, "I, whose father had been raised by a branded slave, would open his door. And Mr. Lincoln, looking at my white hand, was satisfied." Lincoln would smile and tip Powell a dollar each night.[20]

Powell was a regular patron at the exclusive, white-owned Harlem Cotton Club, and he was able to enter (because of his appearance) without notice. It was here that he first saw Isabel Washington, one of the infamous Cotton Club dancers, who was later to be his wife. She was the sister of acclaimed actress Fredi Washington of the film *Imitation of Life*. Isabel later met Powell while starring in the Broadway play *Harlem*. Powell was instantly smitten. But his father disapproved of the relationship, believing that his son was destined for the pulpit and should not be courting a dancer. Determined to split them up, his parents sent him on a long trip to Europe, the Holy Land, and Egypt as a college graduation gift. But the trip away only deepened his love for Isabel. In 1933, upon his return, he asked her to marry him. He adopted her son, Preston, by a previous marriage.[21]

Powell briefly attended the Union Theological Seminary and later entered Columbia University Teachers College, where he earned a master's degree in religious education. While working on his postgraduate studies,

Powell helped thousands of poor blacks in Harlem. He set up a homeless shelter that provided a food pantry, literacy classes, job training, referrals, and professional clothes for employment. His generosity became legendary in Harlem. Powell once took off his own shoes and gave them to a homeless man for whom the church clothing bin had no suitable shoe sizes.[22] It was estimated that Abyssinian Baptist Church of Harlem gave away over thirty thousand free meals over the course of four months. The Great Depression had devastated the country, especially those people in black communities. Between 1929 and 1932, the median income for black families in Harlem fell by 50 percent, and over forty thousand blacks were unemployed.

On May 10, 1931, Adam Clayton Powell, Jr. delivered his first sermon as head pastor in the crowded Abyssinian Baptist Church. His father had taken ill. Most of the congregation had watched Powell grow up in this church, and he had been doted on by women parishioners as a child.[23] Famed poet Alice Dunbar-Nelson was in the audience that day. Afterward, she wrote a note about the young preacher to a friend: "The boy is handsome, graceful, and has a marvelous personality and control of the massive congregation, only 22 or 23, ordained without any divinity training, but he can handle the people."[24]

Powell used the church not only as a religious base, but also as a political base to stress black solidarity and incite the Harlem community toward social change. He rallied for black voting participation and built a formidable public following through his job crusades, his fight for fair housing for the poor, and his support for a federal anti-lynching bill. He also began his "Don't Buy Where You Can't Work" campaign against New York's stores, successfully breaking hiring barriers. He pressured utility companies to lower prices and organized strikes against New York City's transportation, resulting in quotas for minority hiring.[25] When asked by the *New York Post* to comment on the Harlem Riot of 1935, he obliged with a scathing attack on discrimination and police brutality. These articles resulted in a regular "Soap Box" column in the *New York Amsterdam News* and later in the *People's Voice*, which Powell founded and published from 1942 to 1946. Through marches to City Hall and Harlem Hospital, he protested racist policies in healthcare services.

In 1941, Powell ran as an independent for the New York City council. He won by a landslide, receiving 90 percent of the eligible votes and becoming the city's first black councilman. After the election, Powell said, "I am fighting for the chance to give my people the best representation in the affairs of their city, to help make Harlem the number one community in New York." He continued to target discrimination in all sectors, including New York's public schools.

Around this time, Powell began an affair with Hazel Scott, a singer who had a steady gig at Café Society, a posh club in the New York's Village, where Powell socialized regularly with singer Frank Sinatra, author Lillian Hellman, and journalist Heywood Broun. The affair landed him in Walter Winchell's gossip column. Isabel Washington Powell filed for divorce. "I have since learned," she said in her suit, "that my husband had lost interest in our marriage because of his infatuation with another woman. This woman is a nightclub performer."[26] After his divorce from Isabel, Powell married Hazel Scott in 1945 and had a son, but this marriage ended in divorce. He married Yvette Diago in 1960 and had another son before their divorce. Both sons were Powell's namesake.

In 1943, a new congressional district was established in Harlem that would almost certainly produce the state's first black representative to Congress. Powell undertook an ambitious campaign for the seat, winning the support of Democrats, Republicans, and Communists. Poet Langston Hughes wrote Powell's campaign song. Powell promised that if elected to Congress, he would push for a range of improvements: an Omnibus Bill for civil rights, fair racial practices, the end of restrictive covenants and housing discrimination, a national Fair Employment Practices Commission, the eradication of the poll tax and segregated facilities, a bolstering of the 13th, 14th, and 15th Amendments to the Constitution, the end of the defamation of any minority, a protest against every form of imperialism and colonialism, and passage of a bill to make lynching a federal crime.[27] He declared he would not be denied a Congressional seat, nor would he suffer again what had happened two years prior when he was stopped at gunpoint from entering the House chambers, during a march on Capitol Hill.[28]

"I'm the first bad Negro they've had in Congress."[29]
– Adam Clayton Powell, Jr.

Powell was elected to the U.S. House of Representatives. He was the first black representative from New York. The *New York Herald Tribune* reported that on December 17, 1944, thousands came to the Golden Gate Auditorium in New York City to send Powell off to Congress. On January 3, 1945, Powell took the oath of office on the floor of the House, joining the 79th Congress. He swore to uphold the Constitution and the Bill of Rights but said the dream of the Founding Fathers was becoming a faint mirage and that "these truths" were no longer self-evident. Under the current administration of Eisenhower, blacks and whites were segregated, even in the armed forces. Powell felt that the Constitution was being dishonored, saying later, "There was an evil there in Washington on January 3, 1945— the evil that comes when one preaches and fails to practice, when one proclaims and does not act, when the outside is clean and the inside is filled with filth. This was Washington, D.C., capital of the 'sweet land of liberty.'"[30] Out of four hundred thirty-four members, only two were black. The other, William Dawson of Chicago, was seen but rarely heard. Powell was different. He was not afraid to upset the status quo. Almost immediately, he tore into Congress for allowing Negro lynching to continue in America. He argued against the southern practice of charging black voters a poll tax and lobbied for the desegregation of public schools, the military, and even the U.S. Capitol.

> *"When I came here, no downtown hotel would rent me a room. No downtown theater would even let a Negro sit in the balcony. When I heard that the dining room for Representatives' staff was off-limits to Negroes, I told my secretary and clerks to go down there and eat whether they were hungry or not!"*[31]
>
> – *Adam Clayton Powell, Jr.*

His approach to civil rights reform was often confrontational. Established white congressmen didn't know what to make of his "in your face" style of activism. Annoying yet likeable, he was both hated and respected by most of his colleagues. Powell would boldly strut into the congressional dining room, fully aware that blacks were not allowed, and demand service.[32] At times, he would invite other black friends to join him. When he needed a haircut, he would walk into the "white only" congressional barber shop and take a seat. He all but harassed racist congressmen, demanding they stop their flagrant use of the word "nigger" in congressional assemblies, and he campaigned to desegregate the press galleries.[33]

> *"High above Washington on the great dome of the Capitol, was the statue of Freedom, and yet below that statue there was no true freedom for people with the 'wrong' skin color."*[34]
>
> – *Adam Clayton Powell, Jr.*

Powell's aggressive stance on discrimination led to several confrontations with Congressman John Elliot Rankin, a Democrat from Mississippi. Rankin believed in segregation and hated Jews and blacks. He objected to any attempts to integrate the Capitol, describing the 1943 protest to do so by saying, "That gang of communistic Jews and Negroes . . . tried to storm the House restaurant and went around here arm in arm with each other." He once yelled on the House floor, "I said Niggra! Just as I have said since I have been able to talk and shall continue to say."[35] It was not uncommon for Rankin to use the word "nigger." After doing so in describing actor Paul Robeson, both Powell and Congressman Vito Marcantonio sought to put an end to this slur. Marcantonio protested to House Speaker Sam Rayburn, saying, "The gentleman from Mississippi used the word 'nigger.' I ask that the word be taken down and stricken from the record, inasmuch as there are two members of this House of Negro race."[36]

> *"No one can afford to be a slave to anything—neither physical colonialism, nor a mindset. Anyone who doesn't have an open mind is a slave."* [37]
>
> – *Adam Clayton Powell, Jr.*

Rankin made it clear that he did not want to sit anywhere near a Negro in Congress. Powell made it a point to sit as close to Rankin as possible. Rankin changed his seat five times in a futile attempt to get away from Powell. Powell retorted, "I am happy that Rankin will not sit by me, because that makes it mutual. The only people with whom he is qualified to sit by are Hitler and Mussolini."[38] But their feud did not end there. Powell spoke out on the House floor, condemning Rankin's racist attack against Jewish journalist Walter Winchell, saying:

> Last week democracy was shamed by the uncalled for and unfounded condemnation of one of America's great minorities . . . I am not a member of that great minority, but I will always oppose anyone who tries to besmirch any group because of race, creed, or color. Let us give leadership to this nation in terms of racial and religious tolerance and stop petty bickering in this body.[39]

Powell's unique ability to garner respect from his congressional colleagues was apparent immediately. Only days after Powell took office, Speaker of the House Sam Rayburn of Texas said, "Adam, everybody down here expects you to come with a bomb in both hands. Now don't you do that . . . Oh, I know all about you, and I know you can't be quiet for very long . . . Take your time. Freshmen members of Congress are supposed not to be heard and not even to be seen too much . . . Get re-elected a few more times, and then start moving." Powell responded, "Mr. Speaker, I've got a bomb in each hand, and I'm going to throw them right away." Rayburn exploded with laughter (while chewing on a wad of tobacco), and the two were friends from that moment on.[40]

In his first year, Powell denounced First Lady Bess Truman for her affiliation with the Daughters of the American Revolution, which then had racially discriminatory policies. President Harry S. Truman was outraged.[41] In Congress, Powell styled himself as "the irritant," because he berated both Republicans and his fellow Democrats for failing to ensure civil rights for blacks. He attached to bill after bill what became known as the "Powell Amendment." This amendment would deny federal funding to any state or local agencies if they were found to be discriminatory in any way against blacks. Even schools in the rural South would have to submit to an open policy to hire black teachers and admit black students, or risk losing funds. In 1964, the Powell Amendment became law as Title VI of the Civil Rights Act.[42]

Adam Clayton Powell, Jr., A. Phillip Randolph, Walter White, Roy

Wilkins, and other distinguished black leaders called for both President Roosevelt and President Truman to end discriminatory practices in the American armed services. They had the backing of the black press, the NAACP, and other civil rights organizations. Randolph raised the specter of civil disobedience, pledging that "From coast to coast in my travels, I shall call upon all Negro veterans to join this civil disobedience and to recruit their younger brothers in an organized refusal to register and be drafted." Randolph declared that he would "openly counsel, aid, and abet youth, both white and Negro, to quarantine any Jim Crow conscription system."[43] Senator Wayne Morse warned Randolph that in times of national emergency, his statements could be viewed as treason. Randolph replied that by fighting for their rights, Negroes were serving the cause of American democracy. This point elevated the debate, prompting government advisor Truman Gibson, a member of the presidential "black cabinet," to express "shock and disgust" at Randolph's statements. Gibson predicted that Negroes would continue to participate in the country's defense efforts. For Gibson's open dissent against Randolph, Powell stepped in and publicly branded Gibson "a rubber stamp Uncle Tom."[44]

Powell also advocated for the rights of service women. When asked about the status of women in the Navy, Powell stated that the administration was practicing "not merely discrimination, segregation, and Jim Crowism, but total exclusion."[45] The persistent pressure of black leaders such as Powell on the Truman administration to address these minority issues culminated in victory. On July 26, 1948, President Harry S. Truman signed Executive Order 9981, which abolished segregation in the armed forces and established equal opportunity for blacks.

Powell was never afraid to go straight to the top in addressing pressing issues concerning minorities. If any president (including Truman, Eisenhower, Kennedy, or Johnson) refused to grant him a personal session to discuss civil rights, Powell would make public statements or send embarrassing "open" telegrams to the press describing those The insensitivity of those presidents. describing He said of his tactics, "Whenever a person keeps prodding, keeps them squirming . . . it serves a purpose. It may not in contemporary history look so good, but future historians will say, 'They served a purpose.'"[46] Powell was known to hold Democratic leaders just as accountable as Republicans if he saw unfairness. There were times when he was so disgusted by some Democratic policies that Powell would declare he was going to throw his weight behind a Republican candidate. Just the mere threat that he would endorse one candidate over another could sway the black vote up to thirty percent, indicative of how much power Powell had.[47]

He was keenly aware of the good 'ole boy system that permeated Capitol Hill and the stalwart racial barriers in which he was operating. When renowned black contralto Marian Anderson sang at Eisenhower's inaugural festivities, Powell kissed her hand in front of the crowd. North Carolina Congressman Basil Whitener had taken a southern friend to the event, who said of the gesture, "Well look at that. You don't see that kind of thing back home, a White man kissing a colored woman." "That's no white man," Whitener said. "That's Adam Clayton Powell."[48]

Powell's natural charisma kept him shielded for most of his congressional career, despite his fundamental approach to rid America of its outdated policies. Even Republicans sometimes confessed their fondness and reverence for him. Herbert Brownell, Jr., Sherman Adams, and Maxwell M. Rabb, members of Republican President Dwight D. Eisenhower's cabinet, held Powell in high regard, in spite of Powell's back and forth support and denouncement of Eisenhower. Author Wil Haygood says in *King of the Cats: The Life and Times of Adam Clayton Powell, Jr.*, "Brownell and Rabb, the two members of Eisenhower's administration he knew best, came to realize just why they admired Powell so—he took such gambles, gambles that he made look like sheer gallantry, and he seemed to enjoy life as much as they sometimes enjoyed politics."[49]

U.S. Attorney General Brownell had once been in Germany at Berchtesgaden, Hitler's hideaway. Powell was "the first person I walked into when we were sightseeing," said Brownell. White House Chief of Staff Sherman Adams had been in Germany in 1955, near the Austrian border, in an occupied area. "One of the amenities I was given," he explained, "was the right to catch some fish. I went out to this pond. I was casting. I looked up above this dam, and who do you suppose was sitting there? Powell. He had a bottle." Cabinet Secretary Rabb admitted he enjoyed watching Powell descend the stairs of the Capitol in the evenings. "He had on his camel's hair coat . . . He was feared. He was a power. You knew he was there . . . You couldn't control Adam Clayton Powell."[50]

Representative Adam Clayton Powell, Jr. talks to the press outside the U.S. Capitol after being ousted as Chairman of the Committee on Education and Labor. He called the action a lynching, northern style. *(Source: Bettmann/Corbis/AP Images)*

Powell fishing in Oak Bluffs, Martha's Vineyard, c. 1942. *(Source: Isabel Powell/ Courtesy of the Powell Family)*

Adam and his first wife Isabel Powell, 1934. *(Source: Isabel Powell/Courtesy of the Powell Family)*

Powell being sworn in to the New York City Council by Mayor Fiorella La Guardia in 1942. Also present: mother Mattie Powell, wife Isabel Powell, and father Adam Clayton Powell, Sr. *(Source: Isabel Powell/Courtesy of the Powell Family)*

Adam Clayton Powell, Jr. with second wife Hazel Scott and
son Adam "Skipper", c. 1948 *(Source: James J. Kriegsmann)*

Hazel Scott was an extraordinarily talented jazz musician
and classical pianist, who was given scholarships from the
age of eight to study at Julliard. Scott traveled around the
world captivating audiences. After their divorce, friends
close to the couple described their union as a clash between
two titanic personalities.

With 3rd wife, Yvette Diago Powell, and son Adam IV. in San Juan, 1962. *(Source: Yvette Powell/Courtesy of the Powell Family)*

Congressman Powell's Washington staff, 1962. *(Source: Daniel Crosby)*

Stumping for President Eisenhower at a press conference on October 11, 1956. Powell's declaration to endorse one political candidate over another could sway the black vote up to 30 percent. *(Source: The National Park Service/Dwight D. Eisenhower Presidential Library & Museum)*

President John F. Kennedy hands Powell his pen after signing the Manpower Development and Training Act on March 15, 1962. (*Source: Abbie Rowe, White House Photographs, John F. Kennedy Presidential Library and Museum*)

Powell visits with President Kennedy, Senator Joseph S. Clark, and Congressman Elmer J. Holland in the Oval Office. (*Source: Abbie Rowe, White House Photographs, John F. Kennedy Presidential Library and Museum*)

Powell with President Lyndon B. Johnson (right) at the White House, 1965.
(Source: LBJ Presidential Library)

Adam Clayton Powell Jr. talks with President Johnson in the Oval Office.
(Source: LBJ Presidential Library)

Powell calls a press conference on March 24, 1968 to discuss concerns. His avid lieutenants stand behind him in support. *(Source: Bettmann/Corbis/AP Images)*

Civil rights icons, Adam Clayton Powell, Jr. and Malcolm X. The leaders speak prior to a boycott of New York City public schools. More than 165,000 students attended this anti-segregation protest on March 16, 1964. *(Source: Bettmann/Corbis/AP Images)*

Harlem Congressman Adam Clayton Powell, Jr. addresses a crowd in the Watts section of Los Angeles, January 10, 1968. *(Source: UPI/Bettmann Archive)*

"Keep the faith, baby; spread it gently and walk together, children!" [51]

– Adam Clayton Powell, Jr.

As a twelve-term congressman, Powell's legislative leadership significantly expanded opportunities for blacks in America. He made his greatest contribution as chair of the Education and Labor Committee. This position gave him an enormous amount of power to effect change. Powell and his constituents initiated proposals worth billions of dollars, passed bills that gave blacks access to higher education through the National Defense Education Act, enacted the monumental Anti-Poverty Bill, and increased the minimum wage. [52] These decisions affected millions of Americans, hundreds of schools, employment policies, and labor unions. Powell supervised the passage of social programs such as President Kennedy's "New Frontier" and President Johnson's "Great Society." Under Johnson's administration, almost sixty pieces of major legislation were directly influenced by Adam Clayton Powell, Jr.

"As a member of Congress, I have done nothing more than any other member and, by the grace of God, I intend to do not one bit less." [53]

– Adam Clayton Powell, Jr.

His unapologetic opposition to racism combined with his flamboyant lifestyle eventually proved too unnerving to his racist colleagues. Despite their secret admiration for him and applause for his tenacity, he made them uncomfortable. It was something they were not used to, and so they sought to bring him down. Powell did not behave like most Negro politicians, but he was not in politics to win a popularity contest; his focus was to advance the welfare of his people through the passing of civil rights legislation.

In May of 1958, Powell was indicted for income tax invasion, accused of pocketing congressional employment paychecks to his wife, and taking junkets abroad with female staffers. The trial ended in a hung jury. In 1960, he was sued by a woman who claimed he had falsely accused her of collecting police graft. He was cited for contempt of court in 1966 for refusing to pay damages awarded by the suit. In 1967, the House of Representatives voted to remove Powell from his congressional seat. He was, nevertheless, re-elected in his district in 1968. But rejected by his colleagues in the House, his committee chairmanship and seniority were taken away.

This did not dissuade Powell from any of his positions on civil rights. In the latter 1960s, the Black Power movement emerged with Stokely Carmichael at its helm. Carmichael was the leader of the Student Nonviolent Coordinating Committee (SNCC). Though Powell did not coin the term "black power," he used it on May 29, 1966, during a baccalaureate address at Howard University, saying, "To demand these God-given rights is to seek black power."[54] The speech resonated with many in the community. Soon, internal divisions within the civil rights movement began to emerge among black leaders. Two factions were formed: those who embraced King's nonviolent protests, and those such as Carmichael, who preferred a more aggressive and militant stance.[55] Powell briefly allied with Carmichael and the "new black militants." He defined Black Power as "a new philosophy for the tough, proud young Negroes who categorically refuse to compromise any longer for their rights."[56]

Powell's fight to retain his seat continued and was taken to the U.S. Supreme Court. During this time, Reverend Martin Luther King, Jr. wrote Powell, saying in part:

> For many years you have been a militant champion of justice,
> not only as a Congressman from Harlem, but necessarily as
> a spokesman for disenfranchised millions in the South. You
> are now being assailed with desperate weapons of political
> destruction because you exercised independence and acted with
> militant singleness of purpose . . . I feel the unity of all decent
> thinking Americans is an obligation, when a calloused effort
> is made to single out an individual leader who symbolizes the
> Negroes' determination to realize full equality in every aspect
> of American life . . . While I cannot speak for the leaders of the
> South, nor for all the people, I can assure you that you have my
> wholehearted support.[57]

In 1969, the High Court ruled that the action taken by the House against Powell had been unconstitutional. But by then, Powell's health was failing, and he was defeated in the Democratic primary election of 1970. He thereafter resigned as pastor of Abyssinian Baptist Church and retired to the island of Bimini in the Bahamas. On April 4, 1972, Adam Clayton Powell, Jr. died of prostate cancer at the age of 63, while in Miami, Florida. He was cremated, and his ashes were spread over South Bimini.

Congressman Adam Clayton Powell, Jr. stands amid hundreds of supporters on the steps of the U.S. Capitol on January 10, 1967. Powell addresses the crowd, after being denied his seat in the House of Representatives, pending an investigation. He was ultimately re-seated. *(Source: AP Photo/Charles Tasnadi)*

Robert Purvis was the President of the Underground Railroad. It is estimated that Purvis helped nearly 11,000 slaves obtain freedom. *(Source: Boston Public Library, Rare Books Department)*

3

ROBERT PURVIS
1810–1898

Underground Railroad, Abolitionist

Robert Purvis was "President of the Underground Railroad."[1] He was a giant in the American abolitionist movement. Like Harriet Tubman, the "female Moses," Purvis assisted thousands of fugitive slaves on their perilous journey from bondage to freedom. Records from his personal journal indicate that Purvis helped an average of one runaway slave a day for thirty years. It is estimated that from 1831 to 1861, Purvis helped nearly eleven thousand slaves achieve freedom.[2] He used his large, antebellum house as a station on the Underground Railroad and risked his very life to support this systematic passage to liberty.

The Underground Railroad was not a railroad at all, but rather a network of hidden routes and safe houses from the South to the free North. Fugitive slaves traveled through woods, swamps, rivers, and dirt roads, by foot, boats, trains, and wagons.[3] Slaves were hidden in homes, barns, stables, caves, basements, vaults, attics, secret chambers, root cellars, hay stacks, and churches.

Purvis was a dedicated abolitionist, who allied with powerful, white anti-slavery leaders to generate sympathy in the North and abroad for the eradication of slavery in America. He was president of the highly influential Pennsylvania Anti-Slavery Society and was an active member of the American Anti-Slavery Society. He fought for the rights of free blacks as well as those in bondage. As chair of a seven-man committee, he campaigned to repeal a Pennsylvania law barring free blacks from voting. In 1838, he drafted a powerful protest document called "Appeal of Forty Thousand Citizens, Threatened with Disenfranchisement, to the People of Pennsylvania."[4] Purvis was also a proponent of women's rights, prison reform, and prohibition. He served as the first vice president of the Women's Suffrage Society, founded by famous abolitionist and feminist Lucretia Mott.

His home was a welcomed way station on the Underground Railroad. By the time slaves reached the Purvis house, they had often traveled several hundred miles. Purvis housed fugitive slaves overnight, or longer if necessary. The runaways were hidden in a secret room that could only be accessed via a trapdoor. Some slaves arrived exhausted and near death. Purvis and his wife, Harriet Forten Purvis, were very wealthy and used their means to hire a large staff who were fully attentive to the needs of their guests. Runaways arrived in need of food, water, shelter, rest, and medical attention. In 1837, Purvis founded the Vigilant Association in Philadelphia. The organization provided aid to runaway slaves. The Vigilant Committee was set up as a separate part of the organization in order to elect officials and raise funds "to help colored people in distress."[5] From 1837 to 1844, this group coordinated all slave rescues in the Philadelphia area.

In Still's *Underground Rail Road Records*, William Still describes the extraordinary dedication and sacrifice of Purvis as follows:

> To the cause of the slave's freedom, he [Purvis] gave with all
> his heart, his money, his time, his talents. Fervent in soul,
> eloquent in speech, most gracious in manner, he was a favorite
> on the platform of Anti-slavery meetings. High-toned in moral
> nature, keenly sensitive in all matters pertaining to justice and
> integrity, he was a most valuable coadjutor with the leaders of an
> unpopular reform; and throughout the Anti-slavery conflict, he
> always received, as he always deserved, the highest confidence
> and warm personal regard of his fellow-laborers. His faithful
> labors in aiding fugitive slaves cannot be recorded within the
> limits of this sketch. Throughout that long period of peril to all
> that dared to "remember those in bonds as bound with them," his
> house was a well-known station on the Underground Railroad;
> his horses and carriages and his personal attendants, were ever
> at the service of the [slave] travelers on that road . . . He lived to
> witness the triumph of the great cause to which he devoted his

youth and manhood; to join in the jubilee song of the American slave; and to testify that the work of his life has been one "whose reward is in itself."[6]

Historians believe the Underground Railroad could have begun as early as the 1700s, reaching its peak sometime between 1850 and 1860.[7] It was run by both white and black abolitionists. They strongly believed that all people are created equal and no human should live in bondage. These great men and women would hide, feed, transport, and provide rest and warm shelter to runaway slaves on their journey North. The Underground Railroad was a strong protest against the cruelty of American slavery.

Runaways often traveled hundreds of miles. A strong, healthy slave might have made it to freedom in a few months. For others, especially in bad weather, the trek could have taken over a year. In the years between the American Revolution and the Civil War, it is estimated that as many as one hundred thousand Negro men, women, and children escaped.[8] Moses Grandy, a former slave, described the difficulties that faced runaways. In his 1843 book, *Life of a Slave*, Grandy wrote:

> They hide themselves during the day in the woods and swamps; at night they travel, crossing rivers by swimming, or by boats they may chance to meet with, and passing over hills and meadows which they do not know; in these dangerous journeys they are guided by the north-star, for they only know that the land of freedom is in the north. They subsist on such wild fruit as they can gather, and as they are often very long on their way, they reach the free states almost like skeletons.[9]

Robert Purvis was born free in Charleston, South Carolina, on August 4, 1810. His father, William Purvis, was a wealthy white cotton broker who had come to America from Northumberland in northern England, in 1790. Robert's mother, Harriet Judah, was a mulatto. Harriet's mother was an African named Dido Badaraka. Dido was described as "a very dark-skinned Moor with tightly curled hair," referred to as a "blackamoor." She had been captured from her native land of Morocco at the age of 12 and

Robert Purvis and his wife, Harriet Davy Forten Purvis. Harriet was part of the Forten family, the most powerful black abolitionist family in the United States. The Fortens founded and funded six anti-slavery societies.

James Forten, the father of Harriet Forten Purvis and the head of the Forten Family, was a wealthy abolitionist who used his money towards the eradication of slavery.

sold into slavery in Charleston.[10] After seven years in bondage, Dido was manumitted. She had a son and daughter with Baron Judah, a German Jewish merchant whose family had prospered in Charleston.

Harriet, the daughter of Dido and Baron Judah, married William Purvis. They had three sons: Joseph, William, and Robert. Though Robert was only partially black, his mulatto mother instilled in him an identity as a colored man. Despite suggestions from others to pass as white, Purvis rejected the idea to deny his African heritage.

He recalls as a youth having been with his father and witnessing a slave hiding under a bale of hay, intending to escape. The incident took place when William Purvis had contracted a group of slaves from a nearby plantation to load cotton onboard two of his shipping vessels. Robert asked his father if he was going to tell the owner of the slave, and his father responded, "No," that he did not want to "expose him to a whipping."[11] At the age of nine, Purvis was sent to the Abolition Society's Clarkson School, a private school in Philadelphia, Pennsylvania. Young Purvis showed enormous interest in the crusade against slavery, so his father William provided him with anti-slavery books to read. Purvis later attended Amherst College in Massachusetts.

In 1826, his father died, leaving Purvis and his brothers $250,000—a considerable amount of money for that time. The eldest brother, William, died of tuberculosis not long after, and Robert and Joseph were left to split the estate. Purvis, now a very wealthy man, was determined to use his fortune toward the eradication of slavery. His goal was later confirmed when around 1830 he met and allied with prominent white abolitionists Benjamin Lundy and William Lloyd Garrison. Lundy's paper, *The Genius of Universal Emancipation*, highlighted the works of many abolitionist writers. The paper demanded the immediate release of slaves. Lundy's slogan was "Let Justice Be Done Though the Heavens Should Fall."[12] Garrison's newspaper, *The Liberator*, was also a leading instrument in the fight against slavery. Purvis gave generously to the paper, formed a life-long friendship with Garrison, and traveled throughout the country and abroad with him to raise funds for the anti-slavery cause.

Purvis was described as "a handsome man, six feet tall and graceful, with an erect carriage, dark wavy hair and sideburns, dark eyes, fine brows, high cheekbones, a well-formed mouth and chin, and very light-skinned."

He was "a fine horseman who traveled extensively, usually by horseback or horse and carriage, and sometimes stayed in fashionable places where he was often mistaken for white."[13] American reformer Samuel J. May, who came to know Purvis through the American Anti-Slavery Society, recalled, "He was so nearly white that he was generally taken to be so . . . But rather than forsake his kindred, or try to conceal the secret of his birth, he magnanimously chose to bear the unjust reproach . . ."[14] Reporters who met him speculated that Purvis "had only one-eighth, one-sixteenth or one-thirty-second African blood; but his identification with his grandmother's race was perhaps the strongest element in his sense of identity."[15] Sallie Holley, an abolitionist lecturer who visited Purvis, wrote:

> I am now staying at the elegant country home of Robert Purvis. It may be called "Saints' Rest" for here all the abolitionists find that "the wicked cease from troubling and the weary are at rest". . . Mr. Purvis is a colored man but so light no stranger would suspect it.[16]

On September 13, 1831, Purvis married Harriet Davy Forten, described as "very lady-like in manners and conversation [with] something of the ease and blandness of a Southern lady."[17] She was the daughter of James Forten, the wealthiest black abolitionist in the country, who had amassed a fortune in the sail-making business. The Fortens were dedicated to the anti-slavery movement and had both founded and funded six abolitionist organizations across the United States. They also supported women's rights organizations. In December 1833, the Forten women established the Philadelphia Female Anti-Slavery Society, the first society made up of both black and white women.[18] Notable white members included Elizabeth Cady Stanton, Susan B. Anthony, and Lucretia Mott. Harriet's sister, Sarah Forten, an abolitionist writer, married Robert's brother, Joseph Purvis. Both families gave a lot of their time and money to the American Equal Rights Association and the Pennsylvania State Equal Rights League.

Robert and Harriet purchased a large antebellum home that sat on about one hundred acres of land in Byberry, located in northeast Philadelphia.[19] They redesigned the house with secret rooms, trap doors, and hidden compartments in order to hide runaways. Their sizeable staff provided care

ELIJAH F. PENNYPACKER.
See p. 688

WILLIAM WRIGHT.
See p. 691.

DR. BARTHOLOMEW FUSSELL.
See p. 695.

ROBERT PURVIS.
See p. 711.

STATION MASTERS ON THE ROAD.

The dedication of white abolitionists was essential to the success of the Underground Railroad. Robert Purvis - bottom right. *(Source: Photographs and Prints Division, Schomburg Center for Research in Black Culture, The New York Public Library, Astor, Lenox and Tilden Foundations)*

Robert Purvis. *(Source: Photographs and Prints Division, Schomburg Center for Research in Black Culture, The New York Public Library, Astor, Lenox and Tilden Foundations)*

for the weary slaves, including food, water, clothing, and medicinal salves for open wounds. At times, entire slave families arrived. They were kept as long as was needed for them to eat, bathe, rest, and regain the necessary strength to continue on their journey to freedom. It was custom for slaves to hide out in the woods near a house on the "railroad" station until it was safe. There was often a signal to let the runaways know when it was best to approach.[20]

Purvis spoke briefly to a historian about part of his intricate system for rescuing slaves. He said he had two market women in Baltimore, one white and one black, who would direct slaves to his house. These women had somehow obtained certificates of freedom or "passports," which the slaves used. The passports would later be returned and used over and over again. Purvis also had the loyalty of a slave owner's son in New Bern, North Carolina, who brought runaways to him. There were also two sea captains who shipped wood from New Bern to Philadelphia, who allowed stowaways. Further, he had abolitionists such as Thomas Garrett and Samuel Burris in Delaware and others who transported slaves to his home.[21] The Underground Railroad's survival depended on the dedication of these people, mostly white, throughout the country.

The Purvis mansion was frequently a target of arson attempts by locals, as it was suspected of being a safe haven for fugitive slaves. Huge abolitionist meetings were also held there and strategies were discussed for the rescue of slaves. At times, large mobs would surround his family's home, threatening to kill them.[22] Robert and Harriet had several children; three died young. Their son Charles Burleigh Purvis made history in 1881 as the first physician to provide medical assistance to President James A. Garfield after an assassination attempt in Washington, D.C. Charles was a surgeon and a professor of medicine at Howard University for thirty years. The couple also adopted Harriet's niece, Charlotte Forten Grimké, who became a famous abolitionist poet.

In 1833, Purvis co-founded the Philadelphia Library Company of Colored People. This was the first library for blacks in Philadelphia.[23] That same year, he became fully active in William Lloyd Garrison's American Anti-Slavery Society. His signature is recorded in the society's "Declaration of Sentiments," a testament to his dedication to the eradication of slavery.[24] Purvis opened the first meeting by saying, "I wish to utter a heartfelt thanks to the delegates who have convened for the deliverance of my people."[25] Present at the meeting was poet John G. Whittier. He wrote about this event in his memoirs:

> A young man rose to speak whose appearance at once arrested my attention. I think I never saw a finer face and figure and his manner, words, and bearing were in keeping. "Who is he?" I asked one of the Pennsylvania delegates. "Robert Purvis, of this city, a colored man," was the answer.[26]

Purvis summed up his gratitude to those gathered by saying, "The friends of the colored Americans will be remembered—their exertions and memories will be cherished, when pyramids and monuments shall crumble."

In the spring of 1834, Purvis left for Great Britain upon the urging of Garrison and with the blessing of his wife, who was expecting their second child. His mission was to raise needed funds for the anti-slavery movement. He met with wealthy European abolitionists like George Thompson, Daniel O'Connell, and Sir Thomas Foxwell Buxton, the parliamentary leader of Britain's anti-slavery forces. Purvis also went to rally sentiment against the colonization of Liberia, a growing movement that he vehemently opposed. He stayed in England just long enough to celebrate the emancipation of slaves in the British West Indies on August 1, 1834.[27]

In 1838, Purvis drafted an eighteen-page pamphlet entitled "Appeal of Forty Thousand Citizens, Threatened with Disenfranchisement, to the People of Pennsylvania," which stressed the contributions of Negro citizens to the economic, political, and cultural life of the state and invoked the "no taxation without representation" theme from the Declaration of Independence as precedent in opposing disenfranchisement.[28] Purvis strongly believed that the right to vote for blacks and women should go hand in hand. Despite the vigor and logic of his argument, the appeal failed. But it was widely embraced in anti-slavery circles and cited throughout abolitionist press. Some speculate that its failure was due in part to the longstanding sentiment held by many whites after the Nat Turner slave rebellion in 1831. After this event, many states enacted laws restricting the rights of free blacks.[29]

Purvis served as president of the Pennsylvania Anti-Slavery Society from 1845 to 1850. In 1853, when free Negro children were excluded from Byberry public schools, the wealthy Purvis refused to pay taxes in protest.[30] He asserted publicly that his nonpayment was "a vindication of his rights and personal dignity against an encroachment upon them as contemptibly mean as it was infamously despotic." This courageous act compelled the directors of the public schools to rescind their exclusionary edict, because Purvis paid a large amount of taxes to the county each year.[31]

In the Dred Scott decision of 1857, the United States Supreme Court concluded that no black person, whether free or enslaved, had constitutional rights. Purvis openly denounced the decision, saying that he "owed no allegiance to a government" founded on the proposition that a black man had "no rights a white man was bound to respect."[32] He expressed his disgust in a bold speech made at the 1860 American Anti-Slavery Society saying:

> What is the attitude of your boasting, braggart republic toward the 600,000 free people of color who swell its population and add to its wealth? I have already alluded to the dictum of Judge Taney in the notorious Dred Scott decision. The dictum reveals the animus of the whole government; it is a fair example of the cowardly and malignant spirit that pervades the entire policy of the country. The end of the policy is, undoubtedly, to destroy the colored man, as a man.[33]

This speech, entitled "On American 'Democracy' and the Negro," put forth a withering indictment of the United States government and its failure to extend democracy to blacks, and Purvis delivered the speech on the cusp of the Civil War.[34] Upon the outbreak of the war, Purvis called for widespread enlistment of blacks in the Union Army. He urged President Abraham Lincoln to make emancipation his goal.[35] When the Emancipation Proclamation was issued, only then did Purvis state unequivocally, "I am proud to be an American citizen."[36] Not long after, Purvis was asked by President Andrew Johnson to head the Freedmen's Bureau. But Purvis refused, believing it was a ploy on the part of Johnson to garner black support while attempting to destroy the bureau.[37]

"It is the safeguard of the strongest that he lives under a government which is obliged to respect the voice of the weakest."

– Robert Purvis

On June 11, 1875, Harriet Forten Purvis died of tuberculosis. A few years later, Purvis married Tacy Townsend, a white Quaker abolitionist. In 1883, Purvis presided over the fiftieth anniversary meeting of the American Anti-Slavery Society.

Robert Purvis died of a stroke in Philadelphia on April 15, 1898. The American Negro Historical Society passed a series of accolades on his behalf. *The New York Times* honored Purvis with an eulogistic notice of his death, and the *Washington Bee* editorial stated that Purvis "was one of the few men who deserved to have a monument to his memory."

Gravestone: "Robert Purvis 1810-1898 President of the Underground Railroad." Purvis is buried at the Historic Fair Hill Burial Ground in Philadelphia, PA.

Blanche Kelso Bruce and his wife Josephine Beall Willson
Bruce (below). The Bruces were considered America's First
Black Dynasty. (*Source: Library of Congress Prints and
Photographs Division. Brady-Handy Photograph Collection)*

Josephine Beall Willson Bruce became lady principal of
Tuskegee Institute 1899-1902, after her husband's death.

4   BLANCHE KELSO BRUCE
1841–1898

U.S. Senator, political pioneer

Born a slave, Blanche Kelso Bruce became the first black American to serve a full term in the United States Senate. He served from 1875 to 1881 as the Republican Senator from Mississippi. On February 14, 1879, Bruce presided over the Senate, becoming the first black and the only former slave to do so.[1] As of 2012, he is one of only six blacks to have ever served in the United States Senate. Bruce was also considered for vice president of the United States, receiving eight delegate votes at the 1880 Republican Convention and eleven votes in 1888.[2] He received political appointments under four presidential administrations: Garfield, Arthur, Harrison, and McKinley. In 1881, President James A. Garfield appointed Bruce as the U.S. Register of Treasury. He served in this capacity from 1881–1885, and then again from 1897–1898 under President William McKinley. Hence, this former slave became the first black person to have his name and signature on United States currency.[3]

Bruce was born on a plantation located near Farmville, Virginia on March 1, 1841. His birth name was Branch, but he changed it as a teenager to Blanche.[4] His mother, Polly Bruce, was a slave; and his father, Pettis Perkinson, was her white slave owner. Bruce was the youngest of several children. His father provided for Bruce relatively well, even allowing him to be formally educated by private tutors alongside his white half-brother, William. The two boys were very close. Bruce was highly intelligent and excelled in his studies. But despite favorable treatment by his father, Bruce escaped to Lawrence, Kansas during the Civil War. He attempted to enlist in the Union Army, but his application was denied. Bruce returned to his plantation, but he was not punished. Instead, his father and former slave master manumitted Bruce and sent him to Missouri, where he had arranged for Bruce to acquire a trade.

He studied at Oberlin College in Ohio for two years but could not afford to continue the tuition. Returning to Hannibal, Missouri in 1864, he established the first state school for Negro children. For years, he worked as a steamboat porter on the Mississippi River and saved his earnings. He purchased an abandoned cotton plantation on the Mississippi Delta, in Bolivar County and was eventually able to amass considerable wealth as a planter. Bruce was well-liked by blacks and whites alike and rose quickly in local politics. He was elected sheriff as well as tax collector of the county. He was later appointed conductor of elections by the military governor of Mississippi, Adelbert Ames.[5] When the Republican state board of education appointed him county superintendent of education, Bruce turned the Bolivar County school system into one of the best in the state, creating a segregated but equally funded system. Bruce's efforts were praised by both blacks and whites.

Bruce was described as a tall, heavy-set man, with olive skin and chiseled features. His colleagues admired him for his dignity, elegant manners, and friendly disposition.[6] It was on a trip in 1870 to Jackson, Mississippi that Bruce gained the attention of powerful white Republicans, such as James Lusk Alcorn and Lucius Q. C. Lamar. These well-connected politicians dominated Mississippi's Reconstruction government, and they took a liking to Bruce. They were instrumental in securing him several political appointments, establishing Bruce as the most recognized black politician in the South. This set the stage for his U.S. Senate run. Five years prior to Bruce's election, the Mississippi legislature had sent the Senate its first black member when it elected Hiram Rhodes Revels (sworn in on February 25, 1870). Revels had been the chaplain to an outstanding black regiment in the Union Army. He only served a partial term.[7] Despite being born and raised a slave, Bruce entered the world of white Reconstruction politics with astounding confidence.[8] It had only been twelve years since his manumission when Bruce arrived on the U.S. Senate floor on March 5, 1875. The Senate gallery was packed with spectators to watch the monumental event.[9] According to procedure, the senior Senator from the state of Mississippi, James Alcorn, was supposed to escort Bruce to take his oath of office. But Alcorn denounced political protocol and refused.

As Bruce began walking down the aisle alone, Senator Roscoe Conkling moved to his side ceremoniously. "Excuse me, Mr. Bruce, I did not until this moment see that you were without an escort, permit me. My name is Conkling," he said. He linked his arm with Bruce and completed the journey to the rostrum with him.[9] Bruce would later name his only child after Conkling. He described the day he took his oath in the *National Republican:*

> When I came up to the Senate, I knew no one other than Senator Alcorn, who was my colleague. When the names of the new Senators were called out for them to come out and take the oath, all the others except myself were escorted by their colleagues. Mr. Alcorn made no motion to escort me, but was buried behind a newspaper, and I concluded I would go it alone . . . [Conkling] linked his arm in mine and we marched up to the desk together. I took the oath and then he escorted me back to my seat.[10]

Senator Bruce ultimately gained the respect of many. Senator Lucius Q. C. Lamar of Mississippi described him as "an intelligent man and the best representative of his race in public life."[11] He took on several issues concerning civil rights for all Americans, supporting legislation to combat discrimination against blacks, Native Americans, and Chinese immigrants. He called for the desegregation of the U.S. Army, and fought for fair treatment of black soldiers and veterans.[12] Bruce delivered a speech asking the U.S. War Department to investigate the brutal hazing of black West Point cadet Johnson C. Whittaker. He backed legislation to protect the heirs to the pensions of black Civil War soldiers. In 1879, Bruce submitted a bill to distribute any unclaimed money to five black colleges.[13]

He also debated the Chinese Exclusion Act on the Senate floor. On April 6, 1880, he defended Native American interests against federal management, declaring, "Our Indian policy and administration seem to me to have been inspired and controlled by stern selfishness." Bruce admonished those officials who valued territorial expansion over honoring treaties, saying, "We have in the effort to realize a somewhat intangible ideal, to wit, the preservation of Indian liberty and the administration and exercise of national authority . . . The political system that underlies our

Indian policy . . . is foreign in its character; the individuals and the system of laws are not American."[14] He backed a bill selling federal land to the Ute Indians of Colorado. The bill passed and was approved by President Rutherford Hayes.[15] Bruce introduced legislation that would assist destitute black farmers in Kansas, but it did not pass. He also sought out corruption and fraud in election proceedings, accusing southern Democrats of using deception, intimidation, and violence to stop blacks from voting. He urged the federal government to be more liberal in issuing land grants to blacks. He also made incessant, though ultimately futile attempts, to persuade his fellow senators to seat the former black governor of Louisiana, P.B.S. Pinchback, who had won a seat in both the Senate and the House, but was denied access.

Bruce was assigned to several committees during his term, including the Committee on Manufacturers and the Committee on Education and Labor. During the 45th Congress, he was chairman of the Committee on River Improvements. While serving in this capacity, he established the Mississippi River Improvement Association, a federally funded organization to control river flooding and protect waterfront property through the development of a channel and levee system in the Mississippi Valley.[16]

Because of his personality and good manners, several ladies were vying for his attention in Washington's black elite societies. But on June 24, 1878, Bruce married Josephine Beall Willson, a well-known activist and the first black teacher in Cleveland's public school system. She was the daughter of a prominent dentist (Joseph Willson) and classical pianist (Elizabeth Harnett Willson). Josephine was a favorite in black society pages. Her clothing, elegance, and style were frequently covered in black newspapers around the country. The couple traveled throughout Europe on their four-month honeymoon, before settling in Washington, D.C. Josephine was a linguist and well-versed in American literature and classical music. Their son, Roscoe Conkling Bruce, was born in 1879. He went on to attend the prestigious Phillips Exeter Academy and Harvard University, graduating magna cum laude. From 1902 to 1906, Roscoe served as director of academics at Tuskegee Institute.[17]

The Bruces are often considered the first black American dynasty.[18] The wealthy couple owned two Washington townhouses, a plantation of eight

Blanche Kelso Bruce taken in 1911. *(Source: Photographs and Prints Division, Schomburg Center for Research in Black Culture, The New York Public Library, Astor, Lenox and Tilden Foundations)*

hundred acres in Floreyville, Mississippi, and homes in four states. During Reconstruction, their house was the center for lavish gatherings of both the black and white social elite. They entertained a host of guests, including President Ulysses S. Grant, social reformers Booker T. Washington and Frederick Douglass, and other top Republican politicians. The Bruces were the first black couple to be invited to White House functions. They were frequent guests of President Rutherford B. Hayes.[19] These powerful associations were instrumental in securing Bruce top appointments under four U.S. presidents.

On April 7, 1879, Bruce was appointed chair of a six-member committee to investigate the 1874 collapse of the Freedmen's Savings and Trust Company. The committee uncovered gross incompetency and fraudulent activity on the part of bank officials, and they successfully recovered a portion of the investments made by sixty-one thousand swindled black depositors.

Bruce was well-liked in the Republican Party. At the Republican Convention in Chicago, on the evening of June 8, 1880, eight delegates from the states of Louisiana, Michigan, Wisconsin, and Indiana cast their votes for Bruce for vice president of the United States. Bruce had presided over part of the convention earlier that evening.[20] All but one member of the Mississippi delegation endorsed Bruce for a seat in President James Garfield's cabinet. More delegates wanted to cast their votes, but it appears they could have been talked out of it by Bruce or some of his colleagues.[21] By 1880, the Mississippi legislature had become run by Democrats, and James Z. George was chosen to succeed Bruce.

At the close of Bruce's Senate term on March 3, 1881, President Garfield offered Bruce the post of minister to Brazil, but Bruce declined because slavery was still in existence there. The President attempted to convince Bruce to accept, but he refused in protest. Garfield then hired Bruce as the U.S. Register of Treasury. He became the first black person to ever serve in this position. It was first time a black man's signature appeared on United States currency. He was responsible for the printing of money, minting of coins, and overseeing loans. Bruce served in this capacity from 1881–1885, and then again from 1897–1898 under President William McKinley's administration.[22]

Bruce lectured, wrote magazine articles, and served as superintendent for black achievement at the World's Cotton Exposition in New Orleans in 1884 and 1885. At the Republican Convention in 1888, Bruce once again received votes for vice president, eleven total. He continued to garner political appointments under President Harrison, who appointed him recorder of deeds for the District of Columbia in 1889. He left that position four years later, after receiving an honorary LL.D., and he joined the board of trustees at Howard University.[23]

This former American slave had achieved more than could ever have been imagined. Bruce continued to reside in Washington, D.C. until he succumbed on March 17, 1898 to kidney failure due to complications from diabetes.[24] He is interred at Woodlawn Cemetery in Washington, D.C.

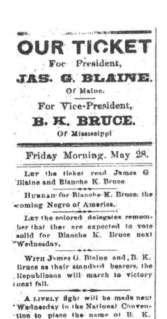

Bruce received 8 votes for Vice President in 1880 and 11 votes in 1888. (*Source: Herald of Kansas, May 28, 1880*)

The Bruce House in Washington, D.C. is a National Historic Landmark. (*Source: Library of Congress*)

Charles W. Chesnutt, in his home library on Lamont Avenue in Cleveland, Ohio, c. 1905.
(Source: Cleveland Public Library, Charles W. Chesnutt Collection)

5

CHARLES W. CHESNUTT
1858–1932

Literary artist, civil rights activist

Charles Waddell Chesnutt was the first nationally recognized black American fiction writer. He earned notoriety for his novels, short stories, and articles during a time when the Negro literary voice was virtually silent. The publication of his works established him as one of the most prominent American fiction writers of the late nineteenth and early twentieth centuries.[1] Chesnutt was a pioneer of racial themes. He boldly addressed issues of slavery and race relations in America, often through the use of satire. Joseph McElrath, Jr. says in *Critical Essays on Charles W. Chesnutt* that Chesnutt was "the first to speak out uncompromisingly, but artistically, on the problems facing his people."[2] His writing, though often controversial, commanded international attention and won widespread critical approval for its artistry.[3] Well-regarded in the literary community, he was a close friend of Ralph Waldo Emerson and Mark Twain, whose seventieth birthday party he attended in 1905.[4] Later in his career, he became an outspoken social and political activist. Chesnutt organized a successful boycott against the racist film *The Birth of a Nation*, leading to the banning of the movie in Cleveland, Ohio. He was highly respected by other black leaders, including Booker T. Washington and W.E.B. Du Bois (who wrote Chesnutt's obituary). In 1928, Chesnutt was awarded the prestigious NAACP Spingarn Award for his literary achievements as "a pioneer novelist, scholar, and writer, who depicted the life and struggles of black Americans." On January 31, 2008, the United States Postal Service honored Charles Waddell Chesnutt with the thirty-first stamp in the Black Heritage Series.

Chesnutt published his first book, *The Conjure Woman*, in 1899. It was a collection of seven stories set in the Cape Fear region of Fayetteville,

North Carolina. Written in southern Negro dialect, the stories are narrated by the character Uncle Julius, a freed slave who entertains a white couple from the North with fantastical tales of plantation life. The stories feature supernatural elements, such as haunting, transfiguration, and conjuring, which were typical of Negro folk tales. While Julius's stories are similar to the Uncle Remus tales published by Joel Chandler Harris, they differ in that they offer oblique or coded commentary on the psychological and social impact of slavery. These entertaining stories are steeped in cultural tradition, including the art of Hoodoo (the American Negro's version of African Voodoo). His accounts include Aunt Peggy's conjure spells in "Mars Jeems's Nightmare," "Po' Sandy," "Sis' Becky's Pickaninny," and "Hot Foot Hannibal," as well as those of free black conjure men in "The Conjurer's Revenge" and "The Gray Wolf's Ha'nt." These superbly written tales reveal moments of active Negro resistance to white oppression, in addition to calculated plots of revenge.[5] This work helped pioneer a literary use of black vernacular culture important to many later writers.

While most writers of his era glorified the Old South, Chesnutt refused to romanticize the slave experience. His works candidly revealed the cruelty of slavery, societal prejudice, and social injustice. He touched upon an array of subjects central to black concerns, such as miscegenation, illegitimacy, passing, and economic advancement. His African ancestry was proudly explored. Yet nationally, his race remained a virtual secret among his early readers.

Despite having primarily Caucasian features, Chesnutt knew that his chances for success in the South were minimal. His mixed racial heritage would continually haunt him. Even as a child, he lamented over the forced estrangement by fellow blacks and spoke frankly about his plight as a Negro who looked white.[6] This entry in Chesnutt's personal journal conveys his opinion about his place in the racist South:

> I occupy here, a position similar to that of Mahomet's Coffin.
> I am neither fish, flesh, nor fowl—neither "nigger," white, nor
> "buckrah." Too "stuck-up" for the colored folks, and, of course,
> not recognized by the whites.

Chesnutt's intimate challenge as a black man who "appeared white" enabled

Charles Waddell Chesnutt at 40. *(Source: Cleveland Public Library, Charles W. Chesnutt Collection)*

Chesnutt, age 16. *(Source: Cleveland Public Library, Charles W. Chesnutt Collection)*

Chesnutt, age 25. This photograph was taken when Chesnutt was the principal of a training school for black teachers. *(Source: Cleveland Public Library, Charles W. Chesnutt Collection)*

Charles Waddell Chesnutt (left) with his younger brother Lewis Chesnutt, c. 1865.
(Source: Cleveland Public Library, Charles W. Chesnutt Collection)

Chesnutt's wife, Susan Perry. *(Source: Cleveland Public Library, Charles W. Chesnutt Collection)*

Chesnutt's youngest daughter, Dorothy, age 3 months. *(Source: Urlin and Beeker, photographers/ Cleveland Public Library, Charles W. Chesnutt Collection)*

Children (L-R): Ethel, Edwin, and Helen.

Daughter, Dorothy Chesnutt, age 7. *(Source: Cleveland Public Library, Charles W. Chesnutt Collection)*

Charles Waddell Chesnutt, c. 1897-1898. *(Source: Cleveland Public Library, Charles W. Chesnutt Collection)*

him to delve into complex issues creating tension between blacks and whites in America. His natural ability to incorporate his unique perspective into his works was welcomed by the mainstream literary community.

In 1899, he published "The Wife of His Youth and Other Stories of the Color Line" in *The Atlantic Monthly*. These essays were a collection of nine stories about a man named Mr. Ryder, the head of the Blue Vein Society, a prestigious social organization made up of fair-skinned blacks. *The House Behind the Cedars* was published in 1900. It examined the psychological and social challenges faced by mixed-race blacks in America and mirrors Chesnutt's own frustration with his life's journey. An incident that took place in his life when he was a young boy appears to have influenced the story line. When Chesnutt was only nine, he saw the lifeless body of a black man lying on the stairs of the Old Market House in Fayetteville. The man had been accused of rape, and his assassins were three white men, who were later acquitted of the murder. It was Chesnutt's awakening to racial injustice in America. The hero in his book recollects an unpunished crime.[7] The novel was praised by influential reviewer William Dean Howells. This helped cement Chesnutt's reputation as a respected novelist. In 1927, the novel was made into a silent movie by famous black director Oscar Micheaux. But many states with white supremacy strongholds like Virginia banned the film, believing it threatened post-war race relations.

Chesnutt's novel *The Marrow of Tradition* was published a year later. It candidly addressed the 1898 Wilmington Race Riot and the violent overthrow of a North Carolina town by white supremacists. Up until now, his readership had consisted largely of white, middle-class readers. Critics, however, felt the plot and characterization of whites was too extreme, so the book was poorly received in some circles. But Eric Sundquist, in his book *To Wake the Nations: Race in the Making of American Literature*, describes the novel as "probably the most astute political–historical novel of its day," both in terms of recounting the massacre and reflecting the complicated social times in which Chesnutt wrote it.[8]

His next novel, *The Colonel's Dream* (1905), was groundbreaking in its storyline, exploring the socioeconomic conditions faced by newly emancipated slaves as seen through the eyes of a Confederate war hero, Colonel French. In 1906, Chesnutt wrote a play in four acts called *Mrs. Darcy's Daughter*. But after failing to find a producer, he put his literary

Chesnutt, age 47. (*Source: Cleveland Public Library, Charles W. Chesnutt Collection*)

career aside for a moment and became active in politics. He wrote articles on race and prepared speeches for other black leaders like Booker T. Washington and W.E.B. Du Bois.

Chesnutt had been born in Cleveland, Ohio on June 20, 1858. He was the son of free Negro parents, Andrew Jackson Chesnutt and Anne Maria Sampson. His parents had migrated to Cleveland from Fayetteville, North Carolina due to racial uprising. Both his parents were of mixed ancestry and white in appearance. The 1850 U.S. Census listed them among the four hundred sixty-five free blacks living in that area. His grandfather, Waddell Cade, had been a white slaveholder and a successful tobacco inspector. Chesnutt was described as having "features that barely distinguished him from whites."[9] Yet, under the one-drop rule, his family was legally and socially black.

Chesnutt was eight when his family returned to Fayetteville, North Carolina. He attended the Howard school, a Negro school established by his father and six other men. Chesnutt worked in his father's grocery store, where he heard the latest political developments and stories of superstition and conjuration. He listened intently. What he learned was later incorporated into his stories and novels. Chesnutt had a sharp ear for the dialect spoken by southern Negroes at that time and captured it perfectly in his works. An exceptional student, he pursued private studies in foreign languages, English classics, music, and stenography. But his family's financial troubles forced him to stop education when he was fourteen. So he started teaching. By age twenty-two, he was the principal of the State Colored Normal School (known today as Fayetteville State University). In 1878, he married Susan Perry, a black teacher, and they had four children. After the birth of their first child, Edwin, Chesnutt began writing newspaper articles but found little compensation. In 1883, he resigned as principal and moved to New York City to become a newspaper reporter. He worked for Dow Jones and Company and also began writing a financial news column for the *New York Mail and Express*. Seeking a better environment for his growing family, he returned to Cleveland, Ohio the following year and got a job in the accounting department of Nickel Plate Railroad Company. In his spare time, Chesnutt wrote articles for *Family Fiction* magazine and studied law. In his personal journal, he wrote:

Chesnutt's house in Cleveland, Ohio. *(Source: Cleveland Public Library, Charles W. Chesnutt Collection)*

In Los Angeles, California, with family, Chesnutt receiving the NAACP Spingarn Medal for literary achievement, 1928. *(Source: Cleveland Public Library, Charles W. Chesnutt Collection)*

Chesnutt was a world traveler. He is seen here at the Bridge of Sighs, Venice, Italy, 1912. *(Source: Cleveland Public Library, Charles W. Chesnutt Collection)*

> I think I must write a book. I am almost afraid to undertake
> a book so early and with so little experience in composition.
> But it has been a cherished dream, and I feel an influence that I
> cannot resist calling me to the task . . . The object of my writing
> would not be so much the elevation of the colored people as
> the elevation of the whites—for I consider the unjust spirit of
> caste which is so insidious as to pervade a whole nation, and so
> powerful as to subject a whole race and all those connected with
> it to scorn and social ostracism—I consider this a barrier to the
> moral progress of the American people: and I would be one of the
> first to head a determined, organized crusade against it.[10]

Very early in his literary career, Chesnutt wrote a short story called "Uncle Peter's House," which was published in the *Cleveland News* and the *Herald*. "The Goophered Grapevine" followed, and it was published in the *Atlantic Monthly* magazine. It explored black resistance and the relationship between slaves and their masters. It was the first literary piece written by a black American to be published in this prestigious magazine.[11] After studying law for some time, he sat for the Ohio Bar Exam in 1887 and passed with the highest score. He joined the law offices of Henderson, Kline, and Tolles; but not long after, he decided to start his own stenography business and law firm. Chesnutt began employing a large number of black attorneys who could not find jobs elsewhere. Feeling overwhelmed with juggling both writing and a law practice, Chesnutt decided to go on a two-month vacation to Europe to put his career goals in perspective. Upon returning, he closed his law firm and began writing full-time.

His works were soon to appear in periodicals around the country, such as *Family Fiction, The Overland Monthly, Puck, The Southern Workman,* and *Youth's Companion*. His writings reflected with raw candor the social nuances of being black. Chesnutt's topic, race relations in America, was delivered through the use of subtle humor and irony, and in a manner that did not alienate white readers. Some inquiry was later made as to why the publishers of his first book did not mention his race. Chesnutt responded, "Indeed, my race was never mentioned by the publishers in announcing or advertising the book. From my own viewpoint it was a personal matter. It never occurred to me to claim any merit because of it, and I have always resented the denial of anything on account of it."[12]

His short story "A Matter of Principle" examined color prejudice within the black middle-class in Cleveland, Ohio. Another short story, "The Passing of Grandison," debunked the myth of the faithful slave servant, revealing that beneath the mask of a docile slave is a wise and crafty individual, much more committed to the welfare of himself and his family than to his master.[13]

Chesnutt's writings are examples of American realism. The maturation of Chesnutt (as a world-class novelist and a voice for the American Negro) can be broken down into three elements: criticism, analysis, and sympathy for the Negro plight.[14] Chesnutt used realist strategies to attack racism and motivate his readers to participate in civil rights reform. In *Chesnutt and Realism: A Study of the Novels*, author Ryan Simmons asserts that "central to Chesnutt's realism is the conviction that understanding reality rightly requires action," thereby denying the mutual exclusivity of realism and political directive.[15]

When asked in 1904 about "the Negro problem," Chesnutt responded, "I should say that it is a continuing problem which assumes some new stage every now and then, and will probably continue to vex us as long as the Negro in this country exists in the public consciousness as something distinct from the ordinary citizen, and whose rights, privileges and opportunities are to be measured by some different standard from that applied to the rest of the community."[16]

Chesnutt focused his later days on civil rights and public protests. The NAACP started a nationwide boycott of the racist film *The Birth of a Nation* (1917), and black leaders in each community were urged to assist.[17] Chesnutt was instrumental in banning the film in Ohio. Chesnutt soon began using articles to promote racial equality. He appeared on the lecture circuit with other nationally known black activists. His political views fell somewhere between those of W. E. B. Du Bois and Booker T. Washington. Thus, he was able to work closely with both of them, publishing numerous short stories and essays for the NAACP's magazine. He was the author of a biography on Frederick Douglass (1899) and was asked to write a chapter in Booker T. Washington's book, *The Negro Problem: A Series of Articles by Representative American Negroes of Today* (1903). Chesnutt's chapter was entitled "The Disenfranchisement of the Negro." In it, he makes a strong argument against strategic moves by southern states to prevent blacks from voting, citing specific civil rights abuses:

> The right of American citizens of African descent, commonly
> called Negroes, to vote upon the same terms as other citizens
> of the United States, is plainly declared and firmly fixed by the
> Constitution . . . This disenfranchisement is accomplished by
> various methods, devised with much transparent ingenuity, the
> effort being in each instance to violate the spirit of the Federal
> Constitution by disfranchising the Negro, while seeming to
> respect its letter by avoiding the mention of race or color.[18]

Chesnutt was an early member of the National Association for the Advancement of Colored People, and he served on its general committee. In a speech he delivered to the Boston Historical and Literary Association in 1905 (later published as an essay entitled "Race Prejudice: Its Causes and Its Cure"), Chesnutt imagined a "stone by stone" dismantling of racial antagonism, which he felt would take place as the black middle class grew larger.[19] He discussed black poverty, chronicled black achievements, and called for blacks to have full rights as citizens. Chesnutt's speech was made fifty-eight years before Martin Luther King, Jr.'s "I Have a Dream" speech, with the following idealistic remarks:

> Looking down the vista of time, I see an epoch in our nation's
> history, not in my time or yours, but in the not so distant future,
> when there shall be in the United States but one people, molded
> by the same culture, swayed by the same patriotic ideals, holding
> their citizenship in such high esteem that for another to share
> it is of itself to entitle him to fraternal regard; when men will
> be esteemed and honored for their character and talents. When
> hand in hand and heart with heart all the people of this nation
> will join to preserve to all and to each of them for all future time,
> that ideal of human liberty which the fathers of the republic set
> out in the Declaration of Independence, which declared that
> all men are created equal, the ideal for which [William Lloyd]

Garrison and [Wendell] Phillips and [Senator Charles] Sumner lived and worked; the ideal for which [Abraham] Lincoln died, the ideal embodied in the words of the Book which the slave mother learned by stealth to read, with slow-moving finger and faltering speech, and which I fear that some of us have forgotten to read at all—the Book which declares that "God is no respecter of persons, and that of one blood hath he made all the nations of the earth."[20]

His last novel, *Baxter's Procrustes*, was published in 1905. Between 1906 and 1932, Chesnutt wrote and published very little, except for a few short stories and essays such as "The Doll" (1912), featured in the NAACP's *The Crisis*. In 1928, he was awarded the NAACP's Spingarn Medal for promoting awareness of the black struggle.[21]

Charles Waddell Chesnutt died at home of arteriosclerosis on November 15, 1932, and he is buried in the beautiful Lake View Cemetery in Cleveland, Ohio. W.E.B. Du Bois wrote Chesnutt's obituary, which was published in *The Crisis* in January 1933. In 2002, the Library of America published a major collection of Chesnutt's works in its American Author Series. On January 31, 2008, the U.S. Postal Service honored Charles Waddell Chesnutt with the thirty-first stamp in the Black Heritage Series.

6

PINCKNEY BENTON STEWART PINCHBACK (P.B.S. PINCHBACK)
1837–1921

Governor, political first

"I am groping about through this American forest of prejudice and proscription, determined to find some form of civilization where all men will be accepted for what they are worth."

— *P.B.S. Pinchback*

Pinckney Benton Stewart Pinchback (P.B.S. Pinchback) was the first black governor of a U.S. state. On December 9, 1872, amid much controversy, he became the twenty-fourth governor of Louisiana. He served as acting governor for thirty-five days.[1] His accomplishments were many. Prior to this historic achievement, he had served as lieutenant governor of Louisiana. Prominent in education, he was on the Louisiana Board of Education. In 1879, he pushed for a black college in Louisiana at the Constitutional Convention, which led to the founding of Southern University, a historically black college still in existence today. He was also a lawyer, the publisher of *The Louisianan* newspaper, a U.S. Marshall, and the only black captain in the Union Army during the American Civil War. After his governorship, Pinchback went on to claim seats in both the U.S. House of Representatives and the U.S. Senate. In his later years, he worked as an Internal Revenue agent and was a member of Southern University's Board of Trustees. By turns a lieutenant governor, a governor, and a senator, Pinchback held more major offices than any other black person in U.S. history.[2]

Pinchback was a radical for most of his life, refusing to succumb to discrimination and segregation. A century before Rosa Parks, Pinchback would sit in the white section of the segregated street cars and refuse to move. It would cause quite a stir, and the conductor would be forced to clear the car of all white people, and Pinchback would ride alone. Once, after being denied service in a saloon, he started a protest against the owner in *The Louisianan*. And in 1874, when his wife was denied a seat on the Jackson Railroad (despite purchasing a ticket), he sued the company.[3] In September of 1868, an assassination attempt was made on his life as he walked down the streets of New Orleans. As author James Haskins notes in his book *Pinckney Benton Stewart Pinchback*, "A turning point came for Pinchback at this time; he would continue to work for his people and for himself, but he would no longer trust any whites, and he would take anything he could get from them."[4]

But perhaps the most astounding facet of P.B.S. Pinchback's life is the fact that prior to his rise to political prominence during the Reconstruction Era, he had been a gambler, a charlatan, a thief, and a jack of all trades. He had even been convicted at the age of twenty-four of assault with attempt to murder and was sentenced to two years in a New Orleans' jail.[5]

Pinchback was born Pinckney Benton Stewart on May 10, 1837 in Macon, Georgia. He did not adopt the surname of Pinchback until later in life. His mother, Eliza Stewart, was a slave. She was of African, Cherokee, Welsh, and German descent.[6] His father, William Pinchback, was her former slave master, who freed Eliza right before Pinchback was born. His parents were in love, but the law prohibited marriages between blacks and whites. Nevertheless, they lived together as husband and wife, and the couple had several children. Pinchback was the youngest of eight.[7]

Not long after he was born, his father purchased a large plantation in Mississippi and moved the family there. His father was a wealthy man who took good care of Pinchback and his siblings. At a young age, Pinchback and his older brother, Napoleon, were sent to Ohio to receive a formal education from Cincinnati's Gilmore School.

In 1848, his father died, leaving behind his common-law wife and children. Because Pinchback's paternal relatives were racists and resentful of his parents' union, they attempted to seize all inheritance left to his mother Eliza. Fearing that her late husband's relatives would also try to legally appropriate her children as slave property, she fled with them to Cincinnati, Ohio. His father's death took a heavy toll on the family. His

P.B.S. Pinchback, first black Governor of a U.S. state. Photograph taken between 1870-1880. (*Source: Library of Congress*)

mother suffered greatly from the possibility of being put back into bondage; and his older brother, Napoleon, became mentally ill, leaving twelve-year-old Pinckney as the sole provider for his mother and siblings.

To support his family, Pinchback worked for many years on gambling boats that traveled the Ohio and Mississippi Rivers. He started off as a cabin boy and worked his way up to a steward. He made eight dollars a month, and sent most of the money back home to his mother and siblings. While he was a servant to several white gamblers, they taught him the tricks of the trade. Pinchback soon became known as a riverboat gambler and skilled swindler. He often got into brawls and even had two known duels to settle a dispute. He was rumored to be a ladies' man and had several female friends. One relationship ended poorly, and the woman's brother stabbed Pinchback. In early May of 1862, Pinchback was again attacked, on the streets of New Orleans by his sister's husband, and a knife fight ensued.[8] Pinchback stabbed his brother-in-law and was arrested. He was sentenced to two years in a prison workhouse, but he only served two months before being released. In the book *Pinckney Benton Stewart Pinchback*, author James Haskins quotes prison records that described Pinchback at the time: "Age, 24; height, 5 ft. 9 1/2 inches; color of hair, black; color of eyes, black; where born, Georgia; education, educated; occupation, laborer; habits, intemperate."

His grandson, writer Jean Toomer, describes him best. Toomer relates that Pinchback did everything "with dash and flair," and that he was "masculine, active, daring, full of energy, vital, never ill, hearty eating, hearty laughing, drink enjoying, able to command, clean, upstanding, forceful, intelligent, well-dressed, well-kept, well-off, noble in bearing, serious, fun-loving, stormy if need be, full of feeling, a grand speaker, a center of influence and attraction, having many friends, much exciting business, and an air of adventure."[9]

The majority of his life, Pinchback found himself in difficult circumstances due to his mixed-race heritage. His appearance was of a white man, which afforded him a substantial education, business opportunities, and financial comforts—benefits generally reserved for whites only. Nevertheless, because Pinchback refused to deny his heritage, he was often subjected to vicious discrimination. Once he was asked which heritage he was more prideful of. Pinchback replied, "I don't think the question is a

HON. PINCKNEY B. S. PINCHBACK,
United States Senator.

Born May, 1837—Educated at Gilmon High School, Cincinnati, Ohio—Captain Co.
A, 2d Regiment, Louisiana Volunteers—Member of Constitutional
Convention of Louisiana—State Senator—Lieutenant-Gover-
nor—Editor and Lawyer—Able as a Statesman,
Eloquent as an Advocate, and Unflinch-
ing in Defense of Equal Justice.

legitimate one, as I have no control over the matter. A man's pride, I regard, as born of his associations, and mine is, perhaps, no exception to the rule." His sister, Adeline B. Saffold, even urged Pinchback to make use of his appearance and pass as white. She advised him in a letter dated April 30, 1863, to strongly consider the option. She wrote:

> If I were you Pink I would not let my ambition die. I would seek to rise and not in that class either but I would take my possession in the world as a white man as you are and let the other go, for be assured of this as the other you will never get your rights. Know this that mobs are constantly breaking out in different parts of the north and even in Canada against the oppressed colored race. Right in Cincinnati they can hardly walk the streets but they are attacked . . . Reuben established his position here as a white man, voted as one and volunteered in the services of his country as one. He was insulted by the negroes here right at the public hotel and called every insulting name . . . I have nothing to do with the negroes—am *not* one of them. Take my advice *dear* brother and do the same.[10]

Pinchback did not take the advice of his sister and was said to have stood up for his race at all times.[11] Author James Haskins says, "P.B.S. Pinchback, or Pinch as he was affectionately called is a one-man answer as to whether or not black people are lazy, shif'less, good-for-nothings without ambition, happy in a subservient position, unreliable, always late and unwilling to fight for their rights."

When the Civil War broke out, Pinchback enrolled to fight on the side of the North, enlisting in a white military company, the First Louisiana Volunteer Infantry. Pinchback began recruiting Negro soldiers for the Union Army, establishing several units of the Corps d'Afrique (African Corps), which were comprised of free blacks and former slaves from the second regiment of the Louisiana Native Guard.[12] Pinchback was the captain, becoming the only Negro officer in the Union Army. But he was denied his commission on the grounds of being a black man; and after being passed over twice for a promotion after what he believed were discriminatory reasons, and suffering enormous humiliations after

The Negro In Our History

THREE SURVIVORS OF THE RECONSTRUCTION

M. W. GIBBS   P. B. S. PINCHBACK   JAMES LEWIS

M. W. Gibbs was municipal judge in Arkansas. P. B. S. Pinchback was elected lieutenant governor of Louisiana, served a short period as acting governor, was elected United States senator, but was not seated. James Lewis was for some years the collector of New Orleans' port.

protesting against racial prejudices toward Negro soldiers, Pinchback found it necessary to resign.[13]

When he was twenty-three, he married Nina Emily Hawthorne, a sixteen year old from Memphis, Tennessee; they later had four children. At the end of the war, the couple moved to Alabama briefly, believing the climate had changed for blacks. But racial tensions had escalated and southern blacks were now under restrictive "Black Codes." Pinchback appeared on public platforms in Alabama, protesting the maltreatment of newly freed slaves.[14] He encouraged blacks to unite politically. White politicians were determined to prevent emancipated slaves from gaining any political voice. It was out of this hostile climate that Pinchback's political career was born. Angered by the many injustices, he became more outspoken against the southern establishment. He moved his family to New Orleans and joined the Republican Party, originally established as an anti-slavery party. Pinchback organized the Fourth Ward Republican Club and served as a delegate to the convention. The convention established a new constitution for Louisiana. After speaking before the assembly, Pinchback was placed on the Republican's central executive committee. In 1867, he ran for Louisiana State Senate. Despite a vigorous campaign, he narrowly lost his bid for the seat. He immediately charged voter fraud. The newly convened legislature agreed with the charge, and Pinchback was permitted to take his oath of office in 1868. He joined a progressive legislature, which already had forty-two representatives of Negro descent (half of the chamber).

He fought hard for Negro rights and was publicly targeted by some of Louisiana's most racist Democrats. He made many bitter enemies and was under constant attack from Democratic newspapers, who believed he was unfit to hold public office. Pinchback argued that if Negroes were citizens, they should be allowed to vote; and if they were not citizens, they should not be drafted. In a speech advocating fair treatment, Pinchback said:

> What would be the result of a man's being refused any of these
> privileges because he was an Irishman, German, Italian, or Jew?
> Nearly every paper in the land would condemn the act. Yet there
> are daily occurrences of outrages of this character perpetrated
> on colored men, and instead of condemnation the act receives

Regular National
REPUBLICAN TICKET
FOR PRESIDENT
Gen. U. S. GRANT
FOR VICE PRESIDENT.
Henry Wilson.

PRESIDENTIAL ELECTORS
— AT LARGE —
M. F. Bonzano, Jules Lanabere, Chas. E. Halstead.

1st DISTRICT	L. C. ROUDANEZ.
2nd "	A. E. JOHNSON.
3rd "	MILTON MORRIS.
4th "	JOSEPH T. TAYLOR.
5th "	JOHN RAY.

STATE TICKET.
— ELECTION, NOVEMBER 4th, 1872. —
For Governor
William Pitt Kellogg.
For Lieutenant Governor
C. C. Antoine.
For Auditor of Public Accounts
Charles Clinton.
Secretary of State
P. G. Deslonde.
Attorney General
A. P. Field.
Superintendent of Public Education
W. G. Brown.
Congress at Large
P. B. S. Pinchback.

HON. P. B. S. PINCHBACK
OF LOUISIANA

Lieutenant-Governor 1871 - 72, and afterward Congressman

applause. It is this that has fostered and perpetuated the prejudice which causes the act and makes the law necessary.

In 1871, Oscar Dunn, Louisiana's lieutenant governor, died suddenly of pneumonia. Dunn, a black physician, had been the first black lieutenant governor of a U.S. state. Upon his death, the Louisiana Governor Henry Clay Warmoth suggested P. B. S. Pinchback as a possible replacement for Dunn, and subsequently Pinchback was elected by a narrow margin. The lieutenant governorship also brought with it the post of president pro tempore of the State Senate. Thus, he had climbed to the second-highest political office in the state of Louisiana, during a time when the political climate was volatile. There had been threats of brutality by the Ku Klux Klan and the Knights of the White Camelia against several Negro politicians, including Pinchback.[15]

At a national convention of black politicians in 1872, Pinchback had a public dispute with Congressman Jeremiah Haralson of Alabama. Congressman James T. Rapier had submitted a motion for convention attendees to denounce any Republican who had opposed President Grant in that year's election.[16] Haralson backed the motion; but Pinchback opposed it because it included Massachusetts Senator Charles Sumner, a well-known anti-slavery crusader.

By the fall of 1872, Louisiana's incumbent governor, Henry Warmoth, was facing impeachment charges. The Customs house senate, a second legislature, had convened. It consisted of mostly Democrats, who had long sought his impeachment. Warmoth called for a special extended legislative session to settle the issue; but on November 21, 1872, a House majority ejected him from his governor's post. He was ordered by law to step down until the conclusion of an investigation. A huge political conundrum developed in which armed thugs were hired to prevent a coup and the removal of the Speaker of the House George W. Carter, a conspirer with several Democrats to remove Warmoth.[17] Warmoth reached out to several, including Pinchback, to unite with him. Pinchback wrote the governor, "I have slept on the proposition you made last night and have resolved to do my duty to my state, party, and race, and I therefore respectfully decline to accept your proposition. I am truly sorry for you, but I cannot help you."[18] As it related to Warmoth's post, Pinchback had been smug in his ambitions, once stating, "I had a good many friends under Warmoth in office and was comfortably housed myself. I concluded that I would drive along with him, until I could get a convenient jumping-off place. I wanted to see what his plans were so as to defeat them."[19]

Warmoth was forced to relinquish his position, and on December 9, 1872, Pinchback became the first black governor in American history. He was to hold the office until the end of Warmoth's term or until a decision was reached on the impeachment charges. Democrats were furious to have a man of African descent in the governor's chair. They challenged the decision. But Louisiana's Supreme Court upheld the legality of Pinchback's ascension. Pinchback served as governor from December 9, 1872 to January 13, 1873, during which time he received death threats and hate mail from around the country. Warmoth himself threatened to use the state militia to regain the office, but President Ulysses S. Grant instructed federal troops to recognize Pinchback's authority, and he assumed control of the state of Louisiana. Charges against Warmoth were later dropped, but Pinchback's short term had made U.S. history.

Pinchback continued his political career, and once again made history when he was elected to the U.S. House of Representatives in 1874 and the U.S. Senate in 1876. His opponents charged that laws had been violated in both elections.[20] Pinchback went to Washington and addressed the Senate, "Sir, I demand simple justice. I am not here as a beggar. I do not care as far as I am personally concerned whether you give me my seat or not. I will go back to my people . . . but I tell you to preserve your own consistency. Do not make fish of me while you make flesh of everybody else."[21] A reporter sketching the Senate at this time described Pinchback respectfully:

> It seems as though the thorn which must rage within him at the sight of the dirty, ignorant men from the South who affect to look down upon him on account of his color, finds play imperceptibly about his lips. His manner is reserved but polite, exhibiting a modesty rarely seen in a successful politician—a model indeed of good breeding to those Texas and Louisiana yahoos who shout "nigger, nigger, nigger," in default of common sense or logic. Mr. Pinchback is the best dressed Southern man we have had in

Congress from the South since the days when gentleman were Democrats.[22]

In 1882, President Chester A. Arthur appointed Pinchback as surveyor of customs in New Orleans. Pinchback began studying law at Straight University (now Dillard University) and passed the Louisiana bar exam in 1886. He moved to New York a few years later and became a U.S. Marshal. He retired some years later in Washington, D.C. Black Nationalist Bruce Grit made the following remarks at the former Louisiana governor's eightieth birthday celebration:

> The equality we seek is not to come to us by gift, but by struggle, not physical but intellectual . . . The civic and political experiences of Governor Pinchback should serve as a guide to our young men in the future and help them to break down the barriers which were set up by designing White men of his own political faith . . . He [Pinchback] is one among the last of the old guard and he has fought a good fight.[23]

Pinchback died on December 21, 1921 in Washington, D.C. and is buried in Metairie Ridge Cemetery in New Orleans. There would not be another black governor of a U.S. state until 1990, when Douglas Wilder became Governor of Virginia.

Harriet Ann Jacobs

7

HARRIET ANN JACOBS
(pen name Linda Brent)
1813-1897

Author, reformer, feminist, abolitionist, relief worker.

"If God has bestowed beauty upon her, it will prove her greatest curse. That which commands admiration in the white woman only hastens the degradation of the female slave." [1]

– Harriet Ann Jacobs

Harriet Ann Jacobs was a writer, reformer, feminist, and abolitionist. Her autobiography, *Incidents in the Life of a Slave Girl*, received worldwide attention because of its explicit account of sexual harassment and the institutionalized rape of female slaves at the hands of their oppressors.[2] This was the first slave narrative ever published that dealt with both sexual and racial oppression. It not only spoke of the devastating effects of this inhumanity on Negro women and their families, but also on white women and their families. Published in 1861 (with the help of prominent white feminists and under the pen name "Linda Brent"), this profound record was instrumental in building Northern empathy towards emancipation. It became one of the most influential books of that period.

"When he told me that I was made for his use, made to obey his command in every thing; that I was nothing but a slave, whose will must and should surrender to his, never before had my puny arm felt half so strong." [3]

– Harriet Ann Jacobs

Harriet Ann Jacobs was born a slave in Edenton, North Carolina in

1813. Like many slaves, the exact date of her birth is unknown. Both of her parents, Elijah and Delilah, were of mixed ancestry. Elijah was a skilled carpenter who was owned by Dr. Andrew Knox.[4] Because of his expertise, he was contracted out to neighboring towns to make money for his slave master. Her mother, Delilah, was a mulatto slave on the plantation of a tavern keeper named John Horniblow. She died in 1819, when Harriet was only six.[5] The child was taken into the home of her mistress, Margaret Horniblow, who taught her how to read, write, and sew. Because Horniblow was openly fond of her, Harriet believed she would set her free one day. But when her mistress died in 1825, she bequeathed Harriet to her five-year old niece, Mary Matilda Norcom. Harriet was now the legal property of this small child and went to live in the Norcom home. The child's father, Dr. James Norcom, became sexually obsessed with Harriet, and Norcom was relentless in his advances. Repeatedly rebuffed, the doctor grew angrier and angrier. She attempted to get married, to escape the hostile environment, but Norcom refused to grant her permission. Harriet states in her autobiography, *Incidents in the Life of a Slave Girl*:

> But I now entered on my fifteenth year—a sad epoch in the life of
> a slave girl. My master, Dr. Flint [Norcom], began to whisper foul
> words in my ear. Young as I was, I could not remain ignorant of
> their import. I tried to treat them with indifference or contempt.
> The master's age, my extreme youth, and the fear that his conduct
> would be reported to my grandmother, made him bear this
> treatment for many months. He was a crafty man, and resorted
> to many means to accomplish his purposes. Sometimes he had
> stormy, terrific ways that made his victims tremble; sometimes
> he assumed a gentleness that he thought must surely subdue.
> Of the two, I preferred his stormy moods, although they left me
> trembling . . . He tried his utmost to corrupt the pure principles
> my grandmother had instilled. He peopled my young mind with
> unclean images, such as only a vile monster could think of. I
> turned from him with disgust and hatred. But he was my master.
> I was compelled to live under the same roof with him—where I
> saw a man forty years my senior daily violating the most sacred
> commandments of nature. He told me I was his property; that I

must be subject to his will in all things. My soul revolted against the mean tyranny. But where could I turn for protection? No matter whether the slave girl be as black as ebony or as fair as her mistress. In either case, there is no shadow of law to protect her from insult, from violence, or even from death; all these are inflicted by fiends who bear the shape of men.[6]

Sometime later, Harriet began a long-term, consensual liaison with Samuel Tredwell Sawyer, a white lawyer, who was an acquaintance of her owner. Sawyer would later become a U.S. congressman. The couple had two children, Joseph and Louisa Matilda. This infuriated Dr. Norcom. Harriet was a slave and as far as he was concerned, she had no choice but to submit to him sexually. Incensed by her continued defiance, his encounters became more and more violent. The brutality was great; but Harriet, who was small in stature, repeatedly fought him off. Bitter at rejection, Dr. Norcom threatened on several occasions to sell her children if she did not submit. Worse yet, his wife, aware of her husband's obsession, endeavored to make Harriet's life a living hell. Her every waking moment was a nightmare. There was no place safe for her in the house of her mistress. Harriet states in her autobiography:

> The mistress, who ought to protect the helpless victim, has no other feelings towards her but those of jealousy and rage. Even the little child, who is accustomed to wait on her mistress and her children, will learn, before she is twelve years old, why it is that her mistress hates such, and such a one among the slaves.[7]

After numerous thwarted attempts at rape, Norcom sent Harriet to work in the fields of another plantation. He wanted Harriet to be broken as punishment. She feared her master would make her children field slaves to further torment her. In 1835, Harriet escaped the plantation and fled to her grandmother Molly's house. Molly had been born a slave. Although Molly was emancipated at the start of the American Revolution, she was later sold back into slavery as a prize of war. Molly was re-emancipated in 1828. Fearing capture and the wrath of Dr. Norcom, Harriet hid in the space below the front porch of Molly's home for six years and eleven months. She hoped that in her absence, Norcom would sell her children to his comrade, Samuel Sawyer, the children's biological father. Sawyer did purchase his two children, set them free, and arranged for their safe passage North, where he had secured employment for them.

The trials of bondage had rendered Harriet immobile with fear. But in 1842, after almost seven years of hiding, Harriet found the fortitude to escape to the North. When she reached Pennsylvania, she was rescued by abolitionist Robert Purvis and his Philadelphia Vigilant Committee. They helped Harriet get to New York.[8] Once there, she obtained a job as a nursemaid for the abolitionist family of Nathaniel Parker Willis, a famous American poet and the highest-paid magazine writer in America at that time, who also worked with Edgar Allen Poe and Henry Wadsworth Longfellow. A record of Harriet's journey through the Underground Railroad can be found in a letter Robert Purvis wrote to journalist Sydney Gay in 1858 (sixteen years after her flight). He recalls Harriet Ann Jacobs and what he could remember of her escape based on her temporary stay in his Philadelphia home:

> She was a beautiful creature, quadroon in blood, just enough
> of Negro admixture to preserve her beauty from the premature
> ugliness of whites in this country . . . In the loft of her Mother's
> hut—a place of a few feet in dimensions—this poor creature was
> confined for seven years . . . Her long confinement had so affected
> her in feelings that she repeatedly expressed to me—a desire to
> return to the little "dark place"—as she called it—in which she
> had been so long immured.[9]

Harriet soon reunited with her daughter, Louisa, who was in New York working as a waiting maid. Harriet's brother, John, was also there and was very connected with Frederick Douglass and his elite circle of activists. They kept watch for some time to make sure Dr. Norcom never arrived in New York. Around 1846, Harriet traveled with her employer and his daughter Imogene to England as the child's caretaker. Harriet found little to no prejudice in England. In 1849, she returned to the states and joined her brother in Rochester, New York, where she became friends with abolitionist Amy Post and her husband Isaac. They introduced Harriet

$100 REWARD

WILL be given for the apprehension and delivery of my Servant Girl HARRIET. She is a light mulatto, 21 years of age, about 5 feet 4 inches high, of a thick and corpulent habit, having on her head a thick covering of black hair that curls naturally, but which can be easily combed straight. She speaks easily and fluently, and has an agreeable carriage and address. Being a good seamstress, she has been accustomed to dress well, has a variety of very fine clothes, made in the prevailing fashion, and will probably appear, if abroad, tricked out in gay and fashionable finery. As this girl absconded from the plantation of my son without any known cause or provocation, it is probable she designs to transport herself to the North.

The above reward, with all reasonable charges, will be given for apprehending her, or securing her in any prison or jail within the U. States.

All persons are hereby forewarned against harboring or entertaining her, or being in any way instrumental in her escape, under the most rigorous penalties of the law.

JAMES NORCOM.

Edenton, N. C. June 30

Runaway slave notice for Harriet Ann Jacobs.

to the anti-slavery movement, and she became very active in that cause. Upon the enactment of the Fugitive Act of 1850, John headed to California with Harriet's son, Joseph, and they worked in the gold mines during the Gold Rush. Harriet headed back to New York City to be with the Willis family. But on February 29, 1852, women abolitionists learned that Daniel Messmore, the husband of Matilda Norcom (Harriet's legal owner) had checked into a New York hotel. Nathaniel's wife, Cornelia Grinnell Willis, sent Harriet to Massachusetts to hide out with some family members and then went to meet Messmore. Willis paid him $300 for Harriet's freedom.[10]

Abolitionist and pioneering feminist Amy Post encouraged Harriet to write her story and to contact famous author Harriet Beecher Stowe for assistance. In 1856, Harriet's daughter, Louisa, became the governess for James and Sara Payson Willis Parton, also known as the writer "Fanny Fern." She was the sister of Nathaniel Parker Willis and the highest-paid newspaper columnist in the country.[11] Harriet wrote her book, *Incidents in the Life of a Slave Girl*, with the support of all these people and in the Willis family's Idlewild estate, which rested on the Hudson River. Her initial accounts were published in the *New York Tribune*.

> *"Reader it is not to awaken sympathy for myself that I am*
> *telling you truthfully what I suffered. I do it to kindle a flame of*
> *compassion in your hearts for my sisters who are still in bondage."*[12]
> – *Harriet Ann Jacobs*

Lydia Maria Child, a famous white feminist and abolitionist writer, agreed to write the preface to Harriet's autobiography. In 1862, Harriet's book was published in England, under a longer title, *The Deeper Wrong, or Incidents in the Life of a Slave Girl*. It contained some of the explicit sexual violations and details about slavery:

> [No] pen can describe—The degradation, the wrongs, the vices
> that grow out of slavery, are more than I can describe. They are
> greater than you would willingly believe. The world of slavery
> is not a world of humanity or of subjective articulation, but a
> world beyond description. It is a world where both slaves and
> slave masters are inhumane; masters because of their cruelty and

inhumanity, slaves because they have been rendered less than human objects.[13]

Harriet's brother John also decided to publish a condensed version of her narrative in England, called *A True Tale of Slavery*, to persuade the English people to back the Union and oppose slavery. Not long after he published it, the Civil War began.

In America, Harriet and Lydia Child targeted their appeal towards middle-class, white Christian women in the North, focusing on the impact of slavery on women's chastity and virtues. Northern Christian women could empathize with the slave woman's station. Harriet speaks of the religious irony when she says of one of the slaveholders, "He boasted the name and standing of a Christian, though Satan never had a truer follower."

There were others like Harriet who were shining a light on slave rape. Mrs. Margaret Douglass, a white southern educator who was jailed for teaching colored children to read, attempted to spur the religious population, statesmen, and lawmakers to stop the raping of female slaves. She speaks of the secret liaisons, concubinage, and the unsanctioned "amalgamation" among the races, calling it "the one great evil hanging over the Southern slave states, destroying domestic happiness and the peace of thousands." In *Educational Laws of Virginia, The Personal Narrative of Mrs. Margaret Douglass*, Douglass speaks of this "acceptable sin" that Harriet and other female slaves suffered through daily. She tells of the pain caused by these heinous acts and the destruction of lives, not only for the slave victim, but also for the wives of the perpetrator, saying:

> It is impossible to deny that amalgamation prevails to a fearful extent throughout the South . . . Neither is it to be found only in the lower order of the white population. It pervades the entire society. Its followers are to be found among all ranks, occupations and professions. The white mothers and daughters have suffered under it for years—have seen their dearest affections trampled on—their hopes of domestic happiness destroyed and their future lives embittered even to agony, by those who should be all in all to them as husbands, sons and brothers . . . every Southern woman. . . their hearts bleed under its knowledge, however

they may have attempted to conceal their discoveries . . . Father
and son seek the same sources of excitement, and alike gratify
their inhuman propensities, scarcely blushing when detected,
and recklessly defying every command of God and every tie
of morality and human affection . . . Is not chastity a natural
instinct, even among the worse savage nations of the earth? Will
not the natural impulses rebel against what becomes with them
a matter of force? The female slave, however fair she may have
become, by various commingling of her progenitors . . . knows
that she is a slave, and, as such, powerless beneath the whims
or fancies of her master. If he casts upon her a desiring eye, she
knows that she must submit. There is no way of escape . . . She
has parents, brothers and sisters, a lover perhaps, all of whom
suffer through and with her . . . [14]

Harriet's revolutionary book was a brave remonstration against the sexual
degradation endured by women in bondage during the antebellum years.
Harriet was determined to fight for her dignity, despite being the property
of Dr. Norcom. She refused to allow him to rape her without a valiant
struggle. Her book empowered both white and black women to stand firm
against unwanted sexual encounters, during a time in American history
when domesticity and submissiveness were expected of all women.

> *"It seems less degrading to give one's self, than to submit to
> compulsion. There is something akin to freedom in having a
> lover who has no control over you, except that which he gains by
> kindness and attachment."*[15]
>
> *– Harriet Ann Jacobs*

During the Civil War, Harriet and her daughter, Louisa, nursed black
troops and helped transport vital contraband. They also assisted with
emergency relief for black refugees, who were crowding behind Union
Army lines. With the help of wealthy abolitionists, Harriet established the
Jacobs Free School for black children in occupied Alexandria, Virginia. In
1868, mother and daughter traveled to London, England to raise funds for
a black children's orphanage and an old folks' home in Savannah, Georgia.

References of their efforts as reformers were noted in the northern press. Harriet later became quite active in the National Association of Colored Women and was appointed to the executive committee of the feminist Women's Loyal National League. After being confronted with increasing anti-black violence in the South, the mother and daughter team retreated to Massachusetts.

Harriet Ann Jacobs died in 1897. She is buried in Mount Auburn Cemetery in Cambridge, Massachusetts. For over a century, there was much speculation about the true author of this great work, *Incidents in the Life of a Slave Girl*. But in 1987, Harriet was named as the author.

In this excerpt from *Incidents in the Life of a Slave Girl*, Harriet describes the psychological torment of a young slave girl, who has been chosen as the sexual target of her master and the object of jealous rage by her mistress:

> Everywhere the years bring to all enough of sin and sorrow; but in slavery the very dawn of life is darkened by these shadows … She [the slave girl] listens to violent outbreaks of jealous passion, and cannot help understanding what is the cause. She will become prematurely knowing in evil things. Soon she will begin to tremble when she hears her master's foot fall … I cannot tell how much I suffered in the presence of these wrongs, nor how I am still pained by them in retrospect. My master met me at every turn, reminding me that I belonged to him, and swearing by heaven and earth that he would compel me to submit to him. If I went out for a breath of fresh air, after a day of unwearied toil, his footsteps dogged me. If I knelt by my mother's grave, his dark shadow fell on me even there. The light heart which nature had given me became heavy with sad forebodings. The other slaves in my master's house noticed the change. Many of them pitied me; but none dared to ask the cause. They had no need to inquire. They knew too well the guilty practices under that roof; and they were aware that to speak of them was an offense that never went unpunished.[16]

8 DANIEL HALE WILLIAMS
1856–1931

Heart surgeon, medical pioneer

Daniel Hale Williams, the first black American cardiologist, performed the first successful open heart surgery. On July 10, 1893, at Chicago's Provident Hospital, he successfully removed a knife from the heart of a stabbing victim. The patient was a black man named James Cornish, who had been injured in a bar fight.[1] After extracting the weapon, Williams sutured the wound to the pericardium, the fluid sac surrounding the myocardium. The patient recovered and lived for several years afterward. While other doctors had attempted open heart surgery prior to Williams (such as Francisco Romero in 1801, Dominique Jean Larrey in 1842, and Henry Dalton in 1891), none had been successful, and the patients had either died during surgery or immediately following from infection or other complications.[2] The success of Williams set a precedent, and subsequent surgeries were modeled after his technique. On January 23, 1891, Williams founded Provident Hospital, the first black-owned hospital and the first non-segregated hospital in the United States.[3] He dedicated his life to improving black healthcare and the training of black doctors and nurses. He also taught clinical surgery at the prestigious Meharry Medical College in Nashville, Tennessee. In 1893, President Grover Cleveland appointed him surgeon-in-chief of the Freedmen's Hospital in Washington, D.C.

Williams was born in Hollidaysburg, Pennsylvania on January 18, 1856.[4] Both of his parents, Daniel Williams, Jr. and Sarah Price Williams, were free Negroes of mixed-race lineage. His paternal grandmother was Scot-Irish, and his paternal grandfather was black. His maternal grandmother lived on the same plantation as abolitionist Frederick Douglass and may have been related to him. Williams was the fifth of seven children.[5] His family owned land rich in iron ore on Brush Mountain. Both parents emphasized education for their children and introduced them to various trades. Following the Civil War, the family moved briefly to Sarah's hometown of Annapolis, Maryland. It was here that his father took ill and died abruptly of tuberculosis when Williams was only nine.[6]

His mother sent her children to live with various relatives. Williams stayed in Baltimore, began an apprenticeship as a shoemaker, and continued his education. But he had to drop out of high school for a while because he was plagued by heavy chest colds. Williams moved in with various cousins, worked various jobs, and finally settled in Janesville, Wisconsin. He became a prolific bass violinist and joined a string band. He also worked in a barber shop that was patronized by local abolitionists. He would listen to them for hours as they argued their cause. A businessman named Orrin Guernsey, who frequented the shop, took an interest in Williams and often brought him books to read from his personal library.[7]

Williams enrolled back in school at Hare's Classical Academy. Upon graduation in 1878, he entered law school briefly but abandoned the idea after only a few months. His interest in medicine emerged soon after, when he went to work as an assistant to a physician named Dr. Henry Palmer, the town's ex-mayor and Surgeon General of Wisconsin.[8] Palmer became like an adopted father to Williams and was benevolent enough to later finance his entire medical training at Chicago Medical College, which is now Northwestern University's Feinberg School of Medicine. Williams graduated in 1883. Because he was black, he was not allowed to work in a hospital, so he started his own medical practice. At that time, there were only four black doctors practicing in Chicago. Medical procedures were quite primitive during this time. Circumstances sometimes called for Williams to treat patients in their homes, including conducting occasional surgeries on kitchen tables.[9] In doing so, Williams used and perfected the emerging antiseptic and sterilization procedures of the day. He focused on infection prevention. It was at the South Side Dispensary in Chicago that he honed his surgical skills.

In 1889, Williams was appointed to the Illinois State Board of Health. In his spare time, he instructed students at Northwestern University, and he worked as the on-staff physician at Protestant Orphan Asylum. Over the years, Williams observed that blacks often got secondhand medical treatment, and he saw that institutionalized racism made it nearly

DR. DANIEL H. WILLIAMS,
Chicago, Ill., Founder of Provident Hospital and Training
School, Chicago; Appointed by President Cleveland as
Surgeon-in-Chief of the Great Freedman's Hospital, Washington, D. C. By his profession
he has amassed a large fortune; as
Physician and Surgeon he has
few equals of any race
or country.

(Source: Photographs and Prints Division, Schomburg Center for Research in Black Culture, The New York Public Library, Astor, Lenox and Tilden Foundations)

Provident Hospital and Training School for Nurses, Chicago.

The first hospital and school established in this country by colored people for their own race. The founder, Dr. D. H. Williams is one of the best surgeons in the country. 100 graduates have gone out from the school.

Daniel Hale Williams was the first black American cardiologist, and the first person in the world to successfully perform open-heart surgery.

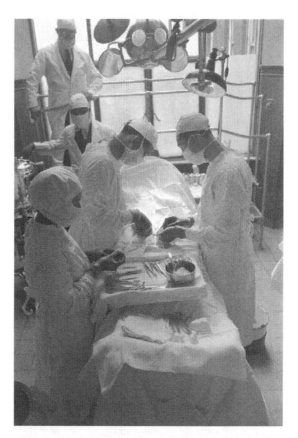

All-black staff performs surgery at Provident Hospital, 1941.
(Source: Library of Congress)

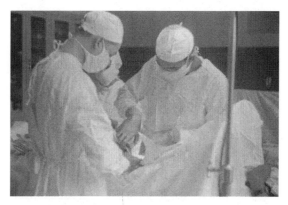

Negro doctors perform a hernia operation at Provident Hospital
in Chicago, Illinois, 1941. *(Source: Library of Congress)*

Daniel Hale Williams established the first Negro nursing school at Provident Hospital. Nurses seen here are in a bacteriology class, March 1942. *(Source: Library of Congress)*

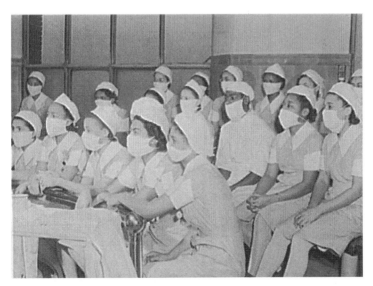

Provident students watch doctors perform a mock operation. *(Source: Library of Congress)*

(Source: Photographs and Prints Division, Schomburg Center for Research in Black Culture, The New York Public Library, Astor, Lenox and Tilden Foundations)

impossible for blacks to get accepted into medical and nursing schools. Williams and a black woman named Emma Reynolds, who had been rejected by every nursing school in the area, started their own hospital.

On January 23, 1891, Williams established Provident Hospital and Training School, a three-story building that held twelve beds and served members of the community. It was the first hospital in the United States owned and operated by blacks. Within its first year, one hundred eighty-nine patients were treated. Of those, one hundred forty-one had a complete recovery, twenty-three had recovered significantly, three had seen a change in their condition, and twenty-two died. That was an 87 percent success rate, unusual for a brand new hospital during that time.[10] Much of the success was attributed to Williams's insistence on the highest standards concerning procedures and sanitary measures. Within the hospital, Williams opened a nursing school, and Reynolds (along with six others) made up the first graduating class.[11] Reynolds later went on to receive her medical degree at Women's Medical College at Northwestern University in 1895.

It was on July 10, 1893, that stabbing victim James Cornish was rushed into Provident Hospital close to death.[12] He had a weak pulse, was in shock, and had lost a tremendous amount of blood. As his condition deteriorated, Williams made the decision to open up Cornish's chest. The surgical team discovered that the man had a pierced blood vessel and a tear to the pericardium tissue surrounding the heart. Williams sutured both of these injuries and effectively stopped the bleeding. This made international news. One newspaper headline reported, "Sewed Up His Heart! Remarkable Surgical Operation on a Colored Man!" Williams was on the front cover of *Time* magazine and was named "Scientist of the Year."[13] James Cornish recovered after fifty-five days and went on to live another twenty years. Williams had performed the first successful open heart surgery.[14]

Williams was also surgeon-in-chief at the Freedmen's Hospital in Washington, D.C. His exceptional organizational skills allowed him to established several different departments within the hospital, each specializing in the treatment of various conditions. Within a short time, Williams had set up surgical, gynecological, obstetrical, dermatological, genitourinary, and throat and chest departments. Two years later, Williams co-founded the National Medical Association for black doctors and became the only black physician in a group of one hundred charter members of the

American College of Surgeons.[15]

In 1898, he married Alice Lee "Darling" Johnson, a school teacher. She was the daughter of famous Jewish sculptor Moses Jacob Ezekiel and a maid of mixed ancestry.[16] Because of his expertise, Williams was frequently invited to speak to medical associations around the country. He spoke primarily on the subject of black healthcare and urged black leaders to establish hospitals in their cities to ensure quality care. He worked at Provident until 1912; and for some time, he was the associate attending surgeon at Saint Luke's Hospital, an all-white hospital in Chicago.

His wife, Alice, died of Parkinson's disease in 1924. Williams retired following a stroke in 1926. He passed away in Idlewild, Michigan, on August 4, 1931. By this time, he had received numerous honors, and he had been awarded honorary degrees from several universities. He established procedural surgical standards that would be implemented for years to come. Williams is mentioned for his extraordinary achievements in musical icon Stevie Wonder's song "Black Man," from the album *Songs in the Key of Life*. In 1970, Congress awarded Dr. Daniel Hale Williams with a commemorative stamp in his honor. His surgical procedures have served as a paradigm, and his pioneering success in cardiology continues to be an inspiration to the medical community.

9

JEAN TOOMER
1894–1967

Harlem Renaissance writer, poet

"Acceptance of prevailing standards often means we have no standards of our own."

– Jean Toomer

Jean Toomer, though not well-known, was possibly the most important figure in the Harlem Renaissance. This era spanned through the 1920s and 1930s and was a cultural flowering also known as the "New Negro Movement." Toomer's book, *Cane* (1923), is credited as giving birth to the movement. The book was a collection of stories, poems, and impressionistic prose sketches about black life in rural Georgia and the urban North. When early Negro writers of the Harlem Renaissance first read *Cane*, in the words of renowned writer Arna Bontemps, "they went quietly mad." No prior literary description of the American Negro experience had reached its level of artistic achievement.[1]

Cane was inspired by Negro folk culture. The stories depicted the Negro experience as marked by frustration and tragedy, but also by a desire for spiritual enlightenment. The work is outstanding in its poetic delivery and evocative images of Southern life and black mysticism.[2] It established Toomer as one of the leading American writers of the 1920s. More importantly, it inspired other towering writers of the Harlem Renaissance. *Cane* became one of the most important seminal works in black artistic and literary expression.[3] It was one of the first times that all Americans were able to intensely identify with the black experience. Leaders like W.E.B. Du Bois and Alain Locke praised Toomer for employing a new way of treating black subjects. American producer Horace Liveright called Toomer "a colored genius." Acclaimed literary critic William Stanley Braithwaite best captured the sentiments held by the literary community at that time:

> Jean Toomer, artist of the race, could write about the Negro without the surrender or the compromise of the artist's vision. He would write just as well about the peasants of Russia or Ireland, had experience given him the knowledge of their existence. *Cane* is a book of gold and Jean Toomer is a bright morning star of a new day of the race in literature. Thus, *Cane* forecasted, by several years, what is now called the Harlem Renaissance and inspired an entire generation of African American writers, beginning with his contemporaries Langston Hughes, Countee Cullen, and Zora Neal Hurston.[4]

But while other artists were raving about his works, Toomer was perhaps his own worst critic. In a letter to famous American writer Waldo Frank, Toomer expressed his frustration about the "Georgia Sketches" in *Cane*, stating that they were "too damn simple."[5] However, some of the anthologized parts of *Cane*, such as the "Song of the Son," "Georgia Dusk," "Karintha," and "Fern" featured a more nostalgic and celebratory aura of the work.[6]

Between 1918 and 1923, Toomer also wrote the short stories "Bona and Paul" and "Withered Skin of Berries," the plays *Natalie Mann* and *Balo*, and poems such as "Five Vignettes," "Skyline," "Poem in C," "Gum," "Banking Coal," "The First American," "Brown River Smile," and "The Blue Meridian." His later works experimented with expressionistic techniques. Expressionism was a style of writing in which the intent was not to reproduce a subject accurately, but rather to portray the subject in such a way as to express the inner state or conflict of the artist. Toomer was a master of expressionism. Distinguished scholar and sociologist Charles S. Johnson says of him:

> Here was triumphantly the Negro artist, detached from propaganda, sensitive only to beauty. Where [Paul Laurence] Dunbar gave to the unnamed Negro peasant a reassuring touch of humanity, Toomer gave to the peasant a passionate charm

Jean Toomer, Harlem Renaissance writer, 1894-1967. (*Source: Photograph of Jean Toomer, undated, Countee Cullen-Harold Jackman Memorial Collection, Atlanta University Center, Robert W. Woodruff Library*)

... More than an artist, he was an experimentalist, and this last
quality has carried him away from what was, perhaps, the most
astonishingly brilliant beginning of any Negro writer of this
generation.[7]

Jean Toomer was born Nathan Eugene Pinchback Toomer on December 26,
1894. He was raised in an upper middle-class black family in Washington,
D.C. His racial heritage was of both African and European descent. Both
of his parents listed themselves on their marriage license as "colored."[8]
His mother was Nina Pinchback Toomer, the daughter of the first black
governor, P. B. S. Pinchback of Louisiana. Toomer's father, Nathan, had
been born a slave. He abandoned his family shortly after the boy's birth,
and Nina and her son went to live with her parents. Toomer described
himself in 1922 as follows:

> Racially, I seem to have (who knows for sure) seven blood
> mixtures: French, Dutch, Welsh, Negro, German, Jewish, and
> Indian. One half of my family is definitely colored. And, I alone,
> as far as I know, have striven for a spiritual fusion analogous to
> the fact of racial intermingling.[9]

Although P. B. S. Pinchback was the primary male figure in his life, Toomer
was careful not to confine himself within the construct of race alone. Rather,
he embraced his individuality and abdicated the labels "white" and "black."
Believing that everyone's physical, emotional, and mental development
was narrowed by society's labeling, he said, "I would liberate myself and
ourselves from the entire machinery of verbal hypnotism ... I am simply of
the human race ... I am of the human nation ... I am of the Earth ... I am of
sex, with male differentiations ... I eliminate the religions. I am religious."[10]
In *The Crock of Problems*, Toomer addresses race and his sense of identity
as a person who was able to live and travel between both worlds. Toomer
says of himself, "I have never lived within the colorline ... Yes I have lived
within the Negro group ... But I have also lived within the white group ..
. And have passed from the one to the other quite naturally, with no loss of
my own identity and integrity ..."[11]

Toomer attended Garnet Elementary, an all-black school. He missed a lot of school due to chronic illness. As a young child, he suffered greatly from stomach ailments. He also showed great strength early on when faced with adversity from other children and even adults. Jean writes in *Wayward and Seeking*, "I had an attitude towards myself that I was superior to wrong-doing and above criticism and reproach . . . I seemed to induce in the grownups, an attitude which made them keep their hands off me; keep, as it were, a respectable distance."[12]

In 1906, Toomer's mother remarried, and the family moved with her new husband to New Rochelle, New York. They resided in a white neighborhood, and Toomer attended a white school for the first time. His mother died three years later, and he returned to Washington, D.C. to live with his maternal grandparents. They enrolled him in Dunbar High School, an exceptional black school, where some of the faculty had graduate degrees. Toomer traveled after high school and studied in six institutions of higher learning in a period of less than four years. And though he attended University of Wisconsin, University of Chicago, City College of New York, New York University, and others, he never earned a degree. Toomer speaks about this part of his character, saying, "I have lived by turn in Washington, New York, Chicago, and Sparta (Georgia) . . . I have worked, it seems to me, at everything: selling papers, delivery boy, soda clerk, salesman, shipyard worker, librarian-assistant, physical director, school teacher, grocery clerk, and God knows what all. Neither the universities of Wisconsin or New York gave me what I wanted, so I quit them."[13]

It was in Chicago that Toomer's interest in literature began. He was particularly interested in the writings of William Shakespeare, George Santayana, Charles Baudelaire, William Blake, Leo Tolstoy, and American writers, especially the imagists. Toomer was influenced by Herman Melville's *Moby Dick* to such a degree that he actually compared himself to the character Ishmael by having "mentally turned failure to triumph." He became enthralled with Victor Hugo's literary character Jean Valjean. He felt "acquainted with" Jean and identified with the character so deeply he began calling himself "Jean" (not Eugene) from that point on.[14]

Around 1919, he wrote three articles: "Ghouls," "Reflections on the Race Riots," and "Americans and Mary Austin" for the *New York Call*. These articles demonstrated his background on political and economic

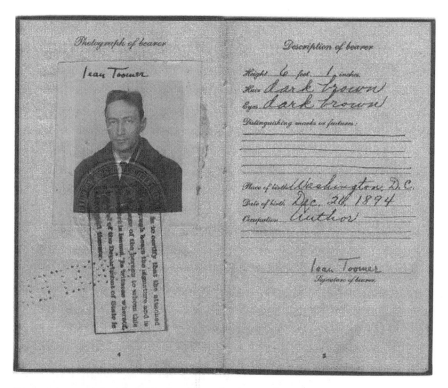

Passport photograph issued to writer Jean Toomer by the United States Government.

thinking, and they remain Toomer's most militant public statements about racial matters in America. In "Reflections on the Race Riots," Toomer prophesies movements of the 1960s, and in "Americans and Mary Austin," he demonstrated his awareness of how prejudice affected race and class. These exceptional articles gave Toomer entry into the social circle of prominent artists such as Waldo Frank, Sherwood Anderson, Kenneth Burke, Hart Crane, Lewis Mumford, Gorham Munson, Georgia O'Keefe, Paul Rosenfeld, Alfred Stieglitz, Margaret Anderson, Rudyard Kipling, Katherine Mansfield, Alexandro Jodorowsky, Peter Brooks, and others.

Toomer and Waldo Frank became very close friends after first meeting at a literary party in New York in 1920, and then again by chance in Central Park, where they talked for hours. The two writers traveled together to the South—both as black men, though Frank was actually a Jewish man with a dark complexion. They shared work, correspondence, thoughts, and intellectual discussions. Unbeknownst to Frank, they even shared his wife, Margaret Naumburg, with whom Toomer had begun an illicit affair. As Frank's marriage began to crumble, Margaret and Toomer began traveling together. She financed Toomer's spiritual quest. As literary critic Gorham Munson said, "All his life he was successful in getting people to support him."[15]

In the 1920s, Toomer joined practitioners of the Gurdjieff system. He was introduced to the system by the editor of the *New Age*, A. R. Orage. George Ivanovich Gurdjieff taught what he said was "the truth found in ancient religions and wisdom teachings relating to self-awareness in people's daily lives and humanity's place in the universe."[16] This process of self-discovery became connected to Toomer for nearly thirty years. Gurdjieff's influence becomes apparent in Toomer's works when he begins using literary forms to inspire human development. Between 1926 and 1931, he publishes *Values and Frictions*, *Gallonwerps*, *Mr. Limp Krok's Famous Ride*, *Transatlantic*, and *Essentials: Definitions and Aphorisms*. The latter was a collection of nearly three hundred aphorisms and definitions largely influenced by Gurdjieff's teachings. The aphorisms are linked together, such as these:

> "I'd rather form a man than form a book."
> "Each of us has in himself a fool who says I am wise."

"Most novices picture themselves as masters and are content with the picture. This is why there are so few masters."
"When I speak, I am persuaded."
"People mistake their limitations for high standards."
"Ordinarily, each person is a cartoon of himself."

Toomer was inspired by one of the aphorisms on the wall of the Prieuré Study House, which read, "You are here having realized that you have only yourself chiefly to contend with. Therefore, thank those who give you the opportunity." Upon reading it, Toomer states:

> The saying took hold of me, found purchase in my very roots; for it crystallized practice that I had engaged in, none too consistently at all, but very earnestly, off and on, ever since that boyhood illness. The new slant was the unmistakable pointing to oneself, the emphasis put on contending with oneself, not with others. The entirely new angle was the allure of actually thanking those who gave us the opportunity . . . Thank everyone who calls out your faults, your anger, your impatience, your egotism; do this consciously, voluntarily . . .[17]

Toomer started a Harlem chapter of Gurdjieff in the spring of 1925, and he began lecturing on the teachings. Many of the Harlem Renaissance artists came to listen to his lectures. Langston Hughes wrote of Toomer in "Gurdjieff in Harlem" (a chapter in the *Big Sea*), "He had an evolved soul and that soul made him feel that nothing mattered not even writing." In 1926, while waiting on a subway, Toomer had an out-of-body experience, which he describes in *Exile to Being*, saying, "My body and my life were in the power of a Power . . . I was losing my life."[18] Finally the Gurdjieff journey led Toomer into isolation from the world. His journey to self-discovery seemed to lead him to understanding and at the same time, to self-doubt. In his final years, Toomer states:

> I do not really know myself, who I am, my selfhood, my spiritual identity, or what I am. I have some information about it, but also some misinformation, some misunderstanding, but much

illusion. Real motivations? What is my aim, assuming that I have but one aim? I do not really know my wife, my child, my closest friends. I do not know anyone or anything.[19]

One of the most well-known women writers of the Harlem Renaissance was Georgia O'Keefe. She became connected with the movement because of her intimate liaison with Jean Toomer and their mutual adoration for spirituality and mysticism. O'Keefe would also become a part of the Gurdjieff group. After being friends for over a decade, they began a love affair around 1933. In a letter to Toomer, O'Keefe writes, "I wish so hotly to feel you hold me very, very tight . . . knowing the feel of your maleness and your laugh." But in 1934, Toomer married Marjorie Content, one of O'Keefe's close friends.[20]

Toomer had been married before. His first marriage was to Marjery Latimer, who died after giving birth to their daughter, Marjery (nicknamed "Argie"). Argie was not informed as a child of any of her racial make-up. And while Toomer never denied his African heritage, he was perplexed by the American fixation on race, as well as the insistence by the literary world to define him in terms of race. "It is clear," he said, "that the world is not going to let me whole-heartedly pursue other interests until I have given it some new facts and creative attitudes towards race."[21] Most of Toomer's writings after *Cane* examined philosophical and psychological problems he saw in Americans.

Author Robert A. Bone, in *The Negro Novel in America*, notes that Toomer participated on equal terms with Gertrude Stein, Ernest Hemingway, Ezra Pound, and T. S. Eliot in the creation of a new, modern idiom during the 1920s. Bone ranks *Cane* with Richard Wright's *Native Son* (1940) and Ralph Ellison's *Invisible Man* (1952).[22] Between 1940 and 1950, Toomer wrote book reviews, essays, stories, novelettes, and poems, such as "The Promise," "They Are Not Missed," "To Gurdjieff Dying," "See the Heart," "Santa Claus Will Not Bring Peace," "The Presence of Love," "Keep the Inward Watch," "Authority," "Inner and Outer," and "Blessing and Curse."

He died on March 30, 1967 in Doylestown, Pennsylvania. Jean Toomer remains an enduring and towering figure in the history and development of black American literary traditions.

Victoria Earle Matthews. *(Source: Photographs and Prints Division, Schomburg Center for Research in Black Culture, The New York Public Library, Astor, Lenox and Tilden Foundations)*

10

VICTORIA EARLE MATTHEWS
1861-1907

Journalist, lecturer, women's advocate, activist, social worker

"And now comes the question, What part shall we women play. . .the ablest intellects of educated colored women, shrinking at no lofty theme, shirking no serious duty, aiming at every possible excellence, and determined to do their part in the future uplifting of the race."

– Victoria Earle Matthews

Victoria Earle Matthews was born a slave in Fort Valley, Georgia on May 27, 1861.[1] She became a writer, journalist, social reformer, civil rights advocate, humanitarian, teacher, and an exceptional lecturer.[2] She served as a surrogate mother and mentor to tens of thousands of young black women after slavery. She inspired women to reach higher despite their circumstances and assisted newly freed black women in their transition from slavery to freedom. She fostered their education and training in skills that allowed them to obtain jobs. Matthews was driven by her belief that the internal devastation suffered by many black women could be converted into external accomplishments.[3]

Matthews started the White Rose Industrial Home for Colored Working Class Girls, also called the White Rose Mission, in 1897. The home was a school and safe haven for poor, downtrodden black girls from the age of three years old and up. The students learned various trades to improve their economic conditions, including domestic work skills: cooking, sewing, and dressmaking. White Rose offered a kindergarten class, job placement, sponsored a visiting district nurse, inaugurated a penny provident program, organized outings to the beach and the circus, and prepared

Thanksgiving and Christmas dinners. The women also received a class in black history that Matthews taught to instill in them a sense of racial pride. She believed self-sufficiency and knowledge of their history would "incite noble thoughts and great ideas."[4] Long before an interest in race literature became common, Matthews was an enthusiast on the subject and placed in the White Rose home a collection of books written by and about Negroes in America, forming, as a white reporter wrote, "One of the most unique special libraries in New York."[5] The books in this library were used by Matthews as a basis for her class on race history. Elegant boarding rooms were available for girls who were homeless.[6] White Rose grew as thousands of girls came to be fed, clothed, sheltered, and guided. Matthews sought to equip each with practical skills for survival and advancement.

Matthews established the home with the conviction that black women were essential to the elevation of the entire Negro race. She strongly believed that these young girls, whose only value in the white world were as maids, could make a difference.[7] As a mentor, she provided them with sound advice, guidance, security, and self-worth. At the end of the school day, Matthews always went outside with the students, who would shower her with love and gratitude before she went home. To them, she was the embodiment of patience, gentleness, and love. She had a positive influence on the lives of countless neglected women, some who were even "walking the streets" for a living. Her organization rescued many girls who had become targets of urban sexual exploitation after migrating from rural areas in the South in hopes of employment opportunities. By 1925, more than 30,000 young women had passed through the doors of White Rose.[8] It was well-organized establishments like White Rose that later influenced the founding of YMCAs.[9]

> *"I shall always feel that the girls will think of the meaning—purity, goodness and virtue and strive to live up to our beautiful name."* [10]
> – *Victoria Earle Matthews*

Matthews was also one of the most active clubwomen and social reformers of the late nineteenth century. In the early 1890s, Matthews, Susan McKinney, and Josephine St. Pierre Ruffin announced plans to form black women's clubs in New York City and Boston.[11] These clubs soon sprang up throughout the United States in major metropolitan cities as well as smaller towns. The groups tackled issues affecting the lives of black women, including suffrage, lynching, education, and occupational advancement.[12] In the fall of 1892, Matthews co-founded the Women's Loyal Union and served as its first president. The organization was initially established to aid Ida B. Wells-Barnett in publishing her account on lynching in the South. The Union's goal was to become a national anti-lynching organization. Working closely with other prominent female leaders, the group presented petitions from fourteen states and Canada in favor of a congressional resolution to investigate lynching. This resulted in Matthews's involvement with the National Federation of Afro-American Women and her appointment as chair of the executive board. Matthews, along with Mary Church Terrell, Josephine St. Pierre Ruffin, and Margaret Murray Washington, would later establish the National Association of Colored Women (1896), a merger of the Federation and the Washington, D.C.-based League of Colored Women. Its purpose was to protect the reputation of black women and improve social conditions within their communities. Matthews became the national organizer, and Terrell served as the first president. By 1916, the NACW had more than a hundred thousand members. It is the oldest black secular organization in existence today.[13]

Matthews was a pioneering journalist who worked for both black and white-owned publications.[14] She was a reporter and regular contributor for several mainstream and Negro newspapers throughout the country, including the *New York Times, Sunday Mercury, New York Herald, Brooklyn Eagle, Boston Advocate, New York Globe, Washington Bee, Richmond Planet, Southern Christian Recorder, Woman's Era, National Leader,* and the *Cleveland Gazette.* She wrote short stories for the *Waverly Magazine* and other publications. She was also the editor for both *Black Belt Diamonds* (a collection of Booker T. Washington's speeches) and *Black Speeches, Addresses, and Talks to Students of Booker T. Washington* (1898).[15]

Her best-known literary work was *Aunt Lindy: A Story Founded on Real Life.* It is a post-Civil War tale about forgiveness, healing, and reconciliation. Aunt Lindy is an ex-slave and nurse who treats a stranger after a fire, unaware at first that it is her former slave master, a man who was cruel to her and had sold all of her children away. Her first thought is to kill him in vengeance; but assuaging her anger, "from the portals of death she brought him, and by healing him, she heals the troubled soul he fostered within her." Her former master provides her with information that leads to the location and ultimate reunion with her eldest son, now a preacher for a local black church; although the rest of her children, she sadly learns, were "sleeping until the morning."[16]

Matthews became increasingly involved in politics and began lecturing on the black struggle. She was particularly interested in the consciousness that left Negroes in psychological bondage. She knew firsthand this plight, as she had been born a slave. As a reformer, she was always aware of both the Negro's desire for equal rights and the consequences of racial activism.

Her exceptional lecturing style bordered on preaching. She can certainly be mentioned alongside other black leaders, such as Frederick Douglass and W.E.B. Du Bois, in shaping nineteenth-century Negro rhetoric. A dynamic orator, she gave passionate deliveries that echoed the verbal patterns of the black pulpit. Matthews often combined cultural rhetoric with scriptural tropes.[17] In 1895, Matthews gave a historic speech entitled, "The Value of Race Literature" at the first National Conference of Colored Women. In the speech, she expressed the importance of literature in challenging racial stereotypes and promoting progress. She encouraged black women to release their "suppressed inner lives" and metaphorically described slavery as a nightmare from which the modern black woman must awake in order to embrace new hope.[18] She also urged them to redeem themselves through domesticity and rallied all women (black and white) to fight for the rights of Negro women. Matthews launched a series of lectures entitled "The Awakening of the Afro-American Woman," which started with an address at the 1897 San Francisco convention of the Society of Christian Endeavor. She stated that it was the responsibility of all Christian women, regardless of color, to join in "elevating the head, the heart, and the soul of Afro-American womanhood."[19] According to the *Washington Post*, Matthews "distinguished herself during the [1896] political campaign by making sound money speeches." She was "the first woman of her race to venture successfully into the financial discussion from a political standpoint."[20]

Matthews was born Victoria Earle Smith to a slave mother named Caroline Smith. Her father was a pitiless slave master. He was so fiercely abusive that as soon as the Civil War began, Caroline escaped and fled for her life to New York, leaving behind Matthews and her siblings. She planned to get enough money to purchase her freedom and that of her children.[21] Around 1869, she returned to Georgia to reunite with her children and pursue custody. Caroline is the first black woman recognized in the Georgia state court system. After receiving legal guardianship, she immediately left with her children and went to Richmond, Virginia and then to Norfolk before settling in New York around 1873.[22]

Matthews was described as "a tall, pale, lanky girl with straight hair and soulful eyes." She was "bright, lovable, gentle and respectful of her elders."[23] She enjoyed devising new games or leading playmates in sports. She was a class leader at school, impressing teachers with precocious questions. As a small child, Matthews was very eccentric and "a lover of woods and fields."[24] She was prone to wander off into the woods on her plantation to commune with the birds and flowers. When her mother would find her, she would explain that she was "listening to nature's teachings." She possessed wisdom beyond her years and would read anything she could get her hands on. Teachers described her as "extremely learned for a colored girl." She was observant of people of all races, pondered injustices in the American system, and voiced her opinions.

When her family moved to New York City, she attended the Grammar 48 School, but the youngster was forced to drop out early to get a job as a maid, in order to help care for her mother and siblings. Her employer had a very large library. She longed to read each book, but she feared the repercussions of touching one, or even asking for permission. One day while dusting the books, she dismissed her fears and opened one. Unconsciously, Matthews slipped into a chair to read and as daylight began to fade, she dropped to the floor near a window. She was so absorbed that she did not hear her employer enter the room. He stumbled over her. A kind man, he felt that any child so eager to learn should be encouraged, and he gave her permission to read any book in his extensive library, whenever time permitted. Matthews would rush to finish her chores early in order to read. She quenched her thirst for knowledge, becoming quite cultured and articulate.[25]

At the age of eighteen, Victoria married William Matthews, a coachman from Petersburg, Virginia. The couple had one child, a son named Larmartine, who died when he was only sixteen. The trauma of his death profoundly affected Matthews, who transformed her grief into vigilance for the social welfare of "other people's boys and girls." She told a reporter for the *New York Sun*:

> Nearly three years ago I lost my only child, a sixteen year old boy, and immediately my heart went out to other people's boys, and girls too, for that matter. I went down to Alabama, visited Tuskegee and several other places, and became much interested in the work that is being done for the colored race in that state. I was being persuaded to go into work there when a minister here wrote, begging me to come back here and start practical work among my people.[26]

In 1897, Matthews started the White Rose Home on the Upper East Side of New York City. As more people began settling in Harlem, the home was moved to a brownstone on West 136th Street.[27] Sharifa Rhodes-Pitts, author of *Harlem is Nowhere: A Journey to the Mecca of Black America*, speaks about the young women who arrived at White Rose:

> Some were well-educated, earnest, of sterling worth, capable and willing to take care of themselves, needing only the advice and encouragement of a good woman. Others were in need of help in many ways. They had no money, no knowledge of the ways of a great city, no friends. They were sheltered, guided, fed, clothed when necessary, many taught to work acceptably in the homes of the Metropolis and many others saved from lives of shame.

To further her missionary work, Matthews secured some much needed assistance from several prominent black pastors with large congregations, such as Reverend Adam Clayton Powell, Sr. of Abyssinian Baptist Church, who became a trustee of the White Rose Mission.[28] Booker T. Washington was also very instrumental in raising funds. It became somewhat of a societal enterprise. In the archives of the White Rose, preserved at the Schomburg Center in New York City, are records of regular garden parties, annual linen showers, "gypsy teas" featuring performances of operettas, and a "tea bag festival" that raised money for general repairs by encouraging invited guests to "drop herein three pennies for every year old."[29]

At a speech for the Hampton Negro Conference (1898), she said:

> The youth of our race . . . will pay with their bright young lives
> . . . for our ignorance, [and] our sinful negligence in watching
> over and protecting our struggling working class . . . Many of the
> dangers confronting our girls from the South in the great cities
> of the North are so perfectly planned, so overwhelming in their
> power to subjugate and destroy . . . Let women and girls become
> enlightened, let them begin to think and stop placing themselves
> voluntarily in the power of strangers.[30]

Matthews spoke regularly before black audiences on the responsibility of self-improvement. She encouraged respect for black women, their work, their struggles, and accomplishments. Matthews was keenly aware of the race and gender issues in the community brought on by racism. She also realized that how blacks defined themselves was greatly influenced by the white power structure. Deeply pensive, Matthews recognized that if the mother of a race was elevated, the entire race would prosper. So, she raised her voice in defense of black women.

She was very concerned about black women who came North in search of employment. Employment agencies went into the rural districts of the South with intriguing stories of New York. Young women were often victimized by procurers and pressured into signing labor contracts, which later led to unscrupulous activities. These black women, who were seeking domestic jobs, were being sent to houses of ill-repute. Matthews established a series of social services from Norfolk to New York to stop this exploitation. She opened the White Rose Travelers' Aid Society, which assigned agents to meet boats at the Old Dominion pier, to insure that inexperienced, young women from the South would not be hoodwinked.

Matthews consistently stressed the need for racial elevation. Like other black reformers, she worried that mainstream society would "take for granted that all black people—all Afro-Americans were naturally low." She strongly believed the black elite had a responsibility to address problems endemic to the black poor and working-class communities.[31]

As her health failed, Matthews passed her duties to her assistants. Victoria Earle Matthews died of tuberculosis at the age of forty-five on March 10, 1907. She is buried in the Maple Grove Cemetery in New York City. At the time of her death, Matthews was one of the most respected black women in the country.[32] Her obituary, published in the *New York Age*, described her as "one of the best-read women in the country . . . a gracious, charming woman, of matchless courage and an indomitable will" and "a leading spirit [in many organizations], spending unstintingly her time and strength for the advancement of the women of the race."[33]

Victoria Earle Matthews. *(Source: Photographs and Prints Division, Schomburg Center for Research in Black Culture, The New York Public Library, Astor, Lenox and Tilden Foundations)*

11

ALEXANDER TWILIGHT
1795–1857

Collegiate pioneer, preacher, educator

Alexander Lucius Twilight was the first black American to receive a college degree. In 1823, he earned a bachelor's degree from Middlebury College in Vermont.[1] He also was the first black person to serve in a state legislature; in 1836, he was elected to the Vermont General Assembly. Twilight was an educator, a minister, and a politician. This pioneer was born in Corinth, Vermont on September 26, 1795.[2] His father, Ichabod, was a free, mixed-race Negro and a veteran of the American Revolutionary War. His mother, Mary, was also born free and was described as "a very fair-skinned mulatto."[3] Twilight was one of six children. He is most recognized for opening colleges and universities to Negro students. He was also ordained in November of 1829 as a congregational preacher by the Presbyterian Church, and he became "acting pastor" of Brownington Congregational Church. He married Mercy Ladd Merrill, who was from a family of some means in Unity, New Hampshire.[4] At the age of thirty-four, he became the principal of the Orleans County Grammar School in Brownington, Vermont, the only high school in a two-county area. In 1836, he built a massive, three-story granite building called the Athenian Hall, originally constructed as a dormitory for the school. It later became Brownington Academy. Today, it is one of the best-preserved institutional buildings of its era in the United States. Twilight died in Brownington, Vermont on June 19, 1857.[5]

TIMOTHY T. FORTUNE.
Editor and Publisher of "New York Age."

Born in Jackson County, Florida, October 6, 1856—Polished and Able—On the Staff of the White Press at Metropolitan Centers—The Most Aggressive and Trenchant Writer of the Negro Press.

(Source: Photographs and Prints Division, Schomburg Center for Research in Black Culture, The New York Public Library, Astor, Lenox and Tilden Foundations)

12

TIMOTHY THOMAS FORTUNE
1856–1928

Militant journalist, national organizer, civil rights activist

"Practically, there is no law in the United States which extends its protecting arm over the black man and his rights ... There is no central or auxiliary authority to which he can appeal for protection. Wherever he turns, he finds the strong arm of constituted authority powerless to protect him." [1]

– Timothy Thomas Fortune

Born a slave in October of 1856 in Marianna, Florida, Timothy Thomas Fortune became the leading Negro journalist of the nineteenth and twentieth centuries.[2] Described as a "militant journalist," he was the owner and editor of three newspapers: the *New York Globe*, the *New York Freeman*, and the *New York Age*. These papers provided a national forum for black people throughout the United States. Known for his fearless and sarcastic journalistic style, Fortune targeted anyone who denied Negroes their full rights as citizens. He waged relentless fights in the press against racist politicians. In 1879, well-known columnist Roi Ottley called Fortune "the dean of black journalism in America." Fortune was the author of more than twenty books and articles, and over three hundred editorials.[3] He is credited with being the first person to coin the term "Afro-American," using it frequently in his columns. In 1890, Fortune founded the National Afro-American League, the first nationwide civil rights organization in the United States and the ideological precursor to the NAACP.

The following excerpt from his book, *Black and White: Land, Labor, and Politics in the South*, was written less than twenty years after slavery was abolished in this country. It is a poignant example of the strong rhetoric and often militant stance Fortune took toward inequality when urging social reform:

> Those who regard the black man in the light of a "ward of the nation," are too narrow-minded, ignorant or ungenerous to deserve my contempt. The people of this country have been made fabulously affluent by legalized robbery of the black man; the coffers of the National Government have overflowed into the channels of subsidy and peculation, enriching sharpers and thieves, with the earnings of slave labor; while nineteen out of every twenty landowners in the South obtained their unjust hold upon the soil by robbing the black man. When the rebellion at last closed, the white people of the South were poor in gold but rich indeed in lands, while the black man was poor in everything, even in manhood, not because of any neglect or improvidence on his part, but because though he labored from the rising to the setting of the sun, he received absolutely nothing for his labor, often being denied adequate food to sustain his physical man and clothing to protect him from the rude inclemency of the weather. He was a bankrupt in purse because the government had robbed him; he was a bankrupt in character, in all the elements of a successful manhood, because the government had placed a premium upon illiteracy and immorality. It was not the individual slave-owner who held the black man in chains; it was the government; for, the government . . . permitted slavery to exist . . .[4]

Fortune was the son of slaves, Emanuel and Sarah Jane Fortune. He was still a boy at the time of Emancipation. His father had learned the rudiments of reading and writing while in bondage, giving him a slight edge over other newly freed Negroes in supporting his family. It was not long before Emanuel became involved in Reconstruction politics. He was so outspoken, he soon became the target of the Ku Klux Klan and sometimes had to flee Florida for months at a time. Nevertheless, he continued to engage in Florida politics. It was not until his closing years that white conservatives grew increasingly hostile toward Emmanuel because of his fundamental

J. Thomas Fortune

Timothy Thomas Fortune, militant journalist, 1902.

fight for racial equality; they sought to purge him from the Republican Party. The threat was so serious, the family had to abandon their home and profitable farmland and move from Marianna to Jacksonville, Florida. Losing everything and having to start a new life took an emotional toll on Fortune's family, especially his mother, Sarah Jane, who died shortly after the move.

Fortune obtained his education through a variety of means, both formal and informal. He attended Staunton Institute briefly, and Howard University. But he was primarily self-educated.[5] In his youth, he attended the Freedmen's Bureau school but spent most of his time working at the *Marianna Courier*, where he learned the printer's trade through observation.[6] At the age of thirteen, Fortune became a page for the Florida state senate. The job allowed him to witness firsthand the political corruption and exploitation of blacks by white politicians. Fortune's distrust for political parties later in life and his attitude toward race relations were largely influenced by his years at the State Capitol. The experience would be the foundation of his successful career in journalism.

His first printing assignment was at the *Jacksonville Daily Times Union*, where he distinguished himself through his workmanship. But the newspaper changed owners, and Fortune found himself unemployed and unable to get work at any other paper because of his color. In 1874, he secured a position as a postal mail agent. His route covered the territory between Jacksonville and the Chattahoochee. Fortune encountered several difficulties on this job because of his race. Like his father, he refused to take a racial insult even from his superior officer; and after a disagreement with the postmaster, he was forced to resign.

In 1875, Fortune was appointed Special Inspector of Customs for the Eastern District of Delaware by Secretary B. H. Bristow. Fortune was offered the position upon the recommendation of William J. Purman, a white congressman from Florida's second district. Fortune was not in the position long before he decided to enter Howard University's law school in 1876. But after only two semesters, he changed his major from law to journalism.

Around this time, he met John Wesley Cromwell, editor of the *People's Advocate*, and worked for him for a while before moving to New York in 1878. He was hired by the *New York Sun*, becoming a respected member of the editorial staff. In 1881, he started his own newspaper, the *New York Globe* (later renamed the *New York Freeman* and finally the *New York Age*). It became the leading Negro journal of opinion and the most widely read black newspaper in the United States. Like other black papers, it was barred from membership in the *Associated Press*. This problem prompted Fortune and Cromwell to call for a convention of black editors and publishers, leading to the establishment of the National Colored Press Association. It was later renamed the National Afro-American Press Association and was largely instrumental in Fortune reaching his apex as a national black spokesperson.[7] Booker T. Washington says in *The Negro in Business*, "His [Fortune's] wide knowledge of conditions in the South has made him a valuable counselor in all movements begun in the interest of the upbuilding of the Negro people. His absolute fearlessness and directness has led him to express his convictions on all subjects with a frankness and vigor that left no uncertainty in regard to his position."

> *"To tell a man he is free when he has neither money nor the opportunity to make it, is simply to mock him. To tell him he has no master when he cannot live except by permission of the man who, under favorable conditions, monopolizes all the land, is to deal in the most tantalizing contradiction of terms."[8]*
> – *Timothy Thomas Fortune*

Fortune's writing style was as distinctive as his manner of speech. Such qualities set him aside from his contemporaries. His high literary standards were essential to his newspaper's success. Seemingly unafraid to speak out on racial matters, his bluntness often sent chills down the spine of the white power base. His position on equal rights was deemed radical by white leaders, but his ideas were widely embraced by blacks throughout the country, and other black leaders rallied behind him. Fortune believed the government had no intention of protecting the rights of blacks, so he began urging black men to "assert their manhood and citizenship." He states in the *Globe*, "We do not counsel violence. We counsel manly retaliation." He was arrested several times for his public outspokenness during organized protests against discrimination. Author Shawn Leigh Alexander says in *T. Thomas Fortune, the Afro-American Agitator*:

The editorship of three prominent black newspapers—the *New York Globe, New York Freeman*, and *New York Age*—provided Fortune with a platform to speak against racism and injustice. For nearly five decades his was one of the most powerful voices in the press. Contemporaries such as Ida B. Wells, W.E.B. Du Bois, and Booker T. Washington considered him an equal, if not a superior, in social and political thought.[9]

In 1884, Fortune published his book, *Black and White: Land, Labor and Politics in the South*, a study which acrimoniously rebuked racism. In it, he states that southern blacks were "more absolutely under the control of the southern whites; they are more systematically robbed of their labor; they are more poorly housed, clothed and fed, than under the slave regime." In discussing the political and industrial problems of southern laborers, he effectually attempts to rally the nation's "common class" to "organization and action." Fortune urges blacks to agitate for their rights, saying, "Let us agitate! Agitate! Agitate! until the protest shall awake the nation from its indifference." He said that to do this would establish the black man as "a new man in black …[who] bears no resemblance to a slave, or a coward, or an ignoramus."[10] This book's rhetoric cemented Fortune's national reputation as a militant civil rights leader. Thus, while he was nationally embraced by blacks, he was widely condemned in the white press as a firebrand.

> *"As an American citizen, I feel it born in my nature to share in the fullest measure all that is American . . . feeling the full force of the fact that while we are classed as Africans, just as the Germans are classed as Germans, we are in all things American citizens . . . We do not ask the American government or people for charity . . . We do not ask any special favor. . . But we do demand impartial justice which is the standard reciprocity between equals."* [11]
>
> *– Timothy Thomas Fortune*

Fortune's 1886 pamphlet *The Negro in Politics* accused the Republican party of treating blacks contemptuously and abandoning black supporters. He openly challenged the dictum of Frederick Douglass that "The Republican Party is the ship. All else is the open sea." Instead, Fortune decreed "Race

1. T. Thomas Fortune, Journalist.   2. Booker T. Washington, Educator.
3. Hon. Frederick Douglass, Statesman.
4. I. Garland Penn, Author, Orator;   5. Miss Ida B. Wells
Chief Commissioner, Atlanta Exposition.   Lecturer, Defender of the Race.

Civil rights activists. (Source: Photographs and Prints Division, Schomburg Center for Research in Black Culture, The New York Public Library, Astor, Lenox and Tilden Foundations) first, then party!"[12] He encouraged freedmen to place their interests before any political party and to stop following leaders who "have swallowed without a grimace every insult to their manhood."

Always promoting black upliftment, Fortune rallied his black readership by asking, "Where is your race pride?— Instead of loving the race," he insisted, "each one of us seeks to get as far away from his African origin as circumstances will permit." He called for blacks to vote intelligently, saying the ballot was their weapon, and they should use it. "The man who possesses the ballot and cringes and fawns upon his equals and spends his days in begging for what is legally his, is a coward who disgraces the dignity of his sovereignty," he declared.[13] Black voters "should cease to be the willing tools of a treacherous and corrupt party . . . cease to be duped by one faction and shot by the other . . . The color of their skin must cease to be an index to their political creed. They must think less of 'the party' and more of themselves; give less heed to a name and more heed to principles," Fortune contended.[14]

He was editor and publisher for the *Washington Sun* for a short while. In 1921, in Memphis, Tennessee, he started a weekly publication called the *Negro Outlook*.[15] Fortune was the chief editorial writer for Marcus Garvey's newspaper, *Negro World*, for several years. He defended Garvey against government charges of stock fraud, and Fortune openly praised Garvey for his skill in securing the allegiance of the masses and the "dramatic element" in Garvey's message.[16]

Fortune also wrote intermittently for the *Norfolk Journal and Guide*, the *Washington Bee*, and *Amsterdam News*. In his article "The Latest Color Line," published both in the *New York Sun* and the *Liberia Bulletin*, Fortune essentially defends the one-drop rule, taking issue with those who seemed to be attempting to create a color caste system in the United States. He begins his critique with a scathing attack on Edward Blyden, a Pan-African Liberian ambassador, who appeared to be stirring dissension within the black race by claiming America's race problem was due more to a conflict between mulattoes and whites, than blacks and whites. Fortune's article cautioned that drawing another color line within the black race would damage the race as a whole. "No friend of the Afro-American race can fail to forget," Fortune said, "that the black and yellow people of the United States will have their problem of manhood further complicated by a color

Timothy Thomas Fortune, national organizer. *(Source: Photographs and Prints Division, Schomburg Center for Research in Black Culture, The New York Public Library, Astor, Lenox and Tilden Foundations)*

line. They have enough trouble as matters stand without borrowing more."[17]

In the early 1880s, Fortune conceived the idea of a national Negro organization to fight for civil and political rights. A few years later, he made mention of it in the May 28, 1887 edition of the *Freeman*, stating in an editorial that there should be an all-black organization modeled after the Irish National League. On January 25, 1890, Fortune put his idea in form and started the National Afro-American League, which focused on civil rights, self-help, and black solidarity. Its mission was to right any wrongs against the American Negro that were authorized and sanction by the federal government. Its objectives were to protect black voters, end lynching, ensure equal distribution of school funds, eradicate chain gangs, convict leases that exploited blacks, end segregation in public transportation, and end discrimination in hotels, inns, and theaters. The league chose to use the term "Afro-American" instead of "black" or "colored" as the name for its constituents. Fortune believed this was the more accurate term for people who were "African in origin, but American by birth."

The league dissolved after four years. It was revived in 1898 by Fortune and A.M.E. Zion Bishop Alexander Walters and renamed the National Afro-American Council. Walters became president of the council, and Fortune was chairman of the executive committee. It provided the first national arena for discussion on issues concerning blacks in America. It attracted support from leaders throughout the country. Heated concerns were the rise in lynchings and disenfranchisement in southern states. The council was designed as an umbrella group, with a large membership, and an executive committee made up of three members from each U.S. state, including one female member from each state.

"The only way to stop it [Southern terror against blacks], is for the colored man to retaliate by the use of the torch and dagger."[18]
– Timothy Thomas Fortune

Later in his career, Fortune formed an unlikely alliance with Booker T. Washington, becoming his good friend and advisor. It was an allegiance that would later cost Fortune national respect as a militant black leader. Booker T. Washington was known as a soft-spoken accommodationist, while Fortune was known throughout the country as a radical agitator. The two were worlds apart in their approach to racial justice, but they had a lot in common. The black community looked to both of them for leadership; they had both been born slaves in the same year; they mutually encouraged the acquisition of land; they both supported women's rights; they both believed education and vocational training would facilitate economic progress and eventually lead to full citizenship rights for Negroes.

Their friendship was quid pro quo. Fortune edited many of Washington's speeches and was the ghostwriter for several books and articles appearing under Washington's name, including *A New Negro for a New Century* and *The Negro in Business*.[19] And because Fortune's newspaper was the most nationally respected and widely distributed black paper in the country, Washington needed Fortune to get his message across to the masses. In turn, Washington provided funding for the publication. Fortune also requested Washington exercise his political influence with President Theodore Roosevelt to secure him an ambassadorship. But all Fortune received was a temporary mission to the Philippines in 1903, as Special Immigrant Agent of the Treasury Department. Upon the end of the term, Washington warned Fortune not to make any politically damaging statements. But Fortune could not hold his peace and openly spoke about the disparaging treatment of the Filipinos by whites.[20]

Fortune became more and more reliant on Washington's financial backing for the circulation of his newspaper and felt obligated to defend Washington publicly against other militants. Soon William Monroe Trotter, W.E.B. Du Bois, and others, who had once seen Fortune as a partner in the black struggle, were now accusing him of being "a mouthpiece for Washington."[21]

His alliance with the more racially compromising Booker T. Washington resulted in his downfall as a reputable reformer. Fortune's personal sullenness in his final years was due to his political decline, which was in large part due to this association. Fortune now butted heads with those of the same vein, his once-avid supporters. Author Emma Lou Thornbrough writes in *T. Thomas Fortune: Militant Journalist* that Fortune was "unable to bend as Washington had, he was broken."

Fortune fell into a deep depression. His marriage to his high school sweetheart, Caroline Smiley, fell apart. His final years were wrought with alcoholism and poverty. In "The Quick and the Dead," an article he published soon after Washington's death, Fortune attempted to assess his own role as a national black leader. He praised his early crusading efforts for civil rights as an editor and founder of the National Afro-American League, attributing his failure to apathy and lack of support in the black community.

Despite his sad end, Fortune had made an indelible mark on the black movement. He pioneered black unity organizations, and his newspapers served as powerful vehicles for black social commentary and black protests, providing solutions to problems facing the race at that time—many of which were still being addressed in the 1970s.

Timothy Thomas Fortune died on June 2, 1928. The Timothy Thomas Fortune House was listed on the National Register of Historic Places on December 8, 1976 and on the New Jersey Register of Historic Places on August 16, 1979.

The following is an excerpt from "Bartow Black," a poem written by Timothy Fortune:

> T'was when the Proclamation came,
> Far in the sixties back,
> He left his lord, and changed his name
> To "Mister Bartow Black."
>
> He learned to think himself a man,
> And privileged, you know,
> To adopt a new and different plan,
> To lay aside the hoe.
>
> He took the lead in politics,
> And handled all the "notes,"
> For he was up to all the tricks
> That gather in the votes;
>
> For when the war came to a close
> And Negroes "took a stand,"
> Young Bartow with the current rose,
> The foremost in command.

His voice upon the "stump" was heard;
He "Yankeedom" did prate;
The "carpet-bagger" he revered;
The Southerner did hate.

He now was greater than the lord
Who used to call him slave,
For he was on the "County Board,"
With every right to rave.

But this amazing run of luck
Was far too good to stand;
And soon the chivalrous "Ku-Klux"
Rose in the Southern land.

Then Bartow got a little note,
T'was very queerly signed,
It simply told him not to vote,
Or be to death resigned.

Young Bartow thought this little game
Was very fine and nice
To bring his courage rare to shame
And knowledge of justice.

"What right have they to think I fear?"
He to himself did say.
"Dare they presume that I do care
How loudly they do bray?

This is my home, and here I die,
Contending for my right!
Then let them come! My colors fly!
I'm ready now to fight!"

– Timothy Thomas Fortune

13

WILLIAM WELLS BROWN
1814-1884

Novelist, playwright, abolitionist lecturer

"It was my great desire, being out of slavery myself, to do what I could for the emancipation of my brethren yet in chains . . ."

– *William Wells Brown*

William Wells Brown was the first black American novelist and playwright.[1] This former slave, with virtually no formal education, became a pioneer in various literary genres, as well as an internationally known author, lecturer, essayist, lyricist, and playwright. He published more than a dozen books, pamphlets, and plays. His novel *Clotel; or, The President's Daughter: A Narrative of Slave Life in the United States* (1853) is regarded as the first full-length novel written and published by a black American.[2] He was still legally a slave at the time of its publication in England. A British couple purchased his freedom in 1854, before he returned to the United States.

Clotel is a story inspired by the purported intimate relationship between Thomas Jefferson and his slave Sally Hemings.[3] Brown fictionalizes the narrative, which describes the perilous antebellum adventures of a young slave named Currer (Sally Hemings) and her mixed-race daughters fathered by Thomas Jefferson and born into slavery. The book includes several subplots relating to other slaves. Currer is described as "a bright mulatto" who gives birth to two "near white" daughters named Clotel and Althesa. They live considerably comfortable lives until Jefferson's death, when they are sold.

Six years prior to *Clotel*, Brown had written his autobiography,

Narrative of William W. Brown, A Fugitive Slave, Written by Himself (1847).
No antislavery work had met with more rapid sale in the United States than
this narrative. The book sold eight thousand copies in eighteen months and
went through four American editions and five British editions before 1850,
earning Brown international fame.[4] Author William L. Andrews says of
Brown's autobiography:

> In popularity, Brown's Narrative rivaled the Narrative written by
> Frederick Douglass two years earlier in 1845. However, the two
> works differed significantly. While Douglass celebrated black
> resistance to slavery and his own rebellion and escape, Brown
> told of the brutal suppression of resistance and rebellion. Brown
> presented himself as a slave trickster, adept at manipulating a
> system designed to oppress him.[5]

Brown was described as "light-complexioned and quick-witted." He spent
his first twenty years mainly in St. Louis, Missouri and its vicinity, working
as a house slave, a field hand, a tavern keeper's assistant, a printer's helper,
an assistant in a medical office, and finally a handyman for James Walker
(a Missouri slave trader with whom Brown made three trips from St. Louis
to the slave ports of New Orleans). Before he escaped from slavery on
New Year's Day in 1834, this unusually well-traveled slave had seen and
experienced slavery from almost every perspective, an education that he
would put to good use throughout his literary career.[6] In the 1840s, he was
a major conductor on the Underground Railroad, transporting fugitive
slaves to Canada, through Lake Erie by steamer.

In 1856, Brown had written his first play, *Experience, or How to Give
a Northern Man a Backbone*, but it was never published. Brown's play *The
Escape, or A Leap for Freedom* (1858) was the first published by a black
American. It was the story of two slaves, Glen and Melinda, who secretly
marry and are determined to gain their freedom, so as not to be torn apart.

Brown was born a slave on November 6, 1816, in Lexington, Kentucky.
According to tradition, his mother, Elizabeth, was the mulatto daughter
of American patriot and famous frontiersman Daniel Boone.[7] Brown had
six other siblings, none of whom had the same father. His father was a
white man named George Higgins, a relative of his slave owner. Higgins

William Wells Brown, 1854.

According to tradition, William Wells Brown
was the biological grandson of American
patriot and frontiersman Daniel Boone, 1835.
(*Source: Library of Congress*)

was aware that Brown was his son and asked his relative not to sell Brown or lend him out for hard labor. But the request was never honored. He was routinely contracted out to work on different plantations, beginning at a very young age.

Brown was born on a plantation that primarily harvested tobacco and hemp. There were about forty slaves, most of whom were field hands. The overseer was Grover Cook, a cruel man who would unvaryingly wake the field slaves up at 4 a.m. every morning by ringing a bell. They were given thirty minutes to eat breakfast and report to the field to begin their daily toil. Any slave who was late automatically received ten lashes. Fortunately for Brown, he was a house slave. They were allowed an extra thirty minutes of sleep, and they were better fed and clothed than the field workers. But his beloved mother was a field slave, so Brown cringed at the sound of the whip issued in the fields. In his youth, he recalls hearing his own mother crying out in the distance, while being whipped by the lash. Powerless to save her, the young man fell to his knees and wept at the front door of his master's house. Brown says of the incident:

> She cried, "Oh! pray—Oh! pray—Oh! pray"—these are generally the words of slaves, when imploring mercy at the hands of their oppressors. I heard her voice, and knew it, and jumped out of my bunk, and went to the door. Though the field was some distance from the house, I could hear every crack of the whip, and every groan and cry of my poor mother. I remained at the door, not daring to venture any further. The cold chills ran over me, and I wept aloud. After giving her ten lashes, the sound of the whip ceased, and I returned to my bed, and found no consolation but in my tears. It was not yet daylight . . . Experience has taught me that nothing can be more heart-rending than for one to see a dear and beloved mother or sister tortured, and to hear their cries, and not be able to render them assistance.[8]

In his teens, Brown was contracted out to the plantation of Mr. Freeland, a gambler and a salacious drunk. He was brutal, had a horrible temper, and was known to hurl chairs and other large objects at his house servants. At times, for his own amusement, he would tie up his servants, hanging them upside down by their feet in the smokehouse and whip them as they gasped for air. This cruel act he called "Virginia Play."[9] After working for Mr. Freeland for several months, Brown could take no more. He says:

> I complained to my master of the treatment which I received from Major Freeland; but it made no difference. He cared nothing about it, so long as he received the money for my labor. After living with Major Freeland five or six months, I ran away, and went into the woods back of the city . . . One day, while in the woods, I heard the barking and howling of dogs, and in a short time they came so near that I knew them to be the bloodhounds . . ."[10]

Brown climbed a tree in an attempt to escape, but the dogs were soon at its base, barking loudly. He was forced down and hung by his wrists to a collar beam and severely whipped to the brink of death. Then Freeland had his son make a fire with tobacco stems and smoked Brown out until his lungs filled up and he was coughing and sneezing.[11] It took him months to recuperate from the ordeal.

The most pleasant of Brown's contracts was as a handyman in the print shop of Elijah P. Lovejoy, a well-known abolitionist and editor of the *St. Louis Times*. Brown later described Lovejoy as a good and humane man. "My work, while with him, was mainly in the printing office, waiting on the hands, working the press, etc. Mr. Lovejoy was a very good man, and decidedly the best master that I had ever had. I am chiefly indebted to him, and to my employment in the printing office, for what little learning I obtained while in slavery."[12]

Brown was then sent to work for a man named James Walker, a speculator who had amassed a large fortune in the slave trade on the ports of New Orleans. Walker would load fifty to sixty slaves on his boat and travel from St. Louis to New Orleans. The slaves were housed in the lower deck. But despite the human cargo being heavily guarded, there were slave escapes when the boat was docked at landing ports. Once the boat arrived in New Orleans, the slaves were placed in a pen, and the strongest slaves were sold first. The remainder were then taken to a public auction and placed on the blocks. Brown was responsible for preparing the older male slaves for auction. Walker demanded Brown cut their hair and pluck out any grey hair. He then had to blacken any remaining hair, a process that made the slaves look ten to fifteen years younger.

To survive slavery, Brown began to morph into a trickster, manipulating the system at times to skirt punishment. In one instance, Brown overfills the wine glasses of Walker's visitors, causing them to spill the contents. The embarrassment enrages Walker, who sends Brown to the Vicksburg jail with a note detailing his prescribed punishment: twenty lashes. But Brown tricks a free man to take the message to the jailer, and he instead is issued the punishment. When the beaten man returns, Brown offers him 50 cents in exchange for the jailer's note, which attests to the given punishment. He takes it back to Walker after wetting his face to fake sweat and tears. Brown later in life expresses his sincere guilt and regret at the hoax that caused another man to suffer, and criticizes the slave institution that "makes its victims lying and mean; for which vices it afterwards reproaches them, and uses them as arguments to prove that they deserve no better fate."[13]

In *Narrative of William W. Brown: A Fugitive Slave*, Brown details his travels with this callous slave trader, even speaking of witnessing infants torn from their mothers by Walker. In one instance, the mother was still breast feeding and could not get her baby to stop crying during their journey to the auction by foot. Walker threatened the mother; but the child, irritated by the hot sun, continued. After a long trek, he put the slaves up at a country inn. The next morning, the child began crying again. Walker grabbed the infant by one arm and offered him to the innkeeper saying, "Madam, I will make you a present of this little nigger, it keeps making such a noise that I can't bear it." The mother flung herself at Walker's feet, crying and pleading with him to give the baby back. Her desperate appeal fell on deaf ears. The infant was left behind, and the mother was shackled to the gang and hauled off, never to see her child again.[14]

Brown tells of a day when droves of slaves boarded the ship headed for the slave market in New Orleans. Among them was a beautiful slave girl, white-skinned, with light, straight hair and blue eyes, bound and prepared for sale. "But it was not the whiteness of her skin that created such a sensation among those who gazed upon her," Brown reveals. "It was her almost unparalleled beauty." The girl, who was no more than twenty years old and obviously a quadroon or an octoroon, sat next to her slave master all the way to the port of New Orleans. Brown recalls the uproar that was caused by her arresting beauty, as white passengers stared at the poor enslaved girl, though they dare not speak to her.[15] He speaks of another incident in which a slave woman, who had been sold away from her husband and children, was so overcome with grief she could not bear it. Somehow she threw off the shackles and flung herself overboard before reaching the Louisiana docks.[16]

Brown's time with Walker was so troubled by his witnessing of unthinkable inhumanities, that he was happy to learn that his slave owner wanted him back. But this joy was short-lived, as he was informed upon returning that his owner was in need of money and planned to sell him, his sister, and two brothers. Because Brown was the blood relative of his slave owner, he was given the courtesy of finding another master of his choice, as opposed to being sold on the public auction block. He set out to the city on this quest, but he was detoured by his desire to locate his recently sold sister. He found her sitting in a room with four other female slaves who had been purchased for one slave owner's own sexual use. Brown was allowed to see her and entered the room. She was so sullen that she did not notice her brother at first. But then she ran to him, threw her arms around his neck, and wept on his chest for some time.[17] She told Brown there was no hope for her, that she would live out the rest of her life as the property of this man. But she made him swear to save their mother and get her to free land. He promised; and after imparting some brotherly advice for the last time, he took off his ring and gave it to her as he bid farewell. Brown says of this agonizing moment, "did ever a fair sister of thine go down to the grave prematurely, if so, perchance thou hast drunk deeply from the cup of sorrow? But how infinitely better it is for a sister 'to go into the silent land' with her honour untarnished and with bright hopes, than for her to be sold to sensual slave-holders."[18]

> "Behind I left the whips and chains, before me were sweet Freedom's plains!"[19]
>
> – William Wells Brown

Brown's next assignment gave him hope that he could one day be free. He was sold to Enoch Price, the captain of a steamboat that traveled the Missouri River. Working as a carriage driver for Price and his wife,

Brown employed his charm on Mrs. Price, who became quite fond of him. To ensure that he would not flee, she became determined to marry Brown to a slave woman, believing he would never abandon a wife. She first attempted to match him with a slave they owned named Maria; but learning his affections were for a slave on a neighboring plantation named Eliza, she purchased her. Brown went along with his mistress's plan, yet never intended to carry it forth. All the while, Brown pretended to detest all free states. The Prices let their guard down and allowed Brown to take a trip on their steamer to Cleveland, Ohio. It was on New Year's Day in 1834 that he seized his opportunity to flee. He stayed on the boat until it reached a Cincinnati dock, then slipped away.

Brown was on his final trek to freedom when he met with inclement weather on the fifth day. The cold rain began falling fast and then froze. His clothes became "one glare of ice."[20] But he traveled on by night through the treacherous wind and freezing rain until he became so cold and his limbs so benumbed that he could not continue. He found shelter in a barn, where he had to pace back and forth for hours in an attempt to raise his body temperature in order to stay alive. Brown says, "Nothing but the providence of God, and that old barn, saved me from freezing to death."[21] He continued his journey for two days straight before developing a cold that settled in his lungs. His feet were frozen for some time before he was unable to walk any further. Brown states in his narrative that he was far more afraid of recapture than of death. He took cover behind logs and brush to recover and wait for a passerby. Brown says, "I thought it probably that I might see some colored person, or, if not, someone who was not a slaveholder; for I had an idea that I should know a slaveholder as far as I could see him."

He saw two men traveling down the road, one with a horse and buggy and the other on horseback. Brown decided not to approach. But he soon saw a third man who was traveling by foot, leading a white horse. He thought that this was the man he had been waiting for. The man asked Brown if he were a slave. Brown responded by asking the stranger if he knew anyone who could help him, as he was sick. The man agreed and asked a second time if he were a slave. When Brown said yes, the stranger cautioned that they were in a very proslavery area; and if Brown would wait, he would go home and return for him with a covered wagon. Brown

agreed and the man traveled out of sight. Brown says, "After he was gone, I meditated whether to wait or not; being apprehensive that he had gone for someone to arrest me. But I finally concluded to remain until he should return."[22] The stranger did not return for almost two hours but came as promised with a two-horse covered wagon and took Brown back to his home where he was nursed and fed by the man and "an old lady." Brown says in the book, *From Fugitive Slave to Free Man: The Autobiographies of William Wells Brown*:

> The only fault I found with them was their being too kind. I had never had a white man treat me as an equal, and the idea of a white lady waiting on me at the table was still worse![23]

After being by the fire for a while, his feet thawed. He then got a high fever and was bedridden. But because he was cared for by the couple, Brown soon regained his strength. He remained with them for twelve to fifteen days, during which time new clothes were made for him and the man bought him a pair of sturdy boots. According to the couple, Brown was about two hundred miles from Cleveland, which was on Lake Erie. He had to get to the lake to catch a steamer to Canada. When his benevolent caretaker asked for his name, he had only one: William. "Since thee has got out of slavery, thee has become a man, and men always have two names," said the man, whose name was Wells Brown. He gave William his name, which William placed behind his own, and from that day on he referred to himself as William Wells Brown.[24] In his narrative, Brown speaks about a slave's given name, the circumstance of illegitimacy, and the discomfort of carrying the name of a slave master, saying:

> But I always detested the idea of being called by the name of either of my masters. And as for my father, I would rather have adopted the name of "Friday," and been known as some servant of Robinson Crusoe, than to have taken his name. So I was not only hunting for my liberty; but also hunting for a name; though I regarded the latter as of little consequence, if I could but gain the former.[25]

Brown continued his arduous journey with little money and limited food and water. He traveled for four days. After going a couple of days or more without food, he could go no longer and decided to approach a house to beg. A man answered and turned Brown away, but the wife intervened and insisted on helping. She boldly pushed her husband aside and made Brown a large meal, at which point he stuffs himself, providing plenty of nourishment to continue. This moment, he later says, impassioned him towards women's rights. The woman gave him ten cents and a note to take to a friend of hers that was some miles down the road. Brown pushed on, and in three days, he was in Cleveland; but, he still desired to reach Canada. The only problem was Lake Eerie was frozen, and navigation was temporarily suspended. It was here that Brown saw his first anti-slavery newspaper: *The Genius of Universal Emancipation*, by Benjamin Lundy.

Brown got a job in Cleveland at the Mansion House as a waiter and stayed on until the spring when his boss secured a job for him on a steamer making twelve dollars a month. Brown soon began transporting fugitive slaves, hiding as many as he could conceal aboard the vessel and insuring their safe passage to Canada.[26] It was not long before he became the primary conductor on the Underground Railroad for the Lake Erie region. Between May and December of 1842, Brown carried sixty-nine fugitives to Canada. On a trip to southern Ontario in 1843, Brown was fortunate enough to renew his acquaintance with many of the men, women, and children he had helped to freedom. He was visiting the village of Malden, in Upper Canada, where he saw seventeen of his former passengers.[27]

Brown's narrative tells of several instances where his cleverness had to be employed to save runaways from recapture. In one case, a dark-skinned male fugitive had made his way to freedom, but he was still being relentlessly pursued by his former slave owner. The claimant and his coadjutors followed the fugitive all the way to the home of a Cleveland abolitionist. They staked out the house, waiting for the slave to emerge. They even set up lookout posts at all the Cleveland ports for days, making it nearly impossible for the man to escape. In this emergency, Brown secured the assistance of a local painter. "In an hour, by my directions, the black man was as white, and with as rosy cheeks, as any of the Anglo-Saxon race, and disguised in the dress of a woman, with a thick veil over her face," says

Brown. He was able to hoodwink the man's prospective captors and place him on the steamer to Canada without being recognized.[28]

Brown met, wooed, and married Elizabeth "Betsey" Schooner. The couple had two daughters, Clarissa and Josephine. During the summer of 1836, Brown moved his family to Buffalo, New York, because it was the terminus for the steamboat line and therefore more reasonable for him to live there. Buffalo had a large, close-knit Negro population. During the off-seasons on the steamer, he could find other employment with relative ease.

Shortly after Brown settled in Buffalo, slave catchers, led by a man named Bacon Tate of Nashville, Tennessee, came to western New York to recapture the Stanfords, a black couple and their six-week-old infant, who had sought refuge in St. Catherines, Ontario.[29] Tate was notorious in Tennessee for "breaking" slaves on the plantation, as well as capturing fugitives and returning them to their owners for a fee. Tate and his posse traveled all the way to Canada with the intent of kidnapping the Stanfords and other fugitives they had been contracted to bring back to the South. They were successful in capturing the family, taking them in the middle of the night. When other blacks in the town discovered the family missing, they sent out word all the way to Buffalo. Blacks everywhere were looking for the family and their captors. Tate and his group began heading south; but upon reaching Hamburg, New York, Brown, along with a heavily armed group of black men, apprehended the party. They took the couple and started back to Buffalo. Tate and the slavers immediately appealed to the county sheriff, who gathered seventy men to go after the couple. When the two groups met, a melée occurred. There was so much commotion that the Stanfords were able to escape. But the black rescuers were arrested for breaking the peace on the Sabbath, and twenty-five of them were found guilty and ordered to pay steep fines up to fifty dollars.[30] The Stanfords were later escorted to Black Rock Ferry and transported back to St. Catherines.

A few years later, Brown met William Lloyd Garrison, and his interest in the abolitionist and temperance movement peaked. Brown built a temperance restoration society of colored men in Buffalo. Within three years, the organization had over five hundred members, out of a population of only seven hundred.[31] A natural orator, Brown began lecturing throughout the North on the anti-slavery movement. Despite having no known formal education, he became a prolific speaker and was highly regarded in the anti-slavery community. There were many times when Brown was not well-received, not provided lodging, and was even pelted with eggs at a speech in East Aurora, New York. On one occasion, while speaking at a public meeting on Cape Cod, along with white abolitionists Parker Pillsbury, Lucy Stone, and S. S. Foster, cries from the crowd included, "haul them out," and "down with them." Some insults were obviously aimed only at Brown: "Tar and feather him!" "Ride him on a rail!" "Where's the darky?" "Pass out that nigger."[32] The incident became known as the "Mob on Cape Cod." A crowd of around twenty-five hundred people had gathered, prompted by the anti-slavery message of the abolitionists. They were also riled by seeing Lucy Stone and Brown walking down the street together ("a woman with a great black Negro," as one man described them).[33] Regardless of many incidences of this sort, where his life was threatened, Brown continued lecturing on the slave institution, his personal experience, and temperance. He was quick to point out the irony in American democracy and the use of religion to psychologically subdue slaves. His sophistication as a speaker and his growing reputation in the anti-slavery community led to an invitation to speak at the annual meeting of the American Anti-Slavery Society in 1844 in New York. Three years later, he spoke again at the Female Anti-Slavery Society's assembly in Salem, Massachusetts. Brown expressed his challenge in fully capturing the horrors of the slave experience in his lecture, saying:

> Were I about to tell you the evils of Slavery, to represent to you the Slave in his lowest degradation, I should wish to take you, one at a time, and whisper it to you. Slavery has never been represented; Slavery never can be represented.

During a lecture to a small audience on October 4, 1854, in Rochester, New York, Brown incidentally relayed his participation in the rescue of a man who had been accused of being a fugitive slave. According to Brown, he and other abolitionists retained Millard Fillmore as counsel "for an alleged fugitive," and Fillmore served without accepting a fee, explaining that he considered it "his duty to help the poor fugitive." This was the same Millard Fillmore, Brown observed, who would later become the president of the United States and sign into law the Fugitive Slave Act of 1850.[34]

Brown's marriage to Elizabeth dissolved around 1845, and he retained custody of his daughters. In 1847, he was hired as a lecture agent by the American Anti-Slavery Society. That same year, he published his autobiography, *Narrative of William W. Brown: A Fugitive Slave*. In 1849, he began a lecture tour in Great Britain. He traveled to Paris, France as a delegate to the International Peace Congress. Brown remained in Europe as an anti-slavery lecturer until 1854. His lengthy stay was partly political and partly personal, in that he was still distraught over the ending of his marriage. His daughters attended school in London during this time. Brown's series of European lectures prompted his travel narrative, *Three Years in Europe; or, Places I Have Seen and People I Have Met* (1852). He speaks of his amazement at the lack of racial prejudice and his impression of European literary figures, statesmen, and institutions, vividly describing the people he encounters, their dress, occupations, and living conditions in London, during the Crystal Palace era, in England's Great Houses, and in laborers' cottages.

The Fugitive Act made it dangerous for him to return to America, so a British couple purchased his freedom in 1854. Brown later married Anna Elizabeth Gray, with whom he had one daughter, named Clotelle.

Brown was the author of several other works about the slave institution, including *The Black Man: His Antecedents, His Genius, and His Achievements* (1863), *The Negro in the American Rebellion* (1867), *The Rising Son* (1873), and *My Southern Home; or, The South and Its People* (1880).

> *"All I demand for the black man, is that the white people shall take their heels off his neck, and let him have a chance to rise by his own effort."* [35]
>
> – *William Wells Brown*

William Wells Brown died on November 6, 1884, at the age of 68, in Chelsea, Massachusetts. He is buried in an unmarked grave in the Cambridge Cemetery in Cambridge, Massachusetts.[36]

After writing *Narrative of William W. Brown: A Fugitive Slave*, Brown sent a copy of his narrative and a letter to the white abolitionist Wells Brown, whose name he had adopted, and to whom he was eternally grateful for assisting him to freedom.

To Wells Brown, of Ohio:

Thirteen years ago, I came to your door, a weary fugitive from chains and stripes. I was a stranger, and you took me in. I was hungry, and you fed me. Naked was I, and you clothed me. Even a name by which to be known among men, slavery had denied me. You bestowed upon me your own. Base indeed should I be, if I ever forget what I owe to you, or do anything to disgrace that honored name!

As a slight testimony of my gratitude to my earliest benefactor, I take the liberty to inscribe to you this little Narrative of the sufferings from which I was fleeing when you had compassion upon me. In the multitude that you have succored, it is very possible that you may not remember me; but until I forget God and myself, I can never forget you.

Your grateful friend,

WILLIAM WELLS BROWN

HON. JOHN M. LANGSTON.

Born in Louisa Country, Va.—Educated at Oberlin, Ohio—Member Board of
Health, District of Columbia in 1871—Minister Resident and Consul-
General to Port-au-Prince, Hayti, 1877—Elected to Congress
from Fourth Congressional District of Virginia in
1890—Author of "Freedom and Citizenship"
and "From the Virginia Plantation
to the National Capitol."

14

JOHN MERCER LANGSTON
1829–1897

Pioneering politician, lawyer, educator, civil rights leader

John Mercer Langston was the only black member of Congress to serve in elected office both before and after the American Civil War.[1] He was the first black American congressman from the state of Virginia. Langston was elected to Congress in 1888; it would be nearly a century before another black politician in Virginia would achieve the same.[2] Early in his career, Langston became the first black public official in the United States, after being elected township clerk for Brownhelm, Ohio, in 1855. He was also the first black American admitted to the Ohio State Bar.[3] He was the first dean of Howard University's law school and helped establish its curriculum. He was the first president of what is now Virginia State University. John Mercer Langston was also the great-uncle of famed American poet and playwright Langston Hughes.

Langston's career as a proponent of civil rights would span nearly five decades. He was one of the most recognized and influential black men in the United States during his time.[4] As an educational inspector, Langston saw that the rights of newly freed slaves were protected.[5] He traveled throughout the South speaking about political and economic equality. He stressed the need for individual responsibility. His message was well received by blacks and whites alike, and Langston was propelled into national prominence.

As a recruiter of Negro servicemen for the Union Army, Langston organized Ohio's first black regiment, as well as the Massachusetts 54th Regiment Volunteer Infantry, the first formal unit made up entirely of black soldiers. This regiment included Charles and Lewis Douglass, the sons of Fredrick Douglass, as well as Harvey Carney, the first black American soldier to receive the Medal of Honor. The movie *Glory*, starring Denzel

John Mercer Langston. (*Source: Library of Congress*)

(*left*) Death of Cleopatra, marble sculpture by Edmonia Lewis, 1876. (*Source: Smithsonian American Art Museum*)

(*right*) Bust of Dr. Dio Lewis, Rome, Italy, sculpture by Edmonia Lewis, 1868. (*Source: The Walters Art Museum*)

Edmonia Lewis, c.1870 (*Source: National Portrait Gallery, Smithsonian Museum*)

Washington and Morgan Freeman, was made about this exceptional fighting unit.[6]

As a lawyer, one of Langston's most famous legal cases was that of Edmonia Lewis, a black student at Oberlin College, who was accused of murder. Langston successfully defended her and she was given a second chance at freedom. Lewis went on to become the first internationally acclaimed black American sculptor, whose works have been sought after by collectors throughout the world. Many of her sculptures have been displayed at the Smithsonian American Art Museum.

Langston was born free on December 14, 1829, in Louisa County, Virginia.[7] He was the son of Lucy Jane Langston, a former slave of African and Native American ancestry, and a white Virginia planter named Ralph Quarles, who was a captain in the Revolutionary War. Lucy had seven children, four belonging to Quarles. Quarles emancipated Lucy and their first child, Maria. Lucy left him immediately after and had three children outside of their relationship: William, Harriet, and Mary. She later reunited with Quarles and had three more children: Gideon, Charles Henry, and John Mercer. Gideon looked so much like his father that he was given his father's surname, Quarles. Because of state law, the couple could not marry; but they remained together until their deaths in 1834. Ralph Quarles left a sizeable inheritance to be divided among his three sons. The children were now orphaned and split up. Langston was only four years old when he and two of his brothers, Charles and Gideon, went to live in Chillicothe, Ohio with William Gooch, a white friend of Quarles. The Gooch family cared for them and provided a good education. In 1835, Gideon and Charles became the first blacks to be admitted into Oberlin College. Three years later, Gooch decided to move his family to Missouri, a slave state. A court ruled that Langston's inheritance would be threatened if he accompanied them, so he moved with his brother Gideon to Cincinnati, who made sure he excelled in school. By age fourteen, Langston began studying at the preparatory department at Oberlin College. He obtained his bachelor's degree in 1849 and a Master of Arts in Theology in 1852.[8]

At the age of eighteen, Langston was selected by the first Black National Convention to head the National Equal Rights League. He spoke at the convention about how to aid fugitive slaves. Langston briefly aligned himself with Free Democrats because they were against the Fugitive Slave

Act. He attempted to become a lawyer, but he was denied entrance by two law schools because of his color. So, he studied law under abolitionist Philemon Bliss in Elyria, Ohio. In September 1854, a district court committee confirmed Langston's knowledge of the law, also deeming him "nearer white than black," and Langston became the first black lawyer in the state of Ohio.[9] He began a law practice in Brownhelm, Ohio. He married his college sweetheart, Caroline Wall, and the couple had five children: Arthur, Ralph, Chinque, Nettie, and Frank. Langston quickly became a leader among free blacks. Together with other black leaders, he organized anti-slavery societies at both the state and local levels. He became active in the Underground Railroad in Ohio, and he fought publicly for women's rights and temperance.[10] In 1855, Langston was elected town clerk of Brownhelm Township, Ohio, becoming the first black person elected to public office in the United States.[11]

Langston served as legal council to Mary Edmonia Lewis, known as "Edmonia," in a prominent legal case. She was half-black, half-Chippewa Indian. ("Edmonia" was a Chippewa name that meant "wild fire.") While studying at Oberlin College, in January 1862, she was accused of poisoning two white female students who boarded at Oberlin trustee John Keep's home. While awaiting trial for murder, Edmonia was seized and beaten so badly she remained incapacitated and bedridden for weeks.[12] Langston successfully defended her in court, and she was acquitted of all charges. Well-liked by her fellow students, she was carried from the courtroom on the shoulders of supportive white friends and resumed her studies.[13] Edmonia went on to become the first black internationally recognized sculptress, crafting exquisite marble sculptures of historical American and world figures.[14]

> "If the Republican Party is not anti-slavery enough, take hold of it and make it so."
>
> – John Mercer Langston

During the Civil War, Langston organized black soldiers to fight for the Union Army. As chief recruiter, he assembled the Massachusetts 54th, the nation's first black regiment.[15] Nearing the end of the war, Langston sought a military commission in order to lead a group of black soldiers into battle. His request was supported by the Army's upper ranks, but the war ended before the order could be carried out. After the war, Langston worked closely with the Republican Party for the redistribution of wealth and power in the country.[16]

At the time of Reconstruction, the Republican Party was the political party most favorable towards blacks. Langston helped shape the character of the party relative to its relationship with black Americans. He organized numerous black political clubs across the country and crusaded for suffrage in Ohio, Kansas, and Missouri.

Langston was appointed dean of Howard University's law school in 1869. But Langston's views on race and his mass recruitment of blacks into the law school troubled the white conservatives on the board of trustees. Believing that the condition of blacks could be elevated if the laws were changed, he wanted as many black lawyers to come out of Howard University as possible. White trustees gradually forced him out in 1876, causing an enormous uproar. Students revolted, and the entire law department resigned in unified protest of Langston's dismissal.

Langston was selected as the U.S. minister to Haiti in 1877. He served for eight years but resigned after a new democratic presidential administration reduced his salary by 30 percent. When he returned to the United States, he ran for Congress as a representative for Virginia and won in 1888. Langston battled for eighteen months to be seated in Congress. Once there, he served only three months because of the constant schemes to steal his seat. Langston spent the remainder of his life in Washington, D.C., where he continued to fight for Negro rights. He died on November 15, 1897.

15

PATRICK FRANCIS HEALY
1830–1910

University president, educational pioneer

Patrick Francis Healy was the first black American to earn a Ph.D., the first to become a Jesuit priest, and the first to become president of a predominantly white university.[1] On July 31, 1874, Healy was inaugurated as the twenty-ninth president of the prestigious Georgetown University in Washington, D.C. He is often considered the institution's "second founder." It was originally founded by Archbishop John Carroll, who began collecting funds for its construction in 1787. But it was Healy who initiated Georgetown's astounding transformation from a small, unknown institution to the internationally renowned university it is today. He strengthened the curriculum, emphasizing science, law, and medicine. Healy founded the Alumni Association and oversaw major construction projects, including the building of Healy Hall.

Healy was born a slave on February 27, 1830, in Macon, Georgia, to Michael Morris Healy (an Irish immigrant) and Mary Eliza Smith (a domestic, mulatto slave) on the plantation of cotton magnate Sam Griswold. Healy was a former Irish soldier who had moved to America from Canada after the War of 1812. After winning 1,300 acres of fertile land in the Georgia Land Lottery, he turned it into a profitable cotton plantation on the banks of the Ocmulgee River near Macon, Georgia. He owned forty-nine slaves.[2] In 1829, Healy purchased Eliza from her slave master after falling in love with her. He was not allowed to legally marry her because she was black, and there were strict laws prohibiting it. A traveling preacher is said to have performed a marriage ceremony for the couple, and they lived as man and wife.[3]

The Healy's had ten children, all of whom were born slaves because of their maternal African ancestry. They were considered the property of their

Patrick Francis Healy, 1830-1910. Healy was the first black president of a predominantly white college, the first black American to earn a Ph.D., and the first black Jesuit priest in the United States.

father. As slaves, they were prohibited from attending Georgia schools, so their parents sent them to the north for their education. Unfortunately, they ran into a considerable amount of bigotry from northern school officials. Their father exhausted himself in an attempt to find his mixed-race children a respectable school that would treat them fairly. A Quaker school in Flushing, New York was willing to admit his three eldest sons, James, Patrick, and Sherwood. Fully embracing Catholicism, the religion of their Irish father, the brothers entered Holy Cross College in Worcester, Massachusetts in 1844. James Healy graduated as the school's valedictorian.

All three brothers pursued priestly vocations, and all were high achievers.[4] Patrick entered a Jesuit order in 1850. He became fluent in Latin, French, Italian, and German, and he studied abroad for several years. In 1858, he entered the University of Leuven in Belgium, where he earned his Ph.D. It was also during this time that he was ordained into the priesthood. In 1866, he returned to the United States and became a professor of philosophy at Georgetown University. He was named Prefect of Studies in 1868. In 1873, the university's board of directors elected him to the position of acting president. The following year, Healy's position as president was confirmed.

Healy Hall at Georgetown University in Washington, D.C.

Each of the Healy children achieved individual renown. James Augustine Healy became the first black Roman Catholic bishop in the United States. Alexander "Sherwood" Healy was ordained a priest and is believed to be the first black American to receive a doctorate in Canon Law.[5] Michael A. Healy became a decorated captain in the United States Coast Guard. He patrolled the Alaskan coastline for more than twenty years, gaining the trust of the inhabitants and the respect of fellow seamen. He helped in the introduction of the Siberian reindeer, which saved many natives from starvation.[6] He was known as "Hell-Roaring Mike," and he is still a legendary figure in Alaska. Commissioned in 1999, the USCGC was named in honor of Michael A. Healy. Three of the Healy sisters became nuns, and one a Mother Superior.

Patrick Healy retired in 1881. He died on January 10, 1910 and is buried in the Jesuit cemetery on Georgetown University's campus. Healy Hall, designed in high Victorian style, was listed on the Inventory of Historic Sites in Washington, D.C. in 1964 and on the National Register of Historic Places in 1971.[7]

16 |  FREDI WASHINGTON
1903–1994

Actress, dancer, civil rights advocate

"I don't want to pass because I can't stand insincerities and shams. I am just as much Negro as any of the others identified with the race." [1]

– Fredi Washington

Fredericka "Fredi" Carolyn Washington was an actress, dancer, casting consultant, journalist, and equal rights advocate. She was one of the first black actresses to gain recognition for her work on stage and in film.[2] She founded the Negro Actors Guild of America in 1937, an organization dedicated to racial reform and securing fair treatment for blacks in theater and film. She served as the organization's first executive secretary. She was a deputy for the Actors Equity Association, and she actively participated in the cultural division of the National Negro Congress and the Committee for Negroes in the Arts. She spearheaded campaigns through the Joint Actors Equity Theater League Committee of Hotel Accommodations, the National Urban League, and the NAACP to secure more black representation in the arts. Washington was an outspoken critic against racial discrimination in Hollywood. She openly stressed that if blacks were cast in films or plays, they should not have to enter the stage from the rear of the building, nor should they be provided substandard living quarters. Washington was a regular on the Jewish radio comedy "The Goldbergs," and she was the principal casting consultant for iconic films like *Carmen* (1953) and *Porgy and Bess* (1959). She was also the entertainment editor for the *People's Voice* newspaper, founded by her brother-in-law Adam Clayton Powell, Jr. She starred in numerous films and stage productions and was often forced to wear makeup to darken her skin. She is best known for her outstanding performance in the Academy Award-nominated film *Imitation of Life* (1934), which *Time* magazine named among the twenty-five most important films on race. Washington was inducted into the Black Filmmakers Hall of Fame in 1975.

She was born on December 23, 1903, in Savannah, Georgia and was the eldest of five children. Both of her parents were black and of notable admixture. Her father, Robert Washington, was a postal worker, and her mother, Harriet Walker Ward Washington, was a dancer. When she was eleven, her mother died, and Fredi became the family's primary caretaker. When her father remarried, he placed Fredi and her sister Isabel in Saint Elizabeth's Convent in Cornwell Heights, Pennsylvania. Not long after, the two sisters were taken in by their grandmother, who lived in New York City. She enrolled them in the Egri School of Dramatic Writing and the Christophe School of Languages. It was at this school that Washington became interested in the performing arts.

At the age of sixteen, Washington made her first cabaret appearance in the city, as a member of the *Happy Honeysuckles*. She worked as a stockroom clerk and a bookkeeper for blues singer W. C. Handy's record company, while pursuing her acting career. In 1922, she made her theatrical debut as a chorus dancer in the Broadway production *Shuffle Along*.[3] Josephine Baker was also a dancer in the production. Baker was taunted by the other dancers, and in one incident, her makeup was dumped in the hallway behind the stage and her clothes were taken from the dressing room. Washington made those responsible return the dancer's belongings and clean up the mess. The two became lifelong friends.[4]

Washington's first onscreen appearance was in 1922 in a relatively unknown film called *Square Joe*. While performing as a dancer at Club Alabam' in New York City, Fredi was spotted by legendary theatrical producer Lee Shubert. He urged her to take a leading role alongside Paul Robeson in *Black Boy*, a 1926 play based on the life of boxer Jack Johnson. Fredi performed this role under the assumed name "Edith Warren."[5] She was cast as a light-skinned black girl named Irene, who decided to pass for white. An article in the *San Francisco News* said, "Washington passed [so] successfully, that a number of playgoers protested to the management about her love scenes with Mr. Robeson."[6] When asked by several filmmakers and

Fredi Washington, publicity photo. *(Source: Maurice Seymour/Courtesy of Ron Seymour)*

reporters why she just did not pass for white, Fredi replied, "Because I'm honest and because you don't have to be white to be good."

As Washington fought to stop typecasting of Negroes off the set, she was subjected to the same fate, and greatly limited by her appearance. She was pale, with straight hair, green eyes, and aquiline features. And though both of her parents were black, Washington was constantly advised to deny her race completely and pass as white, so as not to offend white audiences. Being proud of who she was, she refused. Hollywood executives did not know how to cast her. Several producers continued to encourage her to pass, telling her that with her talent and beauty, they could make her a bigger star than Joan Crawford or Greta Garbo. But Washington resisted. Later, her off-screen activism and public acknowledgment of her Negro heritage made it impossible for her to ever consider playing a white woman in Hollywood. Washington was known to speak openly about the ignorance of Hollywood on race. Fredi said, "If a Negro lady fits the beauty and talent standards of Hollywood, why can't she be a star?" Becoming even more vocal about her dilemma, she said:

> Why should I have to pass for anything but an artist? When I act, I live the role I am assigned to do. If that part calls for me to be a West Indian half caste, a Spanish or Creole maiden, a French woman, a lady of great social distinction or a prostitute—how can I, or anyone, essay such roles with the bugbear of national heritage constantly dangled before my eyes?[7]

There were other black actresses and singers at that time who "rode the color-line" to great success. These entertainers either chose to pass or chose not to mention their race. Ina Ray Hutton was one such performer and singer of the 1930s–1960s. Known as the "blonde bombshell of rhythm," Hutton sang for World War II troops. Young men had posters in their lockers of this classic blonde sex symbol before Marilyn Monroe. Often compared to actress Lana Turner, it was not revealed until later in her career that Hutton, whose birth name was Odessa Cowan, was in fact black and had grown up on the south side of Chicago.[8] Her family was sometimes mentioned in the society pages of black newspapers. Hutton had joined the Ziegfeld Follies at age seventeen. Not long after, she formed her famous

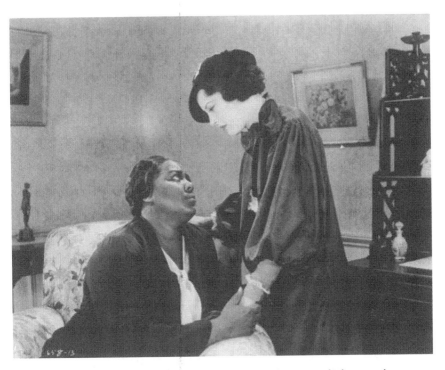

Fredi Washington and Louise Beavers star in the 1934 version of *Imitation of Life*, screen shot. (*Source: Courtesy of Fredi Washington Papers, Amistad Research Center, New Orleans, Louisiana*)

Fredi Washington plays "Peola" in *Imitation of Life*, 1934 screen shot. *(Source: Courtesy of Fredi Washington Papers)*

band the Hutton Melodears, the first all-female swing band to be recorded and filmed. They were all over the television in the 1950s. The popular "Ina Ray Hutton Show" earned an Emmy and aired on the west coast for four years and nationally for one summer on NBC.[9] The Whitman Sisters were also a hit, becoming the highest paid act on the Negro Vaudeville Circuit. These very fair-skinned daughters of a minister began singing at their local church. They were incredible entertainers who could sing, dance, tap, and play the banjo. They were also extraordinary business women who navigated through the constraints of race, gender, and class to become one of the most successful troupes of the 1920s and 1930s. Called "the greatest incubator of dancing talent for Negro shows," the Whitman Sisters were credited with fostering the careers of several black entertainment greats such as Bill "Bojangles" Robinson, Jeni LeGon, Pops and Louis, Ethel Waters, and Count Basie, among others.[10]

But like Dorothy Dandridge and Lena Horne, Washington was continually plagued by the limited roles offered to light-skinned black actresses in American film. All three of these actresses were made to wear makeup to darken their skin on screen. Max Factor even created a makeup called "Little Egyptian" for Horne.[11] This cinematic dilemma brought up issues of race, color, and identity. Stereotypical Hollywood roles for blacks at that time were set. The on-screen caricatures included Toms, Bucks, Mammies, Jezebels, and Tragic Mulattoes. The darker-skinned actresses were cast as maids or mammies; but Washington, Dandridge, and Horne were too light and their features too aquiline to play these roles. They were generally employed to portray tragic mulattoes or beguiling jezebels. To be typecast in these roles was a great vexation to Washington and Dandridge, who both suffered from depression as a result.

In pre-civil rights America, blacks who were light enough to pass for white were intriguing at the box office. The public at this time seemed to love stories about a "tragic mulatto" (usually a female), suffering because of the "dueling bloods running through her veins."[12] This adoption of another identity (to gain access to social privileges otherwise denied)

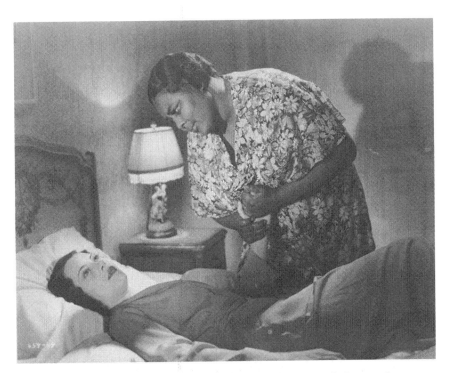

Fredi Washington and Louise Beavers star in the 1934 version of *Imitation of Life*, screen shot. *(Source: Photographs and Prints Division, Schomburg Center for Research in Black Culture, The New York Public Library, Astor, Lenox and Tilden Foundations)*

emerged as a prominent theme. Treatments of the topic in films engaged and overextended coverage in popular black and white media during this period of the phenomenon of "white Negroes."[13] According to Dr. David Pilgrim, professor of sociology at Ferris State University, "The Mulatto was made tragic in the minds of whites who reasoned that the greatest tragedy was to be near-white: so close, yet a racial gulf away. The near-white was to be pitied and shunned." Thus, there existed undoubtedly among lighter-skinned Negroes an incredible sense of marginalization in a country obsessed with race and the colorline.[14]

"I have never tried to pass for white and never had any desire. I am proud of my race." [15]

– Fredi Washington

A frustrated Washington left for Europe with fellow dancer Al Moiret in 1927. Together they formed the ballroom dance duo "Moiret and Fredi." They toured clubs in Paris, Monte Carlo, London, and Berlin for two years. Like her friend Josephine Baker, Washington found freedom from prejudice while abroad. Millionaire Otto Kahn fell in love with Washington and offered to pay for her dramatic education and make her known throughout the continent—if only she would pass as French, but she refused.

Washington returned to America in 1929 and starred in Cab Calloway and Dudley Murphy's musical *Black and Tan Fantasy*. She played the role of Duke Ellington's girlfriend, a dancer who performs despite illness and collapses after her big number. She starred in other stage productions and musical revues like *Hot Chocolates* (1929), *Great Day* (1929), and *Sweet Chariot* (1930), a musical based on Marcus Garvey's Universal Negro Improvement Association. She made other appearances in *Singin' the Blues* (1931) and *Run Little Chillun* (1933).

In 1933, she landed the leading female role as a prostitute in the movie *The Emperor Jones*, alongside Paul Robeson again. After seeing snippets of the independently produced film, the Hays Office demanded the scenes with Robeson and Washington be reshot, fearing public backlash if she were mistaken as white. This time the studio insisted Washington's skin be darkened considerably, so that white moviegoers would not think the popular Robeson was having an onscreen romance with a white woman.

The Hays Office warned that "the sequence would eventually be cut, if the required changes weren't made." So producers reluctantly applied dark makeup to Washington for daily shoots.[16]

Fully aware that her color greatly limited her acting career, she remarked in an interview with the *Pittsburgh Courier* that she wished she had been born with the skin color of actress Nina McKinney, as she would have had greater opportunities if she were darker. The newspaper reporter opined, "Miss Washington is a colored girl and must work as a colored actress. But as a matter of fact, she is not colored. Her skin is white . . . She is too colored for white pictures and too white for colored pictures."[17] The constant focus on her race and her appearance led Washington to say in an interview with the *Chicago Defender*:

> I am an American citizen and by God, we all have inalienable
> rights and whenever and wherever those rights are tampered
> with, there is nothing left to do but fight . . . and I fight. How
> many people do you think there are in this country who do not
> have mixed blood, there's very few if any, what makes us who we
> are, is our culture and experience. No matter how white I look,
> on the inside I feel black. There are many whites who are mixed
> blood, but still go by white, why such a big deal if I go as Negro,
> because people can't believe that I am proud to be a Negro and
> not white. To prove I don't buy white superiority I chose to be a
> Negro.[18]

There was no doubt that Washington was a gifted actress. Typical of the complimentary reviews that followed her performances was one from the *St. Louis Post-Dispatch* in which Calvin McPherson wrote that "Fredi Washington—is perhaps the most talented Negro actress in the business."[19] But all of this did not matter, as Washington's extraordinary talent seemed always overshadowed by her onscreen appearances.

White audiences flocked to see her, partly because of her beauty and partly because they marveled at her "near whiteness." But she was not white, a reality she chose to embrace. Hence, her truncated career was due to the limitations imposed on blacks by society. Despite being an exceptional actress, she never made it to the top like her contemporaries

Fredi Washington with French dancer Al Moiret.
Frustrated by racial typecasting, Washington decided to
travel to Europe with Moiret on a dancing tour.

Ethel Waters, Josephine Baker, and Nina Mae McKinney, simply because she did not look "black enough." She suffered the absurd prejudice against racially ambiguous complexions through typecasting.[20] The *Chicago Defender* said of Washington, "[She] constantly [rages] against the fate that has made her near white even though she is of Negro blood." This dark-haired, green-eyed, ivory-skinned, black beauty perhaps most typically embodied the "uncast-able" in American films. Hollywood failed to define her; or rather, defined her against her will. And though Washington never fully got a chance to develop her craft, she did her best to make memorable impressions in all her performances.[21]

Fredi Washington is best known for her role as Peola in the movie *Imitation of Life* (1934), a film that was nominated for two Academy Awards, for best picture and best sound.[22] The character Peola was a self-loathing Negro girl who looked white. Actress Louise Beavers played the part of her mom, a dark-skinned maid named Delilah Johnson, who raises her pale daughter, Peola, alongside her white employer's daughter, Jesse. The two girls become friends, and Peola longs to have the same opportunities as her playmate. She struggles to reconcile the fact that she is as white as her friend in appearance, but she has been relegated to the bottom of the rung in America's racial and societal hierarchy. So she must inevitably suffer a degrading plight.

The biological father of Peola, we are told in the film, was "almost white," presumably a fair-skinned Negro man, and Peola "came out looking just like him." The character is torn between her love for her Negro mother and her desire to live as a white woman. In the film, Delilah is determined to convince her daughter to accept her fate, saying "He [God] made you Black, honey. Don't be telling him his business. Accept it, honey." But Peola begs her mother to pretend she is not hers and allow her to live as white, stating she wants more for her life than to be a maid; she wants a chance at a good life. Peola decides to leave home and pleads with her mother:

> *"Don't come for me. If you see me in the street, don't speak to me.
> From this moment on I'm White. I am not colored. You have to give
> me up."*

This profound film touched upon the racial dynamics of its time, exploring issues created by the one-drop rule and other American yardsticks in place for racial determination. Peola realized early on the benefits of being a white woman and the humiliation and substandard life allotted to black women. She loves her mother, but she finds her acceptance of "her place" in society contemptible. Determined not to follow in her mother's footsteps, Peola makes it clear that she has no intention of being anyone's mammy. This constant struggle between daughter and mother wears on Delilah, who soon becomes ill and dies of a broken heart. Peola suffers enormous guilt, wondering if it was her choice to pass that hastened her mother's death.

Time magazine said, "Washington gave her greatest performance . . . capturing the inner torment of a young woman who abandons her mother in order to 'pass' as white."[23] The *New York Amsterdam News* told its readers:

> . . . actress though she be, Fredi Washington expresses the
> desire for freedom and equal justice in this picture that is more
> convincing than any mere performer could have voiced. True
> to her own life, the injustices of color and race prejudices have
> retarded and prohibited a fuller life and freedom of expression.

These mulatto roles sustained Fredi, but she continued to loathe them. The fact that Hollywood found her too white-looking to be black (by their standards) ultimately stifled her artistic advancement into mainstream film productions. Bitter about the stereotyping that had crippled her career, Washington leaned toward politics as a source of empowerment. She fought for fair and equal accommodations for blacks and spearheaded several campaigns to stop discrimination in the arts. She used her position as entertainment columnist for the *People's Voice* to wage protests against unfair treatment. She wore a black arm band in support of the NAACP and its campaign against lynching. The *New York Herald Tribune* affirmed Washington's activism, describing her as "a frail, defenseless ingénue, by night—a forthright uncompromising crusader by day." She spoke out against segregation in the military and the treatment of black soldiers, which compelled some white military officers to come out in support of desegregation.[24]

Her public embrace of the civil rights struggle, radical stances, and affiliation with other black activists led to a systematic reduction of her roles in Hollywood. Washington was essentially blacklisted.[25] After *Imitation of Life*, she made one more film as the lead actress in *One Mile from Heaven* (1937), starring Bill "Bojangles" Robinson. Post-Hollywood, she starred in some stage productions, including *Mamba's Daughters* (1939) with Ethel Waters, *Lysistrata* (1946), *A Long Way from Home* (1948), and *How Long Till Summer* (1949). Washington continued to be active in the field of acting, as a registrar for the Henry da Silver School of Acting. She also held a variety of positions in the movie industry as casting consultant for the British film *Cry the Beloved Country* and iconic films like *Carmen Jones* (1943) and *Porgy and Bess* (1959), both starring Dorothy Dandridge.

Interestingly, before the 1960s, it was not uncommon for studios to choose white actors or actresses to play the parts of blacks in mainstream cinema.[26] Films like *Lost Boundaries*, *Pinky*, *Showboat*, *Band of Angels*, *Kings Go Forth*, and *Raintree County* all had white actors playing black roles. Washington had a heated exchange with Alfred Werker, the director of *Lost Boundaries*, after he cast a group of white actors to play the role of a light-skinned black family, the Johnstons. He made comments subsequent to the film's release that only added fuel to the flame. This casting was a bitter disappointment to so many black actors who had hoped the film would supply them with much-needed jobs.[27] In an interview with the *Los Angeles Daily News*, Werker defended his decision, stating that the reason he passed up black actors for the Johnstons was because "the majority of

Negro actors were of the Uncle Tom, Minstrel show, shuffling dancer type of performer."[28] He continued that he had "tried to get a colored cast" but because of the time constraints of the shooting schedule, he was unable to conduct "a thorough canvass of the country for talent to play the lead roles."[29] The black community was incensed, and Washington launched a public attack against the director for these statements, saying:

> I am appalled and not a little fighting mad to think that a so-
> called intelligent adult could be so viciously ignorant . . . I would
> say that Alfred Werker has carved a unique niche for himself
> in the world of picture-making. He now can take the Oscar for
> being Hollywood's number one anti-Negro bigot.[30]

She added, "There are many Negro actors and actresses who are consistently turned down for plays and screen fare on the excuse that they are too fair, too intelligent, and too modern looking." Washington then engaged the efforts of the Committee of the Negro in the Arts to publicize the position of black artists who opposed the practice of casting white actors as black characters.[31]

As secretary of the Negro Actors Guild and deputy of the Actors Equity Association, Washington was keenly aware of the impact of stereotypical images in the media. In 1944, she castigated MGM studios for considering a remake of *Uncle Tom's Cabin*, which she said portrayed Tom as "a selfish, back-bending, white-folks loving yard man." She concedes that "while the book is informative and positive propaganda against the vicious practice of slavery which is still a blot on our country, I most definitely am against any picturization of it by MGM or any other studio."[32] In justifying her position, she recounted the atrocities that blacks had historically suffered and said that the country was still full of potential slave holders. She strongly expressed her reservations in releasing such a movie, saying:

> It would be suicide to show Negroes at that time on the screen
> under the bondage of slavery, illiterate, childlike and docile.
> Conditions for the Negro in the South and in many spots in the
> North are not too far removed from conditions that existed under
> actual slavery. Does not the South still keep the Negro from

voting; from getting an equal education; refuse war contracts because whites refuse to train or work with Negroes; make the Negro soldier ride in the back of their conveyances if at all?[33]

Washington rallied others and the film never materialized after blacks, labor unions, and white liberals vowed to protest the film's release. This was a testament to Washington's political savvy.[34] "When you see how long it took the movie industry to make up its mind to handle the question of anti-Semitism, it gives us an idea of how long we will have to wait for some protest from the screen on Negrophobia in this country."[35]

Washington was very close friends with several black actors and actresses, including Ethel Waters, Paul Robeson, and J. Rosamond Johnson. Johnson was a vaudeville and musical director who was part of the "Johnson Brothers." Many people recognize Johnson as one of the composers of the Negro National Anthem.[36] Also, according to Paul Robeson's son, his father had several extramarital affairs, including a long-term love affair with Fredi Washington.[37]

In 1933, Washington married Lawrence Brown, the trombonist for Duke Ellington's orchestra. The only time Washington was known to "pass as white" was when she was traveling with Ellington's band. Whenever they would travel South, the musicians would ask her to go into the parlors to buy ice cream. The men would wait anxiously outside the store as Washington would enter these establishments with ease and purchase several cones. On some occasions, white patrons leaving the store would see Washington outside, handing out the cones to the group of black men and would scream, "Nigger lover!" Washington divorced Brown many years later and in 1952 wedded a dentist named Anthony H. Bell, to whom she remained married until his death in 1970. Columnist Veronica Chambers pays tribute to Fredi Washington in the *New York Times*, saying:

> In the movies, the tragic mulatto, like a Tolstoy heroine, is always
> punished for her sexuality and her mixed race. Washington,
> however, played the tragedy only onscreen and remained, until
> her death at age 90, black and proud. What she was so keenly
> aware of was, that the tragic mulatto was not so much about
> a light-skinned black who wanted to be white as it was about

a black person who lusted for the life chances that whiteness signified.[38]

On June 28, 1994, Fredi Washington died of pneumonia following a stroke in Stamford, Connecticut. She was ninety years old. During her life, she had received several notable recognitions. The Committee for the Negro in the Arts presented her with a scroll for outstanding contributions by an artist; she was the recipient of the CIRCA Award for lifetime achievement in the performing arts; and she was inducted into the Black Filmmakers Hall of Fame in 1975.[35] But more importantly, Fredi Washington's civil rights efforts on behalf of blacks was monumental, paving the way for future black entertainers to capitalize on opportunities that had been denied her.

Dorothy Maynor, Canada Lee, Fredric March, Fredi Washington and Judge Hubert T. Delany, appeared on Sunday, Feb. 14th for Race-Relations Sunday which was recognized by the National Council of YMCAs, for a dramatization interpreting the part the Negro is playing in the war. (*Source: Photographs and Prints Division, Schomburg Center for Research in Black Culture, The New York Public Library, Astor, Lenox and Tilden Foundations*)

St. Luke Penny Savings Bank, from R.W. Grand Council, Independent Order of St. Luke, Fiftieth Anniversary Golden Jubilee, August 20-24th, 1917, Richmond, VA., Souvenir Booklet. *(Source: Courtesy of the National Park Service, Maggie L. Walker National Historic Site)*

17

MAGGIE LENA WALKER
1864-1934

Pioneering businesswoman, philanthropist

*"I was not born with a silver spoon in my mouth: but instead
with a clothes basket almost upon my head."*

– *Maggie Lena Walker*

Maggie Lena Draper Mitchell Walker was the first female bank president in the United States, as well as the first woman to charter a bank.[1] In 1903, she started St. Luke's Penny Savings Bank (later renamed Consolidated Bank and Trust Company), which is the oldest minority-owned bank in the United States today. She was an astute business woman and a former teacher who devoted herself to civil rights and the feminist movement. Her life was a testament to black economic empowerment and perseverance despite personal challenges. Walker suffered from paralysis later in life and was confined to a wheelchair, but this did not slow her down. And so, she served as an inspiration to disabled persons as well.

She was born Maggie Lena Draper on July 15, 1864, in Richmond, Virginia, during the Civil War.[2] After the war, her mother, Elizabeth Draper, became a domestic servant and assistant cook in the mansion of Civil War spy Elizabeth Van Lew, a wealthy abolitionist who ran a spy operation for the Union Army.[3] Walker's father, Eccles Cuthbert, was a white, Irish-born correspondent for the *New York Herald* and the *Richmond Dispatch*, who frequented the Van Lew estate.[4] "Max," as he was called, was described as a snappy dresser, with a long beard and a heavy Irish accent.[5] Walker did not have a relationship with her father. She described her mother as "a humble, ignorant girl who brought me into life." And yet, she had a deep reverence for her mother, who worked tirelessly scrubbing floors and washing clothes for local whites in order to put Walker and her brother Johnnie through school.

In May of 1868, her mother married William Mitchell, a mulatto butler who worked in the Van Lew mansion. He adopted Walker and gave her his surname, "Mitchell."[6] When her stepfather got a job as head waiter at the Saint Charles Hotel, the family moved into their own home on College Alley off of Broad Street, not far from the Van Lew mansion. The family attended the First African Baptist Church, a large church that was the center of fellowship and social change in the local black community. But not long after the move, her stepfather was tragically murdered, presumably by a robber, and his body was found floating in the James River. Her mother was left to support Walker and her younger brother Johnnie with her laundry business. She assisted her mother and was able to continue her education at the Lancaster School and then the Armstrong Normal School.

In 1883, Walker led her graduating class in a protest against her school's discriminatory policies, after school officials announced that black students would be banned from commencement ceremonies at the Richmond Theater facilities. It is believed to be the first organized college strike by black students, ever. It received national attention and was featured in the June 23, 1883 edition of the *New York Globe*, which reported that "members of this class are already benefactors of their race. They have sent out the decree that they don't intend to be insulted."[7] Walker's biological father showed back up for her graduation with a beautiful dress for her, but her mother, Elizabeth, tossed it into a wood-burning stove. This is believed to be the last time Walker saw her father.[8]

> *"Let us be strong and make big plans."* [9]
>
> – *Maggie Lena Walker*

She taught for three years at the Lancaster School while studying bookkeeping and accounting. On September 14, 1886, she married Armstead Walker, Jr., a highly successful building contractor. Walker was able to stop teaching for some years to care for her family. The couple had three sons, Russell Eccles Talmadge Walker, Melvin DeWitt Walker, and Armstead Mitchell Walker (who died in infancy).[10]

Walker eventually went to work for the Grand United Order of St.

Maggie Lena Walker was the first female bank president of any race to charter a bank in the United States. *(Source: Courtesy of the National Park Service, Maggie L. Walker National Historic Site)*

Maggie Lena Walker as a young woman, c. 1883-1886. *(Source: Courtesy of the National Park Service, Maggie L. Walker National Historic Site)*

Walker and "Grand Officers - Juvenile Department, Independent Order of St. Luke," c. 1917. *(Source: Courtesy of the National Park Service, Maggie L. Walker National Historic Site)*

Seated center row, eighth from the left: Walker with female staffers of the Independent Order of St. Luke, c. 1925. *(Source: Courtesy of the National Park Service, Maggie L. Walker National Historic Site)*

Stenographers at work at the Independent Order of St. Luke, Headquarters, 1917. *(Source: Courtesy of the National Park Service, Maggie L. Walker National Historic Site)*

Interior of St. Luke Penny Savings Bank, 1917. *(Source: Courtesy of the National Park Service, Maggie L. Walker National Historic Site)*

Interior of entrance to Independent Order of St. Luke, headquarters, St. Luke Hall 900 St. James Street, Richmond, VA. *(Source: Courtesy of the National Park Service, Maggie L. Walker National Historic Site)*

Maggie Lena Walker was a very wealthy woman, who was known for her philanthropy, c. 1900-1910. (*Source: Brown Photographer/Courtesy of the National Park Service, Maggie L. Walker National Historic Site*)

Maggie Lena Walker was a community activist. She established several programs for Richmond boys and girls. *(Source: Courtesy of the National Park Service, Maggie L. Walker National Historic Site)*

Seated on first row, fifth from left: Ms. Walker with the Independent Order of St. Luke Board of Trustees, c. 1925-1930. *(Source: Brown photographer/Courtesy of the National Park Service, Maggie L. Walker National Historic Site)*

Walker's granddaughter, Mamie Evelyn Walker. *(Source: Brown photographer/ Courtesy of the National Park Service, Maggie L. Walker National Historic Site)*

Ms. Walker's oldest granddaughter, Maggie Laura. Maggie Laura became a doctor at the age of 22 and resided in Chicago, IL. *(Source: Courtesy of the National Park Service, Maggie L. Walker National Historic Site)*

Four generations of the Walker family: Maggie Lena with her sons, granddaughters, and her mother, Elizabeth Draper Mitchell, seated, c. 1920. *(Source: Courtesy of the National Park Service, Maggie L. Walker National Historic Site)*

Maggie Lena Walker sits in her parlor. *(Source: Courtesy of the National Park Service, Maggie L. Walker National Historic Site)*

Luke (later renamed the Independent Order of St. Luke), an organization she had joined at the age of fourteen. It was a black fraternal order and cooperative insurance society founded in Baltimore in 1867 by Mary Prout, a former slave. The headquarters were later moved to Richmond, Virginia. The primary focus of the order was to promote self-sufficiency and racial solidarity. The members cared for the elderly and sick, and they provided for healthcare and burial arrangements for its members and their families. In 1890, Walker became Right Worthy Grand Chief, the highest ranking volunteer position within the organization.[11] She demonstrated such extraordinary business acumen that in 1899, she was appointed executive secretary-treasurer. The organization was in so much debt that Walker accepted a reduced salary of only eight dollars a month, and she worked hard to advance the black community economically. In 1902, she started the *St. Luke Herald* newspaper, which served as a platform to discuss Jim Crow, mob rule, and the unfair treatment of blacks. There was a section devoted to children, which provided information on the habits of thrift, industry, and personal hygiene. Short stories, articles, and poems written by children in the community were also featured. Walker also established a college fund for deserving students.

> *"Let us have a bank that will take the nickels and turn them into dollars."*
>
> *– Maggie Lena Walker*

While working for the order, Walker discovered that white-owned banks were reluctant to take deposits from a black organization. She saw a need to establish a bank for blacks in the community. And so, in 1903, Maggie Lena Walker founded the St. Luke Penny Savings Bank, becoming the first woman in the United States to establish a banking institution. She started the bank with $9,430 in deposits from members of the fraternal order and served as the bank's first president.[12] The bank facilitated loans and encouraged savings in the black community. Eight years later, the bank moved to a three-story building, lavishly decorated in turn of the century glass and brass, mahogany fixtures, and antique lighting. In 1905, Walker also established a department store called the St. Luke's Emporium, which

(Source: Courtesy of the National Park Service, Maggie L. Walker National Historic Site)

employed fifteen black women as sales clerks. It provided quality goods at affordable prices, and it operated for seven years.[13]

Records indicate that Walker's bank had financed six hundred forty-five homes for blacks whose mortgages had been paid off by the 1930s.[14] The bank grew enormously fast, absorbing other Richmond banks. Even in the midst of the Great Depression, it continued to prosper. St. Luke's Penny Savings Bank later changed its name to the Consolidated Bank and Trust Company, a conglomerate with an insurance agency.[15] It was one of only six black-owned banks in the United States at that time.

Under Walker's administration, the Independent Order of St. Luke's fortunes were completely reversed. Within ten years, the membership had grown to fifty thousand members, with fifteen hundred local chapters, and a staff of fifty working in its Richmond headquarters. Their assets totaled almost $400,000. Over the next twenty-five years, it collected nearly $3.5 million, claimed 100,000 members in twenty-four states, and built up almost $100,000 in reserve.[16]

> *"If our women want to avoid the traps and snares of life, they must . . . organize, . . . put their mites together, put their hands and their brains together and make work and business for themselves."*
>
> *– Maggie Lena Walker*

Walker was the co-founder of the Richmond Council of Colored Women (1912). Serving as president, she helped raise large sums of money for Janie Porter Barrett's Virginia Industrial School for Colored Girls and for other philanthropic agendas. She was a member of the International Council of Women of the Darker Races, the National Association of Wage Earners, the National Urban League, and the Virginia Interracial Committee. Walker also co-founded the Richmond branch of the NAACP. Richmond's black community of Jackson Ward began to flourish, and there were scores of black-owned businesses, largely due to Walker's efforts. The area became known as the "Harlem of the South." According to historian Muriel Branch, co-author of *Pennies to Dollars: The Story of Maggie Lena Walker*, "[Walker] made loans to black businesses, she made loans to students, she made loans to people to buy houses."[17]

Walker's life was a testament to triumph over adversity. She was plagued with several personal tragedies throughout her life. Her stepfather William's untimely death in February of 1876 shattered the family and left them struggling financially. Walker had two very difficult childbirths. During her first delivery, Walker and her son Russell Eccles Talmadge almost died, and afterward Walker was confined to a bed for five months. Her second son Armstead Mitchell Walker only lived for seven months. Her younger half-brother, Johnnie, died as a young man from tuberculosis. These losses were too much for her to bear, so her husband sent for his niece Polly Anderson to live with them, and the couple adopted her. Sadly, Walker's husband was killed in 1915, when her son Russell mistook his father for a prowler and shot him. Although Russell was acquitted of the murder charge, he never recovered mentally from this ordeal and died in 1923. Walker suffered acutely from a knee injury that came from a terrible fall that she had on the front steps of her home in 1907. The damaged nerves and tendons continued to trouble her for the rest of her life. She also had diabetes and by 1928 was confined to a wheelchair.

On December 15, 1934, Maggie Lena Walker died of gangrene from complications of diabetes. In 1985, the house her family occupied in Richmond, Virginia from 1904 to 1934 was made into a museum called the Maggie L. Walker National Historic Site. It is a magnificent twenty-five room mansion with beautiful wallpaper, mahogany furniture, crystal chandeliers, gilded mirrors, a huge library, an elevator, and a richly decorated parlor. It is maintained by the United States National Park Service. As of 2011, Walker's bank, Consolidated Bank and Trust, is still extremely successful, and the majority of its shareholders are black Americans. This black-owned bank has served generations of Richmonders.[18]

ROBERT HARLAN.

18

ROBERT JAMES HARLAN
1816–1897

Businessman, activist, philanthropist

"We are Americans, and let us act as Americans have ever done when denied their rights. Cry aloud and spare not until our injuries are known and our wrongs are redressed and our demands are granted."

– Robert James Harlan

Robert James Harlan was an entrepreneur, businessman, army officer, and civil rights leader. During the California Gold Rush, Harlan accumulated gold worth $90,000, which he invested in real estate in Cincinnati, Ohio. He is credited with building the first school in Cincinnati for Negro children.[1] He became a prominent black politician in both Kentucky and Ohio. Commissioned by President Rutherford B. Hayes as a colonel, he raised a battalion of four hundred Negro soldiers. In 1879, Harlan made a speech before Congress entitled "Migration is the Only Remedy for Our Wrongs."[2]

Robert James Harlan, with his pale skin, blue eyes, red hair, and freckles, was born a slave on the Harlan family plantation in Harrodsburg, Kentucky on December 12, 1816.[3] His beginnings are scarcely recorded, possibly because of the controversy over his paternity.[4] While his mother was a mulatto slave on the plantation, it has long been rumored (and now embraced by historians) that Harlan's father was Judge James Harlan, who was from a very prominent American political family. The Harlan family tree can claim two Supreme Court justices, two members of Congress, a United States senator, and the daughter-in-law of President Abraham Lincoln, among others.[5]

Although Robert James Harlan's name is not listed in the official family records, there are several detailed references of him in the Harlan Papers. Historians now speculate that Robert was actually the half-brother of John Marshall Harlan, the associate justice on the Supreme Court known as the "Great Dissenter," the lone voice of dissent in the landmark 1896 *Plessy v. Ferguson* case.[6] Justice Harlan was described as "a white man who was comfortable around Negroes at a time when most other men of his race were not."[7] He boldly condemned segregation, stating that "the Constitution is color blind." Many surmise that his compassion towards Negroes was due to his closeness to his black brother, Robert.[8]

Although there were several notably mixed slaves on the Harlan plantation, Robert was given special treatment by the Harlans and even allowed to live in the family home.[9] Because there were no schools for Negro children in Kentucky at that time, Harlan was tutored by his two oldest half-brothers. His business acumen was apparent early in life. At eighteen, he opened a barbershop and later a grocery store. Harlan also began trading animal skins with local hunters. At the age of thirty-two, he was permitted to leave the plantation with a group of white men to seek his fortune in the California Gold Rush. Harlan amassed a fortune, wisely investing it in real estate in Cincinnati's Walnut Hills. He also built the first school in Cincinnati, Ohio for Negro children, called the East 17th Street School. Harlan was also a trustee of the local Colored Orphan Asylum.[10]

In 1852, Harlan married Josephine Floyd, the daughter of John B. Floyd (Virginia's once governor and secretary of war under President James B. Buchanan).[11] Harlan and his wife had one son, Robert, Jr. Within months of giving birth, Josephine died. Shortly after this tragedy, Harlan sought to rectify his legal status. Despite all of his success and civic work, he was still legally a slave. He returned to Kentucky briefly to purchase his freedom for $500.[12] Returning to Ohio, Harlan became involved in politics in order to address issues concerning free blacks.

In 1859, after dealing with years of racial prejudice, he moved to England, where he remained for nine years, during which time he raced horses. Upon returning to Cincinnati, he became very active with the Cincinnati Public School system, which captured the attention of leaders in the Republican Party. He served as a delegate-at-large at the 1872 Republican National Convention, which nominated President Ulysses

Grant for a second term. Harlan was appointed by Grant's administration as a special agent for the U.S. Postal Service.

In 1878, Harlan was commissioned as a colonel by President Rutherford B. Hayes to raise a battalion of four hundred Negro soldiers. Harlan's unit was the forerunner of the 94th Ohio Battalion (which was eventually absorbed into the 372nd Infantry Regiment during World War I). In 1884, he was appointed special agent of the Treasury Department by President Chester A. Arthur. Harlan was later elected to the Ohio state legislature, where he fought hard for the repeal of discriminatory "black codes."

During his illustrious 1879 speech "Migration is the Only Remedy for Our Wrongs," made before Congress, Harlan argued for the right of blacks to migrate wherever they wanted to go within the United States. He pointed out that migration was not only a way to escape oppression, but also a strong remonstration against any people who would deny blacks their freedom. Over the next year, six thousand blacks left Mississippi and Louisiana and headed for Kansas. The exodus prompted a congressional hearing. Should blacks leave southern states for better opportunities in the North? Or should they stay in the South and demand their equal rights? Frederick Douglass argued against migration, because he said it left "the whole question of equal rights on the soil of the South open and still to be settled." Douglass believed continued migration "would make freedom and free institutions depend upon migration rather than protection." Robert Harlan joined several other black leaders in opposing Douglass. Harlan's compelling speech on May 8, 1879 said in part:

> Mr. President, as to the present migration movement of the colored people, let it be understood that we have the lawful right to stay or to go wherever we please. The southern country is ours. Our ancestors settled it, and from the wilderness formed the cultivated plantation, and they and we have cleared, improved, and beautified the land. Whatever there is of wealth, of plenty, of greatness, and of glory in the South, the colored man has been, and is, the most important factor. The sweat of his brow, his laborer's toil, his patient endurance under the heat of the semi-tropical sun and the chilling blasts of winter, never deterred the laborer from his work . . . The blood of the colored man has

fertilized the land and has cemented the Union. The Republic owes to every citizen protection for his home and security for his rights. Let this security be given, and until that be done, let us cry aloud against those who refuse it, whether in the North or in the South . . . If the Government shall fail to give protection to our people, it can do no less than aid those who wish to change their habitations to safer and better homes . . . Let us demand that the principles we assert be declared essential, in resolutions of legislatures and conventions, and made a part of our party platform. Let us agitate, even as other classes agitate when their rights and wishes are disregarded. We are Americans, and let us act as Americans have ever done when denied their rights. Cry aloud and spare not until our injuries are known and our wrongs are redressed and our demands are granted.[13]

Robert James Harlan died on September 24, 1897, at the age of 81.

RICHARD T. GREENER
1844–1922

U.S. Diplomat, professor, lawyer

19

Richard Theodore Greener was the first black graduate of Harvard University. He graduated with honors in 1870.[1] He was also the first black person to ever represent the United States abroad in a diplomatic position.[2] He was the first black professor at the University of South Carolina, and he was later appointed dean of Howard University's law school. Greener distinguished himself in the fields of education, oratory, and law. Very active in international affairs, Greener served as a U.S. diplomat during the administrations of President William McKinley and Theodore Roosevelt. From 1885 to 1892, Greener was secretary of the Grant Monument Association and a civil service examiner in New York City. During the 1896 election, he was the head of the Colored Bureau of the National Republican Party. Two years later, he was selected to be the United Consul to Bombay, India by President William McKinley. His most important appointment was as a United States Commercial Agent to Vladivostok, Russia. Greener was the first American (white or black) to ever be posted there, and it was the first time the American flag had been raised on Siberian soil. During his term in Russia, he reported to Washington on the construction of the Trans-Siberian Railroad, the rapid growth of the Russian population in the region, the status of the Jewish population, and the fall-out of China's Boxer Rebellion in 1900. Recognizing Siberia's growing importance to the economic interests of the United States, Greener asked that the U.S. State Department establish a consul-general in Vladivostok; but his request was denied. During the Russo-Japanese War of 1904, Greener supervised the evacuation of the Japanese from Sakhalin Island.[3]

He was awarded the Order of the Double Dragon by the Chinese government for his service during the Boxer Rebellion and for his assistance to the famine victims in Shansi.[4] W.E.B. Du Bois held Greener in very high regard, considered him to be representative of the Negro intelligentsia, and included Greener as part of the "Talented Tenth" (who Du Bois believed could lead and elevate the Negro masses).[5] In *Men of Mark: Eminent, Progressive and Rising*, author William J. Simmons says of Greener:

> The gentleman—is one of the most accomplished scholars in polite literature among us . . . His studies range over a vast field of learning. His taste is aesthetical, and can be compared to the eagle in its flights. He was never known to produce a poor article from his pen. He is an orator of the finest kind . . . He has spent his life among books . . . Mr. Greener has risen to his present status from a poor boy, for he supported a widowed mother by working as a porter while quite a lad.

Greener was born in Philadelphia, Pennsylvania, on January 30, 1844, to Richard Wesley Greener and Mary Ann Le Brune.[6] His family moved to Boston, Massachusetts when he was nine and enrolled him at Broadway Grammar School. His father, Richard, was an adventurous, seafaring man who had been wounded in the Mexican War. As a boy, Greener traveled to Liverpool with his dad, who was the chief steward on a ship called the George Raynes. But his father abandoned the sea and headed to California on a gold-mining expedition and never returned. He was "taken ill and suffered losses" and never heard from again.[7] Greener was forced to drop out of school at fourteen to help support his mother. The young man worked various odd jobs as a night-watchman, a clerk, a hotel porter, and a wood engraver at D. J. Smith and Company. While working at D. J. Smith, there was an incident in which the employer struck him in the face, and Greener walked out of the plant.[8] Fortunately, two of his employers, August E. Batchelder and George Herbert Palmer, were very impressed by his work ethics and sent him to preparatory school at Oberlin College from 1862 to 1864, and Phillips Andover Academy from 1864 to 1865. Batchelder then arranged for Greener's admission into Harvard University. The school (then Harvard College) was conducting an experiment on the education of blacks.

R. T. GREENER.

Greener entered Harvard in the fall of 1865 at the age of twenty-one.[9] Rumors of his background immediately arose among his classmates; he was variously represented as an escaped slave, a genius who had come straight from the cotton field to the college, a scout in the Union Army, the son of a rebel general, and so on.[10] In his sophomore year, he won the Bowdoin Prize for elocution, and then again in his senior year for his English dissertation on the Irish culture called "The Best Way of Crushing the Agitator is to Give Him His Grievance."[11] In 1870, Greener completed Harvard University with honors, becoming the school's first black graduate.[12] He received more awards during his college career than any other student. After leaving, Greener taught for two years at the Institute for Colored Youth in Philadelphia before accepting a job as principal of Sumner High School, a preparatory school for black children in Washington, D.C.[13] Shortly after, he obtained a position at the district attorney's office. It was here that he first began applying himself to the study of law.[14]

On September 24, 1874, Greener married Geneviève Ida Fleet (who later changed her name to Geneviève Van Vliet after the couple divorced). Geneviève came from an elite black family in D.C. The couple had a daughter named Belle Marion Greener, who would later change her name to Belle da Costa Greene (without the "r"). She passed as white, despite her father's known activism and historic achievements as a black man. She would claim a Portuguese lineage to explain her olive skin tone. Belle was known to have several liaisons with very wealthy men who found her quite intriguing, including Renaissance art expert Bernard Berenson and J.P. Morgan, who left her money in his will.[15] She was described as beautiful, stylish, smart, outspoken, and sensual. She enjoyed a Bohemian lifestyle and was able to maneuver comfortably in elite social circles. When asked if she was the mistress of J.P. Morgan, Belle replied, "We tried!" But it was common knowledge that this was the case, and Belle never married. Morgan had hired her as the librarian for his New York library on Madison Avenue. She told him that her goal was to make his library "pre-eminent, especially for incunabula, manuscripts, bindings, and the classics."[16] She turned the library into one of the most outstanding reference libraries for scholars worldwide. Prior to working for Morgan, Belle had been the librarian for Princeton University. Morgan spared no expense, allowing her the privilege of bargaining and acquiring rare art, books, and manuscripts from around the world. Belle became very powerful and was trusted by Morgan with millions. She was at the center of the art trade for forty-three years. Greener had very little contact with his daughter for most of her life, and he later began a family with a Japanese woman.

In 1875, Greener was selected as a member of the Board of Health of Columbia, South Carolina. Around the same time, he joined the state commission to reorganize the common schools. He was asked to fill the professorship of mental and moral philosophy at the University of South Carolina, and he remained there until 1877. He became a member of the American Philological Association; and after several years of study, he graduated with honors from the University of South Carolina school of law, receiving a LL.B. He was admitted to the Supreme Court of South Carolina in 1877 and became a member of the District of Columbia Bar the following year.

Greener was a follower of Frederick Douglass and took every opportunity to attend his lectures. After Greener gained recognition as a black activist, he began speaking at several events organized by Douglass. Greener was one of the orators at the memorial service for abolitionist William Lloyd Garrison, where Douglass delivered the eulogy. In 1879, he was appointed dean of the Howard University's law school. After relinquishing his post in 1882, Greener moved to New York and began his own law firm. He was appointed examiner of the Municipal Civil Service Commission of New York, served as secretary of the Grant Monument Association, and was head of the Colored Bureau for the Republican Party during the 1886 election. After retiring from foreign services in Vladivostok, Russia, Greener settled in Chicago, where he practiced law, worked as an insurance agent, and lectured from time to time. He was conferred an honorary LL.D. by Monrovia College in Liberia, Africa, and also from Howard University in 1907.

Throughout his life, he was a large editorial contributor to journals, reviews, and various works of reference. He delivered numerous addresses, including the following: an inaugural address to the University of South Carolina on "Charles Sumner, the Idealist, Statesman, and Scholar" (June, 1874); "The Eulogy on the Life and Services of William Lloyd Garrison" (June, 1879); "Socrates as a Teacher" (April, 1880); "The Intellectual Position of the Negro" (July, 1880); "Free Speech in Ireland" (October,

1882); "Benjamin Banneker, the Negro Astronomer" (February, 1882); "Henry Highland Garnet" (May, 1882); and "An African Roscius" (June, 1882).

Richard Theodore Greener died of old age on May 2, 1922. The personal papers of Greener, Harvard's first black graduate, were discovered in an abandoned building on Chicago's south side in 2009, and the discovery was released by the press in March of 2012.[17] These papers, which included his Harvard diploma, law license, and various documents pertaining to his diplomatic role in Russia were earlier believed to have been lost or destroyed years prior, possibly by his daughter Belle da Costa Greene (who had burned her own documents in connection with her past before her death, in an effort to conceal her black lineage). The find was described by biographer Heidi Ardizzone as "every historian's dream."[18]

20

CHARLES DREW
1904–1950

Physician, surgeon, medical pioneer

"I feel that the recent ruling of the United States Army and Navy regarding the refusal of colored blood donors is an indefensible one from any point of view. As you know, there is no scientific basis for the separation of the bloods of different races except on the basis of the individual blood types or groups."

– Charles Drew

Charles Richard Drew was a renowned physician, surgeon, medical pioneer, professor and the inventor of the blood bank. He was also the first black American to receive a doctorate in medical science. His revolutionary technique for storing, shipping, and transfusing blood is still used today. Drew's innovative process (which was first launched in Britain during World War II) has saved countless lives. In 1941, Drew established the first American Red Cross blood bank and served as the organization's first director. He organized the first large-scale effort by the American Red Cross, establishing donor stations and mobile blood banks throughout Europe. His work saved the lives of tens of thousands of soldiers and civilians during World War II.[1] In 1943, Drew became the first black surgeon selected to serve as an examiner on the American Board of Surgery.[2]

Charles Drew was born on June 3, 1904 in Washington, D.C. He grew up poor. His father, Richard Thomas Drew, was a carpet layer, and his mother, Nora Rosella Burrell Drew, was a teacher, who stopped teaching

Charles Drew (oldest) with his siblings, c. 1914.
*(Source: Courtesy of Moorland-Spingarn Research Center,
Howard University)*

Graduation photo from Amherst
College, c. 1926.
*(Source: Courtesy of Moorland-
Spingarn Research Center, Howard
University)*

Seated 1st row, 4th from left: Drew with the Amherst College football team. Drew excelled in athletics and was the quarterback for the team, c. 1923.

Seated 1st row, 4th from left: Drew with the Amherst College track team, c. 1923.

Standing far left: Drew with the Dunbar High basketball team, c. 1921.

Charles Drew (standing in the center) with other resident staff at Montreal General Hospital, c. 1935. *(Source: Rice Studios, Ltd. Photographers/Moorland-Spingarn Research Center, Howard University)*

immediately following his birth.[3] Both parents were notably mixed. He was the eldest of five children. Drew's father often told his children, "Do what you believe in. Take a stand and don't get licked."

As a young boy, Drew organized a newspaper business with ten of his friends.[4] He learned how to ride and care for horses at a nearby horse farm. Drew excelled in academics and athletics. He had won four medals in swimming by the time he was eight.[5] He was very active in sports at Mead Mill Elementary School and Paul Laurence Dunbar High School, where he participated in football, baseball, track and field, and basketball. Drew won the James E. Walker Memorial medal for best all-around athlete.

When Drew's sister, Elsie, who had been ailing with tuberculosis, died of pandemic influenza in 1920, he decided to become a doctor.[6] In 1922, he enrolled in Amherst College in Massachusetts, one of the few white colleges that accepted black students. Drew was well-liked and quickly became the leader of the student body, captain of the track team, and quarterback for the football team. The Thomas W. Ashley Memorial trophy was awarded to him in his junior year for the most valuable player. In his senior year, he was awarded the Howard Hill Mossman trophy, which went to the person who contributed the most to Amherst College's athletics. Football Coach McLaughry called Drew the best football player he had ever coached. Drew pledged Omega Psi Phi fraternity. Along with his frat brother Mercer Cook, Drew penned "Omega Dear," the fraternity's official hymn. The fraternity hosts a nationwide blood drive in Drew's honor annually. Drew graduated in 1926 with a B.A. His first job was as a biology teacher and athletic director at Morgan State University. In two years, Drew turned the school's basketball and football teams into collegiate champions.

In 1928, Drew decided to pursue his interest in medicine, enrolling in McGill University in Montreal, Canada. In 1930, he won the neuroanatomical award and was inducted in the honorary fraternity. He met a British professor of medicine named John Beattie, who was studying blood transfusion techniques. Prior to the 1930s, patients often died from a loss of blood after surgery, so several researchers were investigating ways to replace blood through transfusion. Drew saved a man's life with a transfusion while studying under Beattie. Although Dr. Karl Landsteiner had discovered the four different blood types and found that the body would not reject a donor with the same blood type, the problem of finding

Drew sits with his family, c. 1947. *(Source: Harris and Ewing photographers/ Courtesy of Moorland-Spingarn Research Center, Howard University)*

Drew with his wife Lenore, three daughters and son. *(Source: Courtesy of Moorland-Spingarn Research Center, Howard University)*

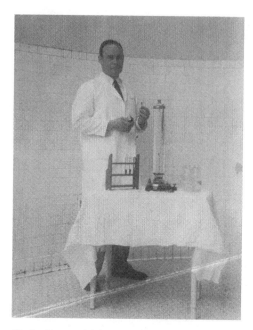

Charles Drew with laboratory apparatus, c. 1940.
(Source: Courtesy Moorland-Spingarn Research Center, Howard University)

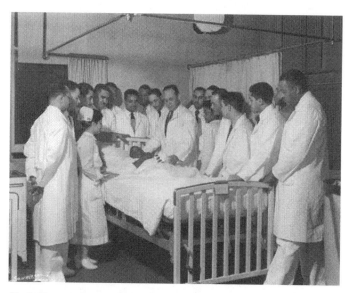

Charles Drew teaching interns at the Freedmen's Hospital, c. 1940.
(Source: Scurlock Studios, Archives Center, National Museum of American History, Smithsonian Institution)

With medical residents at the Freedmen's Hospital. *(Source: Harris and Ewing photographers/ Courtesy of Moorland-Spingarn Research Center, Howard University)*

Charles Drew (center) with staff at the first American Red Cross blood bank, c. 1941. *(Source: Courtesy Moorland-Spingarn Research Center, Howard University)*

a compatible donor in an emergency was unsolved. Drew was interested in resolving this dilemma.[7]

He received his M.D. as well as his Master of Surgery degree from McGill University in Montreal, Canada in 1933. Drew graduated second in his class of one hundred twenty-seven students. He was inducted into the Medical Honorary Society. Drew completed his internship at Royal Victoria Hospital, and worked for a year as a surgical resident at Montreal General Hospital. Drew took a position as a professor of surgery at Howard University College of Medicine in Washington, D.C. A few years later, he was awarded the Rockefeller fellowship and a fellowship from Howard University Medical School to continue his education at Columbia University College of Physicians and Surgeons. Drew was able to greatly expand his research on the storing of blood and transfusions after he was awarded a grant by the Blood Transfusion Association in 1939. This enabled him to open up a blood storage bank at Columbia Presbyterian Hospital. Drew discovered that plasma, the liquid portion of blood, does not contain cells. Therefore, it could be dried and stored for an extended period of time without deterioration. Prior to this, blood could not be stored for more than two days due to the rapid breakdown of red blood cells. Drew found that by separating the plasma from the whole blood and refrigerating them separately, they could be combined over a week later for a blood transfusion. He also discovered that even though people have different blood types (A, B, AB, and O), everyone has the same type of blood plasma.[8] This discovery was so profound that it changed the medical world.

Drew supervised the Blood Transfusion Association for New York City. When World War II broke out in Europe, he was asked to launch the first blood bank in Britain. Drew later became the first director of the American Red Cross Blood Bank but resigned after the U.S. War Department issued a directive that blood taken from black donors should be segregated from that of white donors.

In 1940, Drew graduated from Columbia University and became the first black American to receive a Doctor of Medical Science degree. He was now gaining a reputation worldwide.[9] In 1942, Drew returned to Howard University and served as chief of surgery for the Freedmen's Hospital. In 1948, he was awarded the Spingarn Medal from the National Association

Dr. Charles Richard Drew. *(Source: Courtesy of Moorland-Spingarn Research Center, Howard University)*

for the Advancement of Colored People for his work on blood plasma. He was also presented with the E. S. Jones Award for research in medical science; became the first black person to be appointed an examiner by the American Board of Surgery; received honorary doctorates from Virginia State College and Amherst College; was elected Fellow of the International College of Surgeons; and appointed as the surgical consultant for the U.S. Army's European theater of operations.

Charles Drew died in Tuskegee, Alabama on April 1, 1950, while driving with three colleagues to an annual meeting of the John A. Andrews Clinical Association. His car went out of control, struck the soft shoulder of the road, and overturned. Drew was severely injured and rushed to nearby Alamance County General Hospital in Burlington, North Carolina, but he did not survive.

In 1981, Drew's pioneering achievements in the medical field were commemorated by the U.S. Postal Service, which issued a stamp in his honor as part of the Great Americans Series. Every blood bank in the world is a living memorial to the genius of Dr. Charles Drew and his invaluable gift to mankind. Schools, health clinics, and other facilities throughout the United States have been named in his honor. Drew is considered one of the most respected figures in the field of medicine. His development of the blood plasma bank has given countless people a second chance at life.

21

HENRY WALTON BIBB
1815–1854

Escaped slave, Underground railroad conductor, Newspaper pioneer

"Among other trades, I learned the art of running away to perfection. I made a regular business of it, and never gave it up, until I had broken the bands of slavery." [1]

– Henry Bibb

Henry Walton Bibb, an escaped slave, established the first black-owned and operated newspaper in Canada, called the *Voice of the Fugitive*.[2] The objectives of the paper were "to advocate the cause of human liberty . . . to advocate the immediate and unconditional abolition of chattel slavery everywhere, but especially on American soil . . . to persuade as far as it may be practical every oppressed person of color in the United States to settle in Canada, where the laws make no distinction among men . . . and upon whose soil 'no slave can breathe.'"[3]

Bibb traveled throughout North America and was one of the most effective anti-slavery lecturers of his time. His autobiography, *Narrative of the Life and Adventures of Henry Bibb, An American Slave*, published in 1849, is considered one of the best slave narratives ever written. His testimony and elaborate account of the slave experience was so startling it galvanized the North, strengthening the sentiment toward the eradication of slavery. Bibb's numerous escape attempts and multiple recaptures are chronicled in his narrative. Despite brutal floggings to near death, he remained undeterred in his quest for freedom. He was a young boy when his master began contracting him out. This continued into adulthood. Almost immediately upon arriving on a new plantation, Bibb would plot his escape. What sets Bibb's narrative aside from those of other slaves is his impassioned delivery of the suffering and the devastating impact bondage had on Negro families. Bibb recounts one of his many attempts to free his wife and small child, and their ultimate recapture:

> The wolves kept howling, and were near enough for us to see their glaring eyes, and hear their chattering teeth. I then thought that the hour of death for us was at hand; that we should not live to see the light of another day; for there was no way for our escape. My little family were looking up to me for protection, but I could afford them none. And while I was offering up my prayers to that God who never forsakes those in the hour of danger who trust in him, I thought of Deacon Whitfield; I thought of his profession, and doubted his piety. I thought of his hand-cuffs, of his whips, of his chains, of his stocks, of his thumb-screws, of his slave driver and overseer, and of his religion; I also thought of his opposition to [slave] prayer meetings, and of his five hundred lashes promised me for attending a prayer meeting. I thought of God, thought of the devil, I thought of hell; and I thought of heaven, and wondered whether I should ever see the Deacon there. And I calculated that if heaven was made up of such Deacons, or such persons, it could not be filled with love to all mankind, and with glory and eternal happiness, as we know it is from the truth of the Bible.

Bibb made his final escape from slavery in his twenties, traveling through Missouri, Ohio, and eventually settling in Detroit around 1842, where he became active in the anti-slavery movement. When the Fugitive Slave Act was enacted in 1850, Bibb fled the states and settled in Canada, where he continued to make his mark.

Bibb was born a slave on May 10, 1815, in Shelby County, Kentucky. His mother, Mildred Jackson, was a mulatto slave and the property of attorney David White. His father was a white state senator named James Bibb, who was a friend of his slave owner.[4] Bibb was the eldest of Mildred's seven sons. In his autobiography, Bibb says that although his mother had "the blood of slaveholding flowing through her veins," it was not sufficient enough "to prevent her children from being fathered by slaveholders, from being bought and sold in the slave markets of the South."[5]

He witnessed the selling of each of his younger siblings to different slave owners. He was sold and repurchased by the same owner, as well as contracted out for long stints of time. He spoke of his life on the various slave plantations as "torment," and described his floggings, saying, "I received stripes without number, the object of which was to degrade and keep me in subordination. I can truly say I drunk deeply of the bitter cup of suffering and woe."[6]

When Mrs. White, his slave owner's wife, died suddenly, Bibb became the property of the couple's young daughter, Harriet. This child had been Bibb's playmate, but she was now his legitimate owner. The White family thought it was best to separate Bibb from his mother. Though quite small, he was loaned out for hard labor to various plantations for years at a time. The money he earned went toward the education and care of his new master and childhood friend Harriet White. Bibb says, "It was then that I first commenced to seeing and feeling that I was a wretched slave, compelled to work under the lash without wages."

At the age of ten, he made his first attempt at escape. He was on contract at the Vires family plantation in New Castle, Kentucky. The harsh treatment he endured at the hands of Mrs. Vires was severe. She flogged him daily, boxed him for fun, pulled his ears until they bled, and terrorized him for her own personal enjoyment.[7] Bibb would flee for days at a time to escape her torture, but he would soon be found, caught, and punished. This continued for several years, until the Vires family grew weary of Bibb's escape attempts and gave him back to his owner.

Mr. White was now remarried, and this wife was worse than the first. Bibb described her as a tyrant. She would beat him repeatedly with the lash. Bloodied, and at times beaten to near death, the young man would run into the woods like an animal fleeing to a place to heal. He was under constant labor at her command. His routine duties included rubbing of her feet until she fell asleep, and fanning her the remainder of the night as she slept. He was allowed very little rest. The mistress demanded daily that he scrub the floors, clean the furniture, wash clothes, and rock her in a rocking chair. Bibb said Mrs. White was even "too lazy to scratch her own head," which she demanded of him as well.[8]

In his autobiography, he speaks of the prevalence of conjures and Hoodoo, rooted in African tradition. Many slaves believed these practices could prevent them from floggings. "Such are the superstitious notions of the great masses of southern slaves. It is given to them by tradition, and can never be erased, while the doors of education are bolted and barred against them," said Bibb.

In his twenties, Bibb married a slave named Malinda, whom he described as having "smooth skin, red cheeks and penetrating eyes." They soon had a daughter named Mary Frances. Bibb begins working on thirty-two acres of plantation near Bedford, Kentucky, owned by William Gatewood. Bibb witnessed the brutal beating of his young daughter by Gatewood's wife, a woman he described as "an unmerciful old mistress" who slapped his child "until her little face was left black and blue."[9] After this incident, Bibb was determined to reach free land and formulate a plan to return for his family.

Over the years, he had become skilled at escaping. One thing that he would always take with him was a horse's bridle, so if approached in the woods by fugitive slave hunters, he could claim that he had been sent forth by his master to find a runaway mare. This seemed a plausible explanation to most. Bibb was determined to be free in his lifetime. He says in his autobiography:

> Sometimes standing on the Ohio River bluff, looking over on a free State, and as far north as my eyes could see, I have eagerly gazed upon the blue sky of the free North, which at times constrained me to cry out from the depths of my soul, Oh! Canada, sweet land of rest—Oh! when shall I get there? Oh, that I had the wings of a dove, that I might soar away to where there is no slavery; no clanking of chains, no captives, no lacerating of backs, no parting of husbands and wives; and where man ceases to be the property of his fellow man.[10]

On December 25, 1837, Bibb escaped to Perrysburg, Ohio, via the Underground Railroad. It was his first time making it all the way North. After recovering from the journey and devising a plan, he went back for his wife and daughter; but his plan foiled and he was recaptured in Cincinnati.[11]

Henry Bibb, before 1854.

The entire family was sent to a Louisville jail for several months and then put on the slave auction and sold to a Louisiana farmer named Deacon Whitfield, whose plantation was near the Red River. Whitfield's reputation for slave brutality was notorious. Bibb says the slaves on this plantation were "so much fatigued from labor that they could scarcely get to their lodging places from the field at night."[12]

Bibb knew that his child and wife, who was already becoming ill, could not survive long on this plantation. And after Bibb's attendance at a prayer meeting had been discovered by Whitfield and his overseer, he and his family knew they must flee. They got off the plantation and traveled some distance through the woods and the snake-infested swamps of Louisiana, before bloodhounds and a pack of wolves were dispatched. They were hunted down and cornered. Captured again, Bibb was tortured and whipped within an inch of his life. He describes this beating in his *Narrative*, saying:

> My arms were bound with a cord, my spirit broken, and my little family standing by weeping. I was not allowed to plead my own case . . . He called the field hands to witness my punishment. My clothing was stripped off and I was compelled to lie down with my face to the earth. Four stakes were driven in the ground to which my hands and feet were tied. Then the overseer stood over me with the lash . . . Fifty lashes were laid on before stopping . . . I was marked from my neck to my heels . . . After I was flogged almost to death in this way, a paddle was brought forward and eight or ten blows given me with it, which was by far worse than the lash. My wounds were then washed with salt brine, after which I was let up.[13]

His owner immediately separated the family, selling Bibb to a gang of gamblers, who transported him to Arkansas and then sold him to a Cherokee Indian slaveholder. Bibb attests to the character of this man, saying that he treated him "humanely" and was more sympathetic than his former white owners. The distinction he describes as follows:

> I found this difference between Negro slavery among the Indians,

and the same thing among the White slaveholders of the South. The Indians allow their slaves enough to eat and wear. They have no overseers to whip nor drive them. If a slave offends his master, he sometimes, in a heat of passion, undertakes to chastise him; but it is as often the case as otherwise, that the slave gets the better of the fight, and even flogs his master; for which there is no law to punish him; but when the fight is over that is the last of it. So far as religious instruction is concerned, they have it on terms of equality, the bond and the free; they have no respect of persons, they have neither slave laws nor negro pews. Neither do they separate husbands and wives, nor parents and children. All things considered, if I must be a slave, I had by far, rather be a slave to an Indian, than to a white man, from the experience I have had with both.[14]

Upon the death of this owner, Bibb flees North, arriving in Detroit around 1842. At last free, Bibb was determined to return once more to the South for his wife and child. But he received word that his wife, Malinda, in order to survive, had agreed to be the concubine of a Kentucky slave owner. Bibb decided not to return. To mitigate his grief, he focused his efforts on the anti-slavery cause. A minister in Detroit introduced him to several people in the abolitionist movement, and soon Bibb was making speeches about his slave experiences. Bibb began traveling throughout the North, commanding large audiences. His personal accounts were so riveting, they made national attention. His graphic description of slavery's horrors rallied Northerners to bolster emancipation efforts.

While lecturing in New York, Bibb fell in love with a woman named Mary Miles, whom he had heard was just as dedicated as he was to abolitionism. They married in June of 1848, moved to Dayton, Ohio, and became major conductors on the Underground Railroad. In 1850, the Fugitive Slave Act was passed, which decreed that all runaways could be legally captured and returned to their former slave owners. Bibb openly professed that he preferred death to re-enslavement. And so, Bibb and Mary decided to move to a small town named Sandwich in Ontario, Canada. Bibb says there he was "regarded as a man, and not as a thing."[15]

One year later, Bibb started the first black newspaper in Canada, called *Voice of the Fugitive*. The paper was largely celebrated by emigration advocates. The message of his paper was so far reaching, that three of his brothers, who had been torn away from him during slavery, heard about Bibb's prominent Canadian paper and found him. They had not seen each other since childhood. All three brothers had escaped bondage. The glorious reunion took place just two years before Bibb's death. As slavery had taken its toll, Henry Bibb died in 1854, at the age of thirty-nine.

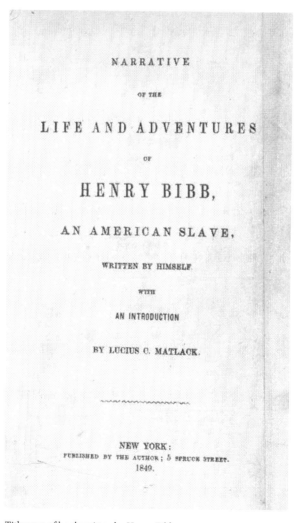

NARRATIVE

OF THE

LIFE AND ADVENTURES

OF

HENRY BIBB,

AN AMERICAN SLAVE,

WRITTEN BY HIMSELF

WITH

AN INTRODUCTION

BY LUCIUS C. MATLACK.

NEW YORK:
PUBLISHED BY THE AUTHOR; 5 SPRUCE STREET.
1849.

Title page of book written by Henry Bibb.

22

HENRIETTE DELILLE
1813–1862

Religious leader, humanitarian

"The crowd gathered for her [Delille's] funeral testified by its sorrow how keenly felt was the loss of her, who for the love of Christ made herself the humble servant of slaves." [1]

– From the Obituary of Henriette Delille

Henriette Delille, is the first black American woman to be considered for sainthood by the Roman Catholic Church.[2] In 1989, the Vatican (under Pope John Paul II) formally opened her case for canonization. On March 27, 2010, Delille was declared venerable by Pope Benedict XVI, and the decree to advance her cause to sainthood was signed. If successful, Delille will become the first black saint born in the United States.[3]

She was born free in 1813, into one of New Orleans' oldest and wealthiest Creole families. At that time, Louisiana Creoles were "free people of color." Delille lived in luxury and grew up on Burgundy Street in the French Quarters. Her parents had a plaçage—a recognized extralegal system in Louisiana at that time in which wealthy French men would enter into common-law marriages with Creole women. This tradition ran deep in Delille's family, like other Creole families, extending back for many generations. Delille was the youngest of four children. Her mother was Marie Josèphe Pouponne Diaz, a free woman of French, African, and Spanish descent. Her father was Jean Baptiste Delille Sarpy, a wealthy white merchant of French and Italian descent, who had been born in Fumel, Lot-et-Garonne, France.[4]

Delille was named after her maternal grandmother, Henriette Dubreuil

Laveau, who was the daughter of an African slave named Marie Anne and a Frenchman named Claude Villars Dubreuil. Her maternal grandfather was a Spanish merchant named John Joseph Diaz. Delille's mother and grandmother were registered quadroons (meaning that they were of one-fourth African ancestry). Delille was described as "a light-skinned French-speaking woman of color" who was fair enough to "passé blanc" (pass for white).[5]

She was groomed early on for a plaçage. As a child, Delille was taught French, literature, music, dancing, and nursing, with the expectation that she would one day become a common-law wife or courtesan of a Frenchman. Her mother taught her how to make medicines from herbs and plants. In antebellum New Orleans, free colored women would attend "quadroon balls" where, if fortunate, they would be courted by a wealthy white "suiter." These women and any children born of the union would be financially cared for and often sent to France to study. There was a favorable social status assigned to such unions, and the women and children were generally protected from many of the racial degradations.

But Delille became an outspoken opponent of such arrangements, believing it violated the Catholic sacrament of marriage. Drawing on her strong faith, she refused to follow in the footsteps of her female ancestors and rebelled against family customs. Her mother was not pleased. In addition, at fourteen, Delille along with some other free, young women of color began teaching slave children religion, as well as how to read and write. This was against the law and punishable under the "Codes Noir" or "Black Codes" in Louisiana.[6] Delille soon renounced her life of luxury in the elite Creole society altogether and became a servant of slaves, the poor, and the oppressed. She devoted herself to serving God in 1836 and became a nun.[7]

> "I believe in God. I hope in God. I love God. I want to live and die for God."[8]
>
> – Henriette Delille

Delille met Sister Marthé Fontier, a nun with the religious order Dames Hospitalier, who had founded a school for young black women. Delille had a deep prayer life, and she had dreams of starting a black order of nuns

COLORED SISTERS OF THE HOLY FAMILY
The Holy Family Convent at New Orleans has eight Catholic Schools in Louisiana and two in Texas. The students are taught Industrial Art, Embroidery, Music, etc., and become very efficient.

The Sisters of the Holy Family in 1917. *(top, Source: Photographs and Prints Division, Schomburg Center for Research in Black Culture, The New York Public Library, Astor, Lenox and Tilden Foundations) (bottom, Source: Library of Congress)*

dedicated to serving the poor and enslaved. Her first two attempts in the 1820s and 1830s were unsuccessful, but she did not give up on her vision. In 1838, Father Père Rousselon was granted permission by the Bishop to form an order of black nuns under the leadership of Delille. The order began with three free women of color. Their mission was to serve God through their service to the needy. They dedicated their time to the aid of slaves and impoverished free blacks. Their efforts conferred hope and dignity to many southern blacks who were touched by their compassion. Under Delille's direction (and with the assistance of devoted friends of the Holy Order such as black philanthropist Thomy Lafon), the Sisters were able to expand their services to form schools, orphanages, and senior homes. For years, they also ran the Lafon Nursing Home in eastern New Orleans.[9] Delille later purchased a home and converted it into a community center where slaves and free blacks could come to socialize and learn the Christian faith.[10] In 1842, Delille, along with two other black women, Juliette Gaudin and Josephine Charles established a sisterhood called "Sisters of the Holy Family." Her biography states Henriette believed that "One day, somehow, she, a woman of African descent, would be a nun in New Orleans, the slave mart of the country, where her people were in distress and no one was going to persuade her to go elsewhere or do anything else."

On October 15, 1852, the three women officially took their vows of poverty, chastity, and obedience to God. Delille's order wore simple black religious uniforms. "The woman who founded our order went to the poorest of the poor, and that is the legacy she left us . . . She was the servant of slaves. You can't get more committed than that," Sister Sylvia Thibodeaux told the Los Angeles Times.[11] Because the sisterhood was made up exclusively of black nuns, they experienced harsh ridicule and many attempts to sabotage their charitable efforts.[12]

Henriette Delille died at the age of fifty on November 17, 1862. Her short life has inspired Catholic women for more than a century. Sisters of the Holy Family continued to serve and grow as an order after her death. In 1870, the Sisterhood was formally recognized by the Roman Catholic Church as a religious community. However, because the order was "colored" and so controversial, the sisters were not allowed to wear traditional Catholic habits until some years later. The Church regarded their work as "harmless" religious education for blacks. Some in New

Orleans, however, regarded their ministry as rebellious. But blacks in New Orleans embraced them as "family," a holy family, who comforted, fed, housed, and educated disinherited slaves and free blacks. By 1950, the order had approximately four hundred fifty members specializing in nursing, education, and social work in several American cities, Belize, and other parts of Central America. In the 1960s, the Sisters began exploring the canonization of Henriette Delille. "We revere her memory and want the universal church to share in the beauty of her life," said Sister Sylvia Thibodeaux. American Catholic Bishops voted unanimously to endorse "the appropriateness and timeliness" of Delille's sainthood. In 2001, actress Vanessa Williams portrayed Sister Henriette Delille in a television movie about her extraordinary life called "The Courage to Love."

The petition for Delille's canonization is still pending with the Roman Catholic Church. If approved, Henriette Delille will become the first black American woman ever bestowed sainthood by the Vatican.

ELLEN CRAFT,

The fugitive Slave.

Ellen Craft, disguised as a slave-holding white man, escaped from slavery with her Negro husband
William. The two lived on different plantations in Georgia.

23

ELLEN CRAFT
1826–1891

Escaped slave, abolitionist

"I had much rather starve in England a free woman, than be a slave for the best man that breathed upon the American continent."

– Ellen Craft

Ellen Craft's escape from slavery was publicized throughout the country and abroad by well-known abolitionists, seeking to gain sympathy and support for the anti-slavery movement. The tale of her journey with her husband still fascinates historians today as one of the most daring flights from American slavery. Ellen, in order to get herself and her beloved husband William to free land, passed as a white man. The couple's quest for self-liberation is one of the most remarkable escapes ever recorded in the Negro slave narrative, in part due to the brazenness of their plan. The Crafts traveled by public transportation all the way from their home in Georgia to the North, even staying in hotels along the way.[1] Their boldness was made possible by the brilliance of their disguise: to mask Ellen (an uneducated, black slave woman) as a wealthy, white, slave-holding man.[2]

Ellen Craft was born a slave in Clinton, Georgia in 1826. Like many slaves, the actual date of her birth is unknown. She could not read or write. Her mother was a mulatto slave named Maria, and her father was a wealthy slave owner, Major James Smith. As a child, Ellen looked so much like her all-white half-siblings (born to Major Smith and his wife), that the wife despised Ellen and sought to get rid of her. When Ellen turned eleven, Mrs. Smith presented Ellen as a wedding gift to her own daughter, Eliza Cromwell Smith. Ellen was now the property of her half-sister, Eliza.

Eliza had married Robert Collins of Macon, Georgia. He was a scion of Macon society: a physician, a financier, an entrepreneur in the railroad business, and a large plantation owner.[3] Collins had authored an essay on the effective control of slaves, and he owned sixty-two slaves and over ten thousand acres.[4] He strictly forbade his slaves to marry slaves from other plantations.

It was on Eliza's plantation that Ellen met William Craft, a dark-skinned Negro slave from a neighboring plantation. He was owned by a man named Ira Taylor. Like Ellen, William had been stripped from his family at an early age. The two fell in love and married when Ellen was twenty. Because they worked on different plantations, they were forbidden to live together. In order to be together, the couple knew they must escape. They considered their plight as slaves, their hard labor, and the prospect of having children who would have to succumb to the same, horrible caste. Ellen vowed that she would never have children as long as she was enslaved.[5]

> *"The fact that another man had the power to tear from our cradle the new-born babe and sell it in the shambles like a brute, and then scourge us if we dare to lift a finger to save it from such a fate, haunted us for years."*[6]
>
> – *William Craft*

The couple concocted a plan for escape. Knowing that Ellen appeared white, William suggested they use this to their advantage by passing as a slave owner and a slave. However, they knew that it was not proper for a white woman to have a male slave accompany her on a long journey North.[7] They determined that Ellen must disguise herself as a white man, and William must pose as her faithful slave servant. The Crafts concluded that December 21st would be the best day to escape, because that was the day that slave masters gave their slaves passes to visit neighboring plantations and spend time with their family and friends. Slaves had to be back on their own plantations the day after Christmas. So the couple had just five days to get to Philadelphia before their absence would be noticed and the bloodhounds dispatched on a hunt for them.[8]

On December 21, 1848, Ellen cut her hair short and donned herself in male attire. William had acquired men's clothes for Ellen to wear, with

WILLIAM CRAFT.

ELLEN CRAFT.

money he had saved up from contracted work. Preparing for all possible occurrences, the couple wrapped Ellen's jaw and neck area with a scarf to conceal her lack of facial hair. The wrap also assisted in her feigning a toothache, which warranted an excuse not to speak frequently to others. Ellen, like most slaves, was illiterate, so she wore a sling around her right arm to save her from being asked to sign any tickets along the way. Along with cross-dressing, Ellen had to convincingly adopt the mannerisms of a man.[9] Her race was easily concealed. William Craft speaks of his wife's white appearance in his book, *Running a Thousand Miles for Freedom; or The Escape of William and Ellen Craft*:

> My wife's first master was her father and her mother his slave—Notwithstanding my wife being of African extraction on her mother's side, she is almost white—in fact, she is so nearly so that the tyrannical old lady to whom she first belonged became so annoyed at finding her frequently mistaken for a child of the family that she gave her when 11 years of age to a daughter, as a wedding gift. This separated my wife from her mother and also from several other dear friends.[10]

Eliza did not treat Ellen as a sister but was protective of her and kinder than most mistresses. Ellen was her "favorite slave," and she even gave her a room of her own, "an astonishing privilege in a culture where sleeping quarters for a female house slave usually meant a corner in the kitchen, a niche near the door way, or a pallet at the foot of the mistress's bed."[11] Eliza also shielded Ellen from some of the more cruel circumstances of slavery. It was not uncommon for mistresses who were angry with their female house slaves to send them to the calybuce sugar house or some similar place for punishment. Here, the women would be subjected to hard labor, severe flogging, and rape.[12] William Craft called the rape of female slaves "the greatest indignity," expressing his feelings about it passionately in his book, *Running a Thousand Miles for Freedom*:

> Oh! If there is any one thing under the wide canopy of heaven, horrible enough to stir a man's soul, and to make his very blood boil, it is the thought of his dear wife, his unprotected sister, or

his young and virtuous daughters, struggling to save themselves from falling a prey to such demons.[13]

As a young man, William had seen his entire family sold away. His old master had decided to sell several slaves to get money to speculate in cotton. While on the auction block, he witnessed his fourteen-year-old sister being sold to a planter who lived some distance away, and placed in a cart. Only sixteen at the time, he begged a bystander to ask the buyer to wait until he got off the auction block so he could say goodbye. But the owner refused, citing that he had a long way to travel. In anguish, William fell to his knees and pleaded with the auctioneer to let him go to his sister to say goodbye; but the auctioneer grabbed him by the neck, and in a commanding voice, said, "Get up! You can do the wench no good; therefore there is no use in you seeing her." As the cart moved slowly off, they stared at each other, brother and sister, for the final time; her hands clasped in despair and tears rolling down her cheeks. Williams says, "It was more than I could bear."[14]

William described his master as a reputed Christian who had no problem separating his older father and mother by selling them to different plantation owners. His parents loved each other very much and had been together for many years. William speaks of the horror of this practice, calling owners who sold couples apart without regard as "reckless traffickers in human flesh and blood, who plunged the poison dagger of separation into those loving hearts which God had for so many years closely joined together—nay, sealed as it were with his own hands for the eternal courts of heaven?"[15] William and Ellen did not want to see their marriage suffer this fate, nor could they accept the possibility of having children who could be sold away from them at any time.

Early on the morning of December 21st, Ellen (disguised as a white man) and William (as her slave) fled from Macon to Savannah, Georgia. The initial leg of the journey was not without an arresting incident. As Ellen sat in the white-only compartment of the train, a male passenger made his way down the aisle to the seat next to her, sat down, and began a conversation. Ellen distinguished this man almost immediately. He was Mr. Cray, a good friend of her slave master. Oddly, he did not recognize her at all in the male disguise, and he insisted on talking. Ellen was sure if she engaged in a discussion she would be found out, so she pretended to be deaf, and the man was soon quieted.[16] This was the first in a series of close calls.

The couple had a plan. They intended to make their way by steamer to Charleston, South Carolina, and from there, take a steamer to Philadelphia. But upon arriving in Charleston, they discovered that the steamer north did not run during the winter, so they had to change course and head swiftly to Wilmington, North Carolina. William had heard of the Overland Mail Route, so they traveled by stagecoach to the Custom House office, where tickets could be purchased to get to Wilmington. William helped "his master" into the building, which was packed with passengers. In a deep voice, Ellen asked for a ticket for herself and her slave. The principal officer gave William a mean look. "Boy, do you belong to that gentleman?" "Yes sir," said William. The man handed the tickets to Ellen. "I wish you to register your name here, sir, and also the name of your nigger, and pay a dollar duty on him." Ellen paid, pointed to her poultice wrapped arm, and requested the officer sign her name. The man shouted, "I shan't do that!"[17] Just as other passengers were taking notice of the ruckus, a military officer, who had been speaking with Ellen on the steamer from Savannah, stepped in and vouched for the couple. The fugitive couple was allowed to board and the captain of the steamer registered the couple. "What is your name?" he asked Ellen. "William Johnson," she replied. He placed their names in the registry as "Mr. Johnson and slave." He then apologized to Ellen for the delay, explaining that Charleston was required to be very strict with their slave property verification, as abolitionists were known to take off with valuable slaves.[18]

The couple reached Wilmington the following morning and boarded a train to Virginia. On this journey, William was questioned by a white man with two daughters as to his master's infirmity. He explained that his master suffered from several unknown conditions and was traveling to Philadelphia with the hope of obtaining a good physician and better medical treatment than he had received in Georgia. The man attested to the physicians in Philadelphia and said, "I reckon your master's father hasn't any more such faithful and smart boys as you." He gave William a ten-cent piece and encouraged him to be good to his master. The daughters of the man had been having a cozy talk with Ellen, who they believed was a white man with inflammatory rheumatism, and with whom they had taken a liking. They covered Ellen with a blanket. One of the sympathetic daughters told her father that she had "never felt so much for a gentleman" in her life.[19] William says in the book *Running a Thousand Miles for Freedom*, "They fell in love with the wrong chap." The father handed Ellen a recipe that was supposed to cure inflammatory rheumatism. Ellen, unable to read, thanked the man and promptly placed it in her waistcoat pocket.

The couple changed trains again, then boarded a steamer headed to Washington, D.C. At the stop in Richmond, a stout, aristocratic lady boarded and sat next to Ellen. When the woman saw William passing on the platform, she sprang up and exclaimed, "Bless my soul! There goes my nigger, Ned!" Ellen said, "No, that's my boy." The woman ignored Ellen, leaned out the window and shouted, "You Ned, come to me, sir, you runaway rascal!" After the confusion was settled, the woman apologized to Ellen, saying, "I beg your pardon sir, I was sure it was my nigger; I never in my life saw two black pigs more alike than your boy and my Ned." Raising her hands, she said, "Oh! I hope, sir, your boy will not turn out to be as worthless as my Ned . . . I was so kind to him as if he had been my own son . . . It grieves me very much to think that after all I did for him, he should go off without having any cause whatever."[20] The woman went on to explain to Ellen and another male passenger that Ned had been married, but his wife had become ill. So she sold her to someone in New Orleans, coldly adding that the woman did not seem grateful that she was being sent to a place where she could restore her health, and oddly seemed more concerned with leaving her husband, Ned, and "their little nigger." She continued by saying that slaves "never know what is best for them." The male passenger then asked, "Was she good-looking?" The woman responded, "Yes, she was very handsome, and much whiter than I am; and therefore will have no trouble in getting another husband."[21]

When they reached Washington, D.C., they hurried to catch a train to Baltimore. This was the final slave port. The Crafts had left Georgia on December 21st, and arrived in Baltimore on December 24th, Christmas Eve. So close to freedom, the couple's adrenaline was high. Excited, but cautious, they knew there was one more critical hurdle to jump. Baltimore was closely guarded, as it was where many slaves crossed into Philadelphia, a free state. As William was helping Ellen into a carriage, he was stopped by "a full-blooded Yankee of the lower order." "Where are you going, boy?" the man asked. William explained that he was traveling to Philadelphia with his master, who was in the adjacent carriage. "Well, I calculate you had better get him out; and be mighty quick about it … It is against my rules to let any man take a slave past here, unless he can satisfy them in the office that he has a right to take them along." William's heart was beating so fast, it seemed as if it was coming through his throat.[22] In the book *Running a Thousand Miles for Freedom*, he says, "But it soon occurred to me that the good God, who had been with us thus far, would not forsake us at the eleventh hour."[23]

When William went to get Ellen and told her the situation, extreme horror instantly fell on her face. The gravity of the situation was enormous. In a moment of despair, she asked her husband if they were doomed to live their lives in bondage. Nevertheless, she was able to regain her composure. She entered the office with seeming calm and asked the head officer what he needed. The passengers began to sympathize with the couple, "not because they thought we were slaves endeavoring to escape," William says, but because they felt the officer was being insensitive to an invalid white man, who needed medical attention.[24] Just when all seemed lost, the bell rang for the train to leave, and seemingly every passenger was attentive to see what the officer would do. He threw up his hands, "I really don't know what to do; I calculate it is all right." He told the clerk to let them aboard. The train left Baltimore at 8 o'clock that evening.

In this region of the country, abolitionism was strong. Two white men began speaking to William, encouraging him to run away from his sick master once he reached Philadelphia. A black gentleman gave William the location of an abolitionist boarding house, in case he decided to take their advice.[25] The train arrived in Philadelphia early the next morning. It was still dark and the cluster of lights from the city could be seen in the distance. When they arrived, William quickly found Ellen, grabbed their luggage, and got a carriage to the boarding house that was recommended. The two were safe and free. Ellen, who had remained remarkably strong throughout the journey, grabbed her husband and broke down crying on his shoulder. They had been through an agonizing ordeal; and Ellen was so drained with emotion, that she could barely stand. Once in the house,

William says:

> . . . there we knelt down, on this Sabbath, and Christmas day—a day that will ever be memorable to us—and poured out our heartfelt gratitude to God, for his goodness in enabling us to overcome so many perilous difficulties, in escaping out of the hands of the wicked.[26]

They had traveled more than a thousand miles to freedom, and their journey was not without close calls from the very beginning. They were now secure in the boarding house of a family of white abolitionists. But the man of the household had an olive-complexion, and was much darker than Ellen. She assumed he was of mixed-blood like her, and spoke to him accordingly. She was surprised to find out he was not a Negro.

Ellen, like most slaves, had been conditioned through suffering to be fearful and distrustful of whites.[27] So when the abolitionist's wife began helping Ellen with her hair bonnet, she became noticeably frightened. The wife said, in a comforting voice, "We would as soon send one of our daughters into slavery as thee; so thou mayest make thyself quite at ease." William writes, "These soft and soothing words fell like balm upon my wife's unstrung nerves, and melted her to tears; her fears and prejudices vanished, and from that day she has firmly believed that there are good and bad persons of every shade of complexion."[28]

The Crafts decided to head even further to Boston, Massachusetts. William was a skilled carpenter and started a furniture business in Boston. Ellen made a living sewing. They connected with the Bostonian abolitionist community and top leaders like William Lloyd Garrison, Wendell Phillips, Theodore Parker, and Barkley Ivens. The community set the Crafts up on the anti-slavery lecturing circuit, and the Crafts began speaking before crowds about their heroic escape. Their journey to freedom was soon published in the *New York Herald*, the *Georgia Journal*, the *Macon Telegraph*, and the *Boston Globe*.

In 1850, the Fugitive Act was passed, allowing slave owners to legally and forcibly recapture fugitive slaves. Slave holders were traveling from the South to the North in search of slaves who had fled their plantations. Word came through underground means that Ellen's former slave master,

Dr. Collins, had sent two slave catchers to hunt her down and bring her back to his plantation. The League of Freedom, an organization consisting of ex-slaves, intervened to protect Ellen and William for some time, but the Crafts thought it wise to flee to England. The couple resided there for eighteen years. During the Civil War they worked with the United Kingdom's anti-slavery movement. The Crafts had five children: Charles Estlin Phillips, William, Brougham, Alfred, and Ellen. The couple gave a series of lectures throughout England about the nightmare of American slavery, and William published the book, *Running a Thousand Miles for Freedom*, in 1860. They both attended Ockham School of Agricultural in Surrey for three years before settling in West London.

After the war, the Crafts moved back to the United States. They had saved up a considerable amount of money during their years in England, and after raising funds from supporters, the couple purchased eighteen hundred acres of land in Byron County near Savannah, Georgia. Here they began a cooperative farm and school for newly freed slaves and their children.[29] In 1870, The Ku Klux Klan targeted the Craft's school for black children and burned their property down to the ground.[30] They were devastated but determined to continue. They opened up another school where they taught seventy-five black children free of charge. Whites in the community sought to close the school and eventually bankrupted the plantation on which the school was built. The couple then moved to Charleston, South Carolina to live with their daughter Ellen and her husband Dr. William D. Crum, who had just been appointed by President Theodore Roosevelt as Collector of the Port of Charleston.[31] Ellen Craft died in 1891, and by her request, she is buried under her favorite tree on her Georgia plantation. William died in 1900.[32]

24

WILLIAM COOPER NELL
1816–1874

Historian and activist

"Our brethren at the South, should not be called slaves, but prisoners of war."

– William Cooper Nell

William Cooper Nell was the first black historian in America. He also became the first black federal employee, when he took a job as a postal clerk in Boston, Massachusetts in 1861.[1] A portrait of blacks in this country cannot be told without the four decades of historical contributions made by Nell. His publications *Services of Colored Americans in the Wars of 1776 and 1812* (1852) and *The Colored Patriots of the American Revolution* (1855), are considered the first research-based, historical compilations of blacks in America. The books are milestones in United States historiography and are still referenced today as primary sources for understanding the presence of blacks in the American Revolution.[2] Nell made the case that equality was owed to blacks because of their contributions to the building of this nation and their dedication to military service. He authored a number of studies chronicling their military valor in American wars.

Nell was also a tireless activist, abolitionist, journalist, lecturer, writer, integrationist, and conductor on the Underground Railroad. He founded several black civic organizations in Boston, Massachusetts, establishing educational and literary groups, including the Garrison Association, the Juvenile Garrison Independent Society, the Adelphic Union Library Association, the New England Freedom Association, the Union Progressive Association, and the Young Men's Literary Society. He also started the Histrionic Club in recognition of literature and theater, and he wrote and directed plays for members.[3] As founder of the Equal School Association, Nell spearheaded a campaign in 1855 that brought an end to segregation in Massachusetts schools.[4]

He also acted as a subscription agent and contributor to many newspapers, including the *National Anti-Slavery Standard, Weekly Elevator, North Star, Provincial Freedman, The Liberator,* and *Pine and Palm.* His articles most often attested to black cultural achievements. Nell also served as publisher at the *North Star* under Frederick Douglass, whenever Douglass was on a speaking tour.[5] But of all these endeavors, his work as a historian was paramount. Nell was one of the most important figures in chronicling the activities of the anti-slavery movement. Author Richard Smith says in *William Cooper Nell: Crusading Black Abolitionist,* "Nell toiled inconspicuously in the anti-slavery garden. Through his letters to William Lloyd Garrison, Wendell Phillips, Amy Kirby Post, and Jeremiah Burke Sanderson, he painted the daily activities of several abolitionists and their visitors in the Anti-slavery office. His breadth of writings included articles, editorial comments, obituaries, biographies, notices of meetings, convention and meeting reports, and pamphlets and books . . ."[6]

> *"I yield to no one in appreciating the propriety and pertinency of every demonstration, on the part of Colored Americans, in all pursuits, which, as members of the human family, it becomes them to share in."* [7]
>
> – *William Cooper Nell*

William Cooper Nell was born in December of 1816 to William Guion Nell and Louise Marshall Cooper Nell. Both of his parents had been born free. His father was a well-known abolitionist who co-founded the Massachusetts General Colored Association, the first black anti-slavery society in Boston. It was composed of some of the most spirited black intellectuals in the area.[8] William Guion was a good friend of David Walker, author of the controversial militant pamphlet, *David Walker's Appeal: To the Colored Citizens of the World,* which advocated slave insurrection as the path to emancipation.[9] In 1810, William Guion became a member of the *Humane and Friendly Society,* which was composed of "free brown men only." He had been born in Charleston, South Carolina and was a steward aboard the

American vessel, the *General Gadsden*, during the War of 1812. When the ship sailed north, he was captured by the British and taken prisoner. After regaining his freedom, he traveled to Boston, settled there, and started a family with Louise.[10]

William Cooper Nell was reared in Beacon Hill in Boston and was the eldest of four children. He was exposed to activism by his father early in life. He attended grammar school in the basement of the Belknap Street Church. In 1829, Nell and two other black students, Charles A. Battiste and Nancy Woodson from the segregated African Meeting House (later called the Abiel Smith School), were recognized as Franklin Medal Scholars for scholastic achievement. Nell was only thirteen years old. But rather than being awarded the silver medal like the white scholars, they received a copy of Benjamin Franklin's biography. Even more insulting was that they were banned from the celebratory banquet hosted by Boston's mayor and held at Faneuil Hall. Nell attended the event, not as a scholar, but as a waiter. The offense ignited in him a yearning for equality. Nell said of the event, "The impression it made on my mind, by this day's experience, deepened into a solemn vow that, God helping me, I would do my best to hasten the day when the color of the skin would be no barrier to equal school rights."[11] The limitations placed on him by racial prejudice continued to trouble him. A couple of years after the Franklin Medal incident, he told his Sunday school teacher, "What's the use in my attempting to improve myself, when, do what I may, I can never be anything but a nigger?"[12] Fortunately, Nell later triumphed over this sentiment and dedicated the remainder of his life to the eradication of racial barriers.[13] He studied law, but he never became a practicing attorney because he refused to pledge allegiance to a Constitution that advocated the enslavement and degradation of blacks.[14]

A second-generation activist, Nell made the case that civil equality was owed to blacks because of their significant contributions to the building of this nation. He endeavored to highlight the largely unrecognized history of black patriotism and military service, and he appealed to white Americans to sponsor the social advancement of blacks.[15]

In 1842, Nell helped establish the New England Freedom Association, which aided and protected runaway slaves. After the passing of the Fugitive Slave Act in 1850, he stepped up his role in Underground Railroad activities.[16]

He formed alliances with top abolitionists Frederick Douglass and William Lloyd Garrison. Nell started writing for Garrison's publication the *The Liberator*. Historian Donald Jacobs says, "Nell was the arch-integrationist, perhaps the most vehement black integrationist in all the free states, and his views fit in well with Garrison's." However, in October of 1847, Frederick Douglass offered Nell a position as acting editor and publisher of *The North Star*. Nell accepted and moved to Rochester, New York. The first issue of *The North Star* made its début on December 3, 1847. *The Liberator*'s review of this issue stated:

> Mr. William C. Nell favorably known to most of our readers from his connection formerly with *The Liberator*, and from his prominence in all efforts for the improvement and advancement of our colored country men, is the publisher of the paper. His connection will, if possible, increase the interest which will be felt in this region, in the success of the undertaking . . . We are happy to hear that the present state of the subscription list is encouraging, and trust that it will become all that its friends can desire.

Nell wrote numerous articles on anti-slavery and segregation for Douglass's paper; but by 1851, their partnership had become contentious. Douglass had begun a feud with Nell's mentor, William Lloyd Garrison, and the growing conflict forced Nell to choose sides.[17] When Douglass gave his support to the Colored National Council and the Manual Labor School, Nell severed all ties with him. Both organizations represented segregated abolitionism, and Nell had always made his position known about abolitionist organizations that allowed segregation within their own groups. He found the contradiction abhorrent.[18] Nell addressed the dispute between Douglass and Garrison on August 2, 1853, at a meeting of the Colored Citizens of Boston, stating, "Now that relation is changed —Douglass' spirit seems more than ever alienated, and in his paper he has made use of language which to many, and certainly to me—seems unkind, ungenerous and ungrateful." Douglass rebutted that Nell was nothing more than Garrison's "contemptible tool" and charged Nell with attempting to discredit him in Boston's black community. Nell defended himself by saying, "What I have said and done, touching this controversy, has been prompted solely by that fidelity which I have cherished for the anti-slavery cause—I have born allegiance to principles, rather than to men."[19] Nell left *The North Star* and returned to *The Liberator*. He was commissioned by the paper to travel the country to assess anti-slavery societies and conduct *The Liberator's* employment bureau for free blacks and fugitive slaves.

Nell was outraged by the 1857 U.S. Supreme Court's ruling in the case of *Dred Scott v. Sandford*, which said that people of African descent brought into the United States and held as slaves, as well as their descendants, had no legal standing or protection under the Constitution and could never be U.S. citizens. The court's opinion was written by Chief Justice Roger B. Taney. Nell wrote an article in response to Taney's decision, which read in part:

> Priests, warriors and statesmen, from Georgia to Maine
> Are mounting the saddle and grasping the reins;
> Right merrily hunting the black man, whose sin
> Is the curl of his hair and the hue of his skin.[20]

In protest of the Dred Scott decision, Nell organized a commemorative festival for black Revolutionary martyr Crispus Attucks at Faneuil Hall on March 5, 1858.[21] Attucks had been the first patriot to fall during the Boston Massacre. The celebration brought fiery speeches by black and white abolitionists, including John Rock, Wendell Phillips, Theodore Parker, William Lloyd Garrison, and Charles Lenox Remond, who were disgusted by the High Court's decision. There was also martial music, displays of Revolutionary War relics, and the recollection of aged black veterans at the festivities.[22] This was the first of seven commemorative celebrations that Nell organized to replace July 4th celebrations for black Bostonians. He proposed the erection of a monument in Attuck's honor, but the Massachusetts legislature denied it. Nell stated that the denial "was to be expected, if we accept the axiom that a colored man never gets justice done him in the United States, except by mistake."[23] That same year, Nell convened the Convention of Colored Citizens of New England. The assembly was made up of blacks only; and while the idea of separatism was contrary to Nell's earlier beliefs, he felt that the Dred Scott decision was such an insult to blacks that they needed to act separately.[24]

Nell worked for legislation to allow blacks into the Massachusetts militia. He did not succeed in this effort, but he lived to see blacks serve in U.S. forces during the Civil War.[25] In 1850, Nell campaigned unsuccessfully for a seat in the Massachusetts Legislature. He ran on the Free Soil Party ticket. When Congress passed the Charles Sumner Bill, which allowed for the integration of the U.S. Postal Service, Nell became the first black American to hold a federal position, when he was hired as a postal clerk. On April 14, 1869, Nell married Frances Ann Ames, daughter of Philip Osgood Ames and Lucy Drake Ames of Nashua, New Hampshire. The couple had two sons, William Cooper Nell, Jr. (1870–1892) and Frank Ames Cooper (1872–1881).[26] Nell died of a stroke on May 25, 1874, at the age of fifty-eight.

The William C. Nell House, National Historic Landmark (Boston, Suffolk County, Massachusetts). *(Source: Photographs and Prints Division, Schomburg Center for Research in Black Culture, The New York Public Library, Astor, Lenox and Tilden Foundations)*

25

MORDECAI WYATT JOHNSON
1890–1976

Educator, civil rights leader, pastor, orator, diplomat

"When the Negro cries with pain from his deep hurt and lays his petition for elemental justice before the nation, he is calling upon the American people to kindle anew about the crucible of race relationships the fires of American faith." [1]

– Mordecai Wyatt Johnson

Mordecai Wyatt Johnson, the son of former slaves, became the first black president of Howard University. On June 26, 1926, at the age of thirty-six, he was elected unanimously, becoming the school's eleventh president.[2] He served in this capacity from 1926 until 1960 and is credited with establishing the university as a vibrant, respected, and internationally known institution. Johnson was awarded the NAACP's Spingarn Medal for his dedication in securing annual federal funds to insure the college's long-term financial stability.[3] Prior to this position, Johnson was pastor of the First Baptist Church in Charleston, West Virginia. He was also active in local politics and founded the Charleston branch of the NAACP.[4]

Throughout his life, Johnson was dedicated to civil rights both nationally and abroad. He was highly influential in Martin Luther King, Jr.'s adoption of nonviolence for social change. Johnson met Mahatma Gandhi in India in 1949. The following year, he preached a sermon on Gandhi's philosophy of nonviolence. This sermon was held at the Fellowship House in Philadelphia and Martin Luther King, Jr. was in attendance. Johnson's speech served as both the catalyst and the foundation for King's nonviolent approach during the 1960s civil rights movement. In a televised interview, King describes how profoundly affected he was by Johnson's preaching, saying:

> In theological seminary days, I had heard of Gandhi. But I remembered hearing a message by the President of Howard University, Dr. Mordecai Johnson, who had just returned from India. He spoke in Philadelphia on his trip to India and the whole philosophy of Gandhi, and passive and non-violent resistance. And I was so deeply moved by the message that I went away and bought several books on Gandhi and Gandhism technique; and at that point, I became deeply influenced by Gandhi, never realizing that I would live in a situation where it would be useful and meaningful.[5]

Johnson was an exceptional speaker, who won several oratory awards. Throughout his career, he was a vocal critic of African colonialism and American militarism.[6] He was the most outspoken university president on behalf of countries under the colonial domination of Britain, France, Belgium, and Holland. In 1951, he was selected to attend a plenary session of the North Atlantic Treaty Organization (NATO) in London. Speaking on behalf of his subcommittee, Johnson petitioned dominant nations to strongly consider the plight of the underprivileged and dispossessed people around the world.[7]

During his administration, Johnson constructed new facilities, developed research centers, revamped programs, and increased faculty salaries at Howard University.[8] He also began heavily recruiting top black intellectuals from around the country. It was under his leadership that Howard University had the greatest collection of black scholars to be found anywhere, and the college soon came to be recognized as the "capstone of Negro education."[9] During the 1930–31 academic year, Johnson added sixty-three members to the staff.[10] Notable scholars at the college included Alain Locke, philosopher and Rhodes Scholar from Harvard University; historian Rayford W. Logan, cell biologist Ernest Everett Just, blood specialist Charles Drew, and chemist Percy Julian. Harlem Renaissance poet Sterling Brown was hired as chair of the English department, and E.

Dr. Mordecai Wyatt Johnson was Howard University's first black president. He was elected president at the age of 36, becoming the university's 11th president. *(Source: Photographs and Prints Division, Schomburg Center for Research in Black Culture, The New York Public Library, Astor, Lenox and Tilden Foundations)*

Franklin Frazier was appointed chair of the sociology department. Frazier later instituted the college's African American Studies program. In 1933, Johnson brought in Howard W. Thurman (as dean of Rankin Chapel) and Benjamin E. Mays (as dean of the school of religion).[11] Johnson also hired Ralph Bunche to head the political science department. Bunche went on to serve in the United Nations; and in 1950, Bunche became the first black American to win the Nobel Peace Prize.

During Johnson's tenure, Howard also boasted an impressive array of recruits to its law school. Between 1926 and 1935, in addition to employing Leon A. Ransom, James N. Nabrit, and William Hastie, Johnson appointed Charles Hamilton Houston as dean of the law school.[12] Houston concentrated the school's attention around research and intense analysis of litigation involving civil rights that had been or might be brought before the High Court.[13]

Some of the notable law students were Spottswood Robinson III, Oliver W. Hill, Robert W. Carter, and Thurgood Marshall. Many of the graduates became important civil rights lawyers, who were prominent in the dismantling of racial segregation in America.[14] It was also during Johnson's helm that Howard's law school was finally granted its sought-after accreditation from the Association of American Law Schools and the American Bar Association.[15] Howard University trained 48 percent of the nation's black physicians, 49 percent of the black dentists, and 96 percent of the black lawyers, under Johnson's leadership.

Johnson was born in 1890 in Paris, Tennessee.[16] Both his parents were former slaves. His father, Wyatt J. Johnson, had been born on a plantation in the middle of Tennessee. Johnson described his father as "a short, muscular, dark-skinned man with a strong body and a booming voice." Like many slaves, the date of Wyatt's birth was not recorded. He worked for several slave masters before Emancipation. He had also been married previously to a woman named Nellie Biass, and they had three children, all of whom died (as well as Nellie).[17] He married Johnson's mother, Carolyn Freeman, some years later. Carolyn was described as a fair-skinned woman who was kind, gentle, intelligent, patient, and had a great deal of love for her family. She enjoyed flowers and stressed education. While in slavery, she had learned to read the Bible. She particularly enjoyed the biblical story of Mordecai, and decided to name her son after this biblical figure

Both of his parents, Wyatt and Carolyn Freeman Johnson, had been slaves. They instilled in Johnson the importance of education and discipline. *(Source: Courtesy of Moorland-Spingarn Research Center Howard University Archives)*

who was "great among the Jews and popular with the multitude of his brethren, for he sought the welfare of his people and spoke peace to all his people." After Emancipation, Carolyn secured employment as a domestic worker for an affluent white family, and Wyatt became a mill worker and a minister at the Mt. Zion Baptist Church in Paris, Tennessee.[18] Strong, reliable, and disciplined, Wyatt was soon promoted to supervisor of the lumberyard and made decent money for that time. He was known to be a strict disciplinarian, who assigned Johnson regular chores and set rigorous standards for his behavior.[19]

After Johnson completed grammar school, his parents enrolled him in Nashville's Academy of Roger Williams University; but the school burned down in 1903. Two years after that event, he entered the preparatory department of Atlanta Baptist College (now Morehouse College), where he concluded his high school studies and received his B.A. at the age of sixteen. Johnson was a distinguished student who excelled in academics. He was also active with the debate team, the glee club, the chorus, and was quarterback of the football team. Johnson was strongly influenced by Morehouse College president John Hope, dean Samuel Howard Archer, and professor Benjamin Brawley.[20] They were so impressed with him that immediately following graduation, Johnson was appointed to the faculty. Johnson taught history, economics, and English, and later served as acting dean of Morehouse College from 1911–1912. The following year, he received another B.A. from the University of Chicago. Johnson's theological training consisted of a bachelor of divinity from Rochester Theological Seminary (1916), a master of theology from Harvard University, and a doctor of divinity from Howard University (1923) and Gammon Theological Seminary (1928).[21]

In 1922, Johnson was selected to give the commencement address at Harvard University, which he titled, "The Faith of the American Negro."[22] In his address, Johnson said:

> The Negro people in America have been with us here for three hundred years. They have cut our forests, tilled our fields, built our railroads, fought our battles, and in all of their trials until now they have manifested a simple faith, a grateful heart, a cheerful spirit, and an undivided loyalty to the nation that

has been a thing of beauty to behold. Now they have come to the place where their faith can no longer feed on the bread of repression and violence. They ask for the bread of liberty, of public equality, and public responsibility. It must not be denied them.[23]

Johnson's speech resulted in a close friendship with Julius Rosenwald, president of the Sears, Roebuck and Company, and philanthropist. Rosenwald would later play a substantial role in helping Johnson realize some of his administrative goals.[24]

After organizing the Charleston, West Virginia branch of the NAACP, Johnson served briefly as secretary of the local YMCA. He ministered as head pastor of the First Baptist Church of Charleston for several years. He married Anna Ethelyn Gardner of Augusta, Georgia, on December 25, 1916. They had five children: Carolyn Elizabeth, Mordecai Wyatt Jr., Archer Clement, William Howard, and Anna Faith.[25] After the death of his first wife, Johnson married Alice Clinton Woodson, and the couple settled in Washington, D.C.

When Johnson was appointed president of Howard University in 1926, it was regarded nationally as a test of whether, in the context of a segregated society, a black president could succeed in leading a high-profile university. All of the leading black colleges at that time—Fisk, Hampton, Spelman, Shaw, Morgan, Talladega, and Lincoln—had white presidents.[26]

Johnson quickly quieted cynics. During his first year as president, he launched a successful campaign to raise money for Howard University's medical school, securing in excess of $250,000 for a new building and $180,000 for medical equipment and educational supplies. This was accomplished with the generous assistance of his friend Julius Rosenwald, solicitations of alumni and faculty, and an endowment from the General Education Board (GEB).[27] Impressed by his leadership and vision for the institution, in 1928, Rep. Louis C. Cramton of Michigan rallied other key lawmakers into pushing a law through Congress that would provide annual funding for the university. This secured Howard's future and Johnson was awarded the NAACP's Spingarn Medal, its highest honor, in recognition of his achievement.

Johnson next focused his efforts on expanding the law school, which at

Dr. Mordecai Wyatt Johnson.
(Source: Portrait by ©Bachrach Photography)

The Johnson family, November, 1958. *(Source: Scurlock Studio Records, Archives Center, National Museum of American History, Smithsonian Institution)*

Dr. Mordecai Wyatt Johnson, first black president of Howard University. *(Source: Harris & Ewing photographers/Photographs and Prints Division, Schomburg Center for Research in Black Culture, The New York Public Library, Astor, Lenox and Tilden Foundations)*

Dr. Mordecai Wyatt Johnson with First Lady Eleanor Roosevelt at Howard University. *(Source: Scurlock Studio Records, Archives Center, National Museum of American History, Smithsonian Institution)*

Professors in robes at Howard University in 1930, under Johnson's administration. *(Source: Scurlock Studio Records, Archives Center, National Museum of American History, Smithsonian Institution)*

Howard University's enrollment increased considerably during Johnson's administration. Howard University Campus, 1942. *(Source: Library of Congress)*

Civil rights leaders: Mordecai Johnson, Congressman Oscar DePriest, and Dr. Emmett J. Scott.
(Source: Scurlock Studio Records, Archives Center, National Museum of American History, Smithsonian Institution)

(Source: Library of Congress)

In his office at Howard University. *(Source: Library of Congress)*

(Source: Library of Congress)

Dr. Johnson was known for mentoring the youth. *(Source: Scurlock Studio Records, Archives Center, National Museum of American History, Smithsonian Institution)*

Speaking with young women visitors on Citizens Week. *(Source: Scurlock Studio Records, Archives Center, National Museum of American History, Smithsonian Institution)*

Mordecai Wyatt Johnson was one of the most effective orators in American history. *(Source: Scurlock Studio Records, Archives Center, National Museum of American History, Smithsonian Institution)*

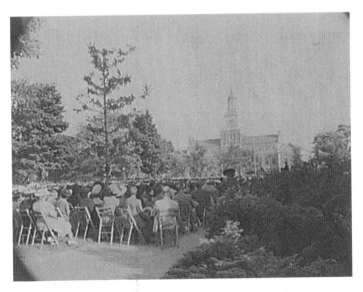

The crowd listens to Mordecai Johnson during Howard University's convocation, June of 1942. *(Source: Gordon Parks/Library of Congress)*

the time he took office, was only a night school. He sought the assistance of Associate Justice Louis D. Brandeis of the U.S. Supreme Court and began contacting top law schools throughout the country for recruitment of their recent black graduates. Brandeis told Johnson that the key to fighting racial discrimination was already embedded in the Constitution. What was needed, Brandeis said, was for lawyers to be prepared to base their arguments before the Court precisely upon the guarantees in the document. This proved to be significant advice not only for the development of the law school at Howard, but also for affecting race relations throughout the country.[28]

Johnson's administration was not without controversy. The Board of Trustees felt he was not qualified, that he was uncompromising, and that he had other detrimental attributes. However, Johnson always had the sponsorship of respected foundations such as the Federation of Jewish Charities and the Julius Rosenwald Fund.

> *"In this worldwide civil war, race prejudice is our most dangerous enemy, for it is a disease at the very root of our democratic life."*
> – *Mordecai Wyatt Johnson*

Johnson represented Howard University throughout the country and abroad and was considered one of the most outstanding orators of his time. He had an extraordinary memory and could speak for forty-five minutes or longer without notes. His speaking style was engaging, and captivated audiences all over the world. Johnson traveled approximately twenty-five thousand miles a year, speaking about racism, segregation, and discrimination. He received ten honorary degrees and was ceremoniously recognized by Liberia and Ethiopia for his global leadership in education.[29]

In 1951, Johnson was one of five people selected to go to London as the American delegation to the North Atlantic Treaty Organization (NATO). He spoke before a large crowd on behalf of the plenary session of the First Atlantic Congress.[30] Because of his fair skin and straight hair, he was frequently mistaken for white, so Johnson began his speech before NATO by defining who and what he was, stating he was a member of the underclass in America and the son of ex-slaves. The revelation sparked instant intrigue among the international audience, who seemed more open to hear his message.[31]

Under Johnson, Howard University became one of this nation's leading universities. During his administration, faculty tripled, salaries doubled, and Congressional appropriations increased to $6,000,000 annually. Perhaps Johnson's greatest contribution was the development of the university's law school as the preeminent source of civil rights attorneys and law professors.[32] At the time of Johnson's arrival, the institution was composed of eight unaccredited schools, had a total enrollment of two thousand, and a budget of $700,000. At his retirement thirty-four years later, Howard University had ten nationally accredited schools, more than ten thousand students, and a budget of $8 million.[33]

Johnson retired at the age of seventy. He died in Washington, D.C. on September 10, 1976, at the age of eighty-six.

Mordecai Wyatt Johnson speaks at an event with Gov. Theodore R. McKeldin of Maryland seated second from the right. One of the most powerful orators of his time, Johnson traveled approximately 25,000 miles a year, speaking on civil rights and race relations. As a young man, Dr. Martin Luther King, Jr. attended a speech made by Dr. Johnson on Gandhi's philosophy of nonviolent resistance. *(Source: Paul Henderson Photograph Collection, Maryland Historical Society)*

ACKNOWLEDGEMENTS

I would like to acknowledge all those who made this book possible and to express my heartfelt gratitude to my family, friends, and supporters who encouraged me to "see it through."

Special thanks to: Adam Clayton Powell, IV.; Jan Hall, Hall Editorial; Janet Green; Robin Krauss, Book Formatters; Valerie Richardson Jackson; Darryl R. Matthews, Sr., 32nd General President of Alpha Phi Alpha Fraternity, Inc.; Darrell Fitzgerald, former President/Chairman of the 100 Black Men of Atlanta; Charles Ward, Executive Director of the Herndon Home Museum; Bernie Lawrence-Watkins, Esq., B. Lawrence Watkins & Associates, PC; Tricia Gesner; Joyce V. Hansen; Andrew Thompson; Juanita Thompson; Linda Looney Bond; Tonya Williams Agenor; Garfield Swaby; Laverne Small; Camille Small-Simon, Esq.; Carlos Pizzino; Norman Smith, Jr.; Alicia Bonner; Shafkat Ahnaf; Sharaya Ceesay; Tazwell Franklin; Tedowros Abebe; Tony Toussaint; Linden Anderson; Stacey Headrick; Cornell German; Guy Bailey; Ron Seymour; Harold L. Brown; Ethan Bullard; and Chris Triplett.

NOTES

Introduction

1.   The One-Drop Rule is a colloquial term to describe a set of laws that were passed by at least eighteen states between 1910 and 1931. These laws were declared unconstitutional in 1967, when the Supreme Court ruled on anti-miscegenation laws in the case of Loving v. Virginia.

2.   Davis, *Who Is Black?*, 1.

3.   Ibid., 15.

4.   Steve Brandt, "One-drop rule persists: Bi-racials viewed as members of their lower-status parent group,"(Harvard Science online, December 9, 2010), retrieved March 3, 2011, http://news.harvard.edu/gazette/story/2010/12/%E2%80%98one-drop-rule%E2%80%99-persists/.

5.   William Walter Hening, ed., *The Statutes at Large: Being a Collection of all the Laws of Virginia from the First Session of the Legislature in the year 1619* (Richmond: Printed by and for Samuel Pleasants, Junior printer to the Commonwealth,1809) 2:170.

6.   Gary B. Nash, *Red White and Black: The Peoples of Early America* (New Jersey: Prentice-Hall, 1974), 289-290.

7.   John Ferdinand Dalziel Smyth, *A Tour in the United States of America: The Present Situation, Population, Agriculture, Commerce, Customs, Manners and a Description of the Indian Nations Vol. 2* (1784; reprint, NY, 1968),181; See also Lawrence Raymond Tenzer, *The Forgotten Cause of the Civil War: A New Look at the Slavery Issue* (Manahawkin NJ: Scholars' Pub. House, 1997), 24.

8.   Jacques-Pierre Brissot de Warville, *New Travels in the United States of America, 1788*, ed. and trans. Durand Echevarria and Mara Socenau Vamons (Cambridge, 1964), 217.

9.   Frederick Marryat, *A Diary in America: With Remarks on its Institutions* (London, UK, 1839), 53-54.

10.   Tenzer, *The Forgotten Cause of the Civil War*, 26-27.

11.   Ibid.

12.   Jesse Torrey, *American Slave Trade* (London: J.M. Cobbett, 1817), 25.

13.   J.C. Furnas, *Goodbye to Uncle Tom* (New York: Apollo, 1956), 149.

14.   Ibid., 42; See Jim Crow Memorabilia, *The Tragic Mulatto Myth*, by Ferris State University.

15.   Testimony of Rev. Francis Hawley of Conn., resident for fourteen years in Carolina; quoted in Theodore Dwight Weld, *American Slavery As It Is: Testimony of a Thousand Witnesses* (New York: American Anti-Slavery Society, 1839), 97.

16.   Lewis Garrard Clarke and Milton Clarke, *Narrative of the Sufferings of Lewis and Milton Clarke* (Boston: Bela Marsh, 1854), 16.

17.   Marli F. Weiner, *Mistresses and Slaves: Plantation Women in South Carolina: 1830-80*, (Champaign: Board of Trustees of University of Illinois, 1998), 97.

18. Lisa Vox, "How Did Slaves Resist Slavery?," African-American History, About.com, retrieved May 14, 2012, http://afroamhistory.about.com/od/slavery/a/How-Did-Slaves-Resist-Slavery_2.htm

19. Walter Hawkins, *From Slavery to Bishopric* (1891).

20. The advertisements are as quoted in Tenzer (1997), 32.

21. Tenzer, *The Forgotten Cause of the Civil War*, 38.

22. Carol Goodman, "As White as Their Masters: Visualizing the Color Line," Memorial University of Newfoundland St. John's, Newfoundland, Canada, retrieved June 3, 2012, http://www.mirrorofrace.org/carol.php

23. Tenzer, *The Forgotten Cause of the Civil War*, xxii-xxiv; "House Divided" speech is one of Lincoln's most famous speeches and was given on June 16, 1858, prior to him becoming President of the United States.

24. James L. Huston. Review of Tenzer, Lawrence R., *The Forgotten Cause of the Civil War: A New Look at the Slavery Issue* and Walvin, James, *Questioning Slavery*. H-CivWar, H-Net Reviews. June, 1998, retrieved June 7, 2012, http://www.h-net. org/reviews/showrev.php?id=2132

25. See Chapter 3 in Tenzer, *The Forgotten Cause of the Civil War*.

26. Davis, *Who Is Black?*, 54.

27. Frank W. Sweet, *Legal History of the Color Line: The Rise and Triumph of the One-drop Rule* (Backintyme, 2005); See back cover.

28. Frank W. Sweet, "The Invention of the One Drop Rule in the 1830s North, Essays on the U.S. Color Line and the One Drop Rule" April 1, 2005, retrieved June 24, 2012, http://essays.backintyme.com/item/15

29. Sweet, *Legal History of the Color Line*, 299-300.

30. Williams v. School District 1834 Ohio (1 Wright 578); Helen Tunnicliff Catterall and James J. Hyden, *Judicial Cases Concerning American Slavery and the Negro* Vol. 2 (New York: Octagon Books, 1968), 4.

31. Ibid.

32. "The Equality of Rights in the Territories: Speech of Harrison G. Blake: Made in the House of Representatives, in committee of the whole, June 12, 1860."

33. See Case: Van Houten v. Morse 162 Mass. 414 (1894), Anna D. Van Houten vs. Asa P. Morse, Suffolk. January 19, 1894.—November 30, 1894. http://chnm.gmu.edu/ aq/photos/texts/162mass414.htm; See also Zebulon Vance Miletsky, "Race on Trial: Passing and the Van Houten Case in Boston" Paper presented at the annual meeting of the 94th Annual Convention, Hilton Cincinnati Netherland Plaza, Cincinnati, Ohio, Sep 30, 2009 <Not Available>. 2012-06-20 <http://www.allacademic.com/ meta/p376718_index.html>.

34. Kevin Johnson, ed., *Mixed Race America and the Law: A Reader* (New York: New York University Press, 2003), 165-166; See also *The Boston Journal*, Oct. 5, 1894.

35. Pauli Murray, ed., *States' Laws on Race and Color* (Athens: University of Georgia, 1997), 428.

36. Ibid., 22, 37, 77, 150, 164; Sweet, *Legal History of the Color Line*, 9

37. Davis, *Who Is Black?*, 6.

38. Ibid., 5; See also Lerone Bennett, Jr., *Before the Mayflower: A History of the Negro in America, 1619-1962* (Chicago: Johnson Publishing Co., 1969), 255.

39. Davis, *Who Is Black?*, 56.

40. A phrase used to describe Henry Ossawa Tanner, a black painter who specialized in biblical themes. See Alan C. Braddock, "Painting the World's Christ: Tanner, Hybridity, and the Blood of the Holy Land," Nineteenth Century Art Worldwide,

retrieved July 15, 2012, http://www.19thc-artworldwide.org/index.php/autumn04/298-painting-the-worlds-christ-tanner-hybridity-and-the-blood-of-the-holy-land

41. Kimberly Davis, "Multiracial Identity Points to Racial Struggle in U.S." News 21 UMD Staff, Aug. 7, 2009, retrieved July 27, 2012, http://thenewvoters.news21.com/mixedrace/multiracial-identity-racial-struggle

42. Davis, *Who Is Black?*, 16.

43. Brandt, "One-drop rule persists."

44. Ibid.

45. Generally speaking, most black Americans, whether consciously or subconsciously, will consider a person black if they "appear" even marginally black (i.e. have one or two "black features"—kinky hair, a brood nose, full lips). Also, if it is known that the person is partially black, they are considered black.

46. See *Ebony* magazine, March 2011 edition. Halle Berry is bi-racial, and her daughter Nahla's father is white. When describing her daughter's racial identity, Berry says in the magazine, "I feel like she's black." Statistics show that most black Americans today also subscribe to this sentiment and feel pride in doing so.

47. Davis, *Who Is Black?*, 15.

48. See Jennifer L. Hochschild, "The Skin Color Paradox and the American Racial Order," The University of North Carolina Press: Social Forces, Volume 86, Number 2 (December, 2007), 643-670. See also [(Swain 1993:21); (Graham 2006); (Davis, F. J. 2001); (Tate 2003)].

49. See (Eugene Genovese, 1976:416) as quoted in Douglas Hales, *A Southern Family in White and Black: The Cuneys of Texas* (College Station, TX: Texas A&M University Press, 2003), 3.

50. (Genovese, 1976:430).

51. Davis, "Multiracial Identity Points to Racial Struggle in U.S."

Walter Francis White

1. Walter White, *A Man Called White: The Autobiography of Walter White* (Athens: University of Georgia Press, 1995), 3.

2. "Walter White: Militant Advocate," *The Crisis* 87, No. 10 (December 1980): 561. Judge John J. Parker's failed confirmation to the U.S. Supreme Court was the first of its kind since 1894. Parker was defeated by one vote in the Senate. The NAACP and labor groups opposed his nomination.

3. Ibid.

4. Ibid.

5. "Walter White (1893–1955)," *New Georgia Encyclopedia: History and Archaeology*, retrieved October 11, 2011, http://www.georgiaencyclopedia.org/nge/Article.jsp?id=h-747

6. See Donald Bogle, *Toms, Coons, Mulattoes, Mammies, and Bucks: An Interpretive History of Blacks in American Films* (New York: Continuum International Publishing Group, 2006).

7. According to the *New Encyclopedia of Georgia*, there were more that 450 documented lynchings in the state of Georgia alone. There may have also been other such tragedies that were not documented or went unrecorded.

8. Amy MacKenzie, "Walter White on Lynching," *The Interracial Review*, September 9, 1936, 134–35.

9. White, *A Man Called White*, 5. The family was so fair that the 1900 Census enumerator mistakenly marked the family down as white. See Robert Whitaker, *On the Laps of Gods: The Red Summer of 1919 and the Struggle for Justice That Remade a Nation* (New York: Crown Publishing Group, 2008), 148.

10. White's mother, Madeline, could trace her heritage back to the 1830s. Madeline's grandmother, Dilsia, bore six of William Henry Harrison's children, prior to him becoming President of the United States. When he decided to run for office, he gave four of Dilsia's children to his brother, believing it would not be tactful to have "bastard slave children." His brother then sold them to a man named Joseph Poythress, one of the largest slaveholders in LaGrange, Georgia. See Kenneth Robert Janken, *Walter White: Mr. NAACP* (Chapel Hill: University of North Carolina Press, 2006), 3.

11. Charles F. Cooney, "Walter White and the Harlem Renaissance," *Journal of Negro History* 57 (July, 1972): 231–240; Janken, *Mr. NAACP*, 2.

12. White, *A Man Called White*, 4.

13. Ibid., 21.

14. John C. Inscoe, *Writing the South through the Self: Explorations in Southern Autobiography* (Athens: The University of Georgia Press, 2011), 48.

15. "Facts of Last Night's Reign of Terror," *The Atlanta Constitution*, September 23, 1906.

16. Charles Crowe, "Racial Massacre in Atlanta," *Journal of Negro History* 54, No. 2 (1969): 154–60; *Atlanta Journal Constitution*, September 23, 1906; see also Glen W. Rainey, "The Race Riot in Atlanta" (Master's Thesis, Emory University, 1929).

17. White, *A Man Called White*, 6. Riots were also prompted by a rise in tension regarding the availability of jobs and the belief that blacks were taking jobs away from whites, as well as the local political climate at that time. See *The Atlanta Journal and Constitution*, September 23, 1906.

18. White, *A Man Called White*, 10.

19. Ibid.

20. White, *A Man Called White*, 11.

21. Ibid, 11-12.

22. Ibid., 19–20.

23. Ibid., 23-24.

24. Edgar A. Toppin, "Walter White and the Atlanta NAACP's Fight for Equal Schools, 1916–1917," *History of Education Quarterly* (Spring, 1967), 3–21.

25. Christopher Waldrep, *African Americans Confront Lynching: Strategies of Resistance from the Civil War to the Civil Rights Era* (London, UK: Rowman and Littlefield Publishers, Inc., 2009), 158.

26. Sondra K. Wilson, *In Search of Democracy: The NAACP Writings of James Weldon Johnson, Walter White, and Roy Wilkins (1920–1977)* (New York: Oxford University Press, 1999), 228.

27. See Vitoria-Zworykin, "Walter Francis White," *Encyclopedia of World Biography* 2nd ed. (Gale Research, 1998), 238; Janken, *The Biography of Walter White*, 2.

28. *The Crisis* (NAACP, May 1918), 17; Waldrep, *African Americans Confront Lynching*, 158–59.

29. *The Crisis* (NAACP, May 1918), 17.

30. Ibid.

31. See Amy MacKenzie, "Walter White on Lynching," *The Interracial Review*, September 9, 1936, 134–35.

32. *The Crisis* (NAACP, May 1918), 17.

33. Ibid., 19. Some accounts of the incident state that McIlherron's penis was burned off, prior to the burning of his entire body. See Whitaker, *On the Laps of Gods*, 150.

34. Waldrep, *African Americans Confront Lynching*, 162; See Ralph Ginzburg, *100 Years of Lynchings* (Baltimore: Black Classic Press, 1988), 164-65.

35. Whitaker, *On the Laps of Gods*, 150.

36. Walter F. White, "I Investigate Lynchings," *American Mercury* (January, 1929): 2-3 accessed January 17, 2012, http://nationalhumanitiescenter.org/pds/maai3/segregation/text2/investigatelynchings.pdf

37. Wilson, *In Search of Democracy*, 229.

38. Ibid., 230.

39. Ibid., 230–231.

40. Whitaker, *On the Laps of Gods*, 147, Walter White's letter to Secretary John Shillady of the NAACP. White's request to investigate this massacre was not long after Shillady (a white man) had been severely beaten by a group of white racists while in Austin, Texas in 1919. He was placed on an outbound train heading North and told not to return by a Texas judge. Governor W. P. Hobby did not object to the incident. See *New York Times*, AP story, August 22, 1919, "Austin Beating Sends Shillady on North Trail," AP story, *Austin American*, August 23, 1919; "Governor Calls Shillady Offender," *New York Age*, August 30, 1919, 2.

41. *Chicago Daily News*, October 18, 1919.

42. Ibid.

43. Janken, *Mr. NAACP*, 51.

44. Walter White, "The Eruption of Tulsa," *The Nation* (June 29, 1921): 909–910.

45. White, "I Investigate Lynchings," 5.

46. Ibid.

47. Ibid, 6.

48. Ibid, 6-7.

49. Ibid.

50. See Columbia University, "Section 6, Plantation to Ghetto: Racial Violence and Terror." *Amistad Digital Resources for Teaching*.

51. White, *A Man Called White*, 56.

52. Walter White and Kenneth Robert Janken, ed., *Rope and Faggot: A Biography of Judge Lynch* (Notre Dame: University of Notre Dame Press, 2002), 30; Wilson, *The Selected Writings of James Weldon Johnson*, 90–91; "Walter White: Militant Advocate," *The Crisis* (December 1980), 561.

53. Ibid.

54. White, "I Investigate Lynchings," 4.

55. White, *A Man Called White*, 59.

56. White, "I Investigate Lynchings," 5.

57. Ibid.

58. Peter F. Lau, *Democracy Rising: South Carolina and the Fight for Black Equality since 1865* (Lexington: The University Press of Kentucky, 2006), 72–73.

59. Nina Mjagkij, ed., *Organizing Black America: An Encyclopedia of African American Associations* (New York: Garland Publishing, 2001), 323.

60. James Madison, *A Lynching in the Heartland: Race and Memory in America* (New York: Palgrave MacMillan, 2003), 36–63; see also David Bradley, "Anatomy of a

Murder," *The Nation*, May 24, 2006; see "Obituary of James Cameron," *Washington Post*, June 12, 2006.

61. Madison, *A Lynching in the Heartland*, 36–63.

62. James Cameron, *A Time of Terror* (Baltimore: Black Classic Press, 1994).

63. *The Nation*, May 24, 2006; some estimates put the mob number as high as 10,000 people.

64. Ibid.

65. Lau, *Democracy Rising*, 73; see also "Critical Period Faces Negro, Walter White Tells Meeting," Press Release, Annual Mass Meeting, January 5, 1931, Part I, Reel 14, *NAACP Papers*.

66. Vann R. Newkirk, *Lynching in North Carolina: A History, 1865–1941* (Jefferson, NC: McFarland and Company, 2009), 121.

67. White, *A Man Called White*, 167–168.

68. Janken, *The Biography of Walter White*, 221.

69. White, *A Man Called White*, 168.

70. Ibid., 169.

71. Ibid., 169–170.

72. Janken, *The Biography of Walter White*, 220.

73. White, *A Man Called White*, 170.

74. Ibid.

75. Linda Greenhouse, "Thurgood Marshall, Civil Rights Hero, Dies at 84," *New York Times*, January 25, 1993, *New York Times On the Web*, 2000.

76. Janken, White: *The Biography of Walter White*, 13.

77. Quote from George S. Schuyler, *Pittsburgh Courier*, September 5, 1942.

78. Dana Stevens, "Caricature Acting," *New York Times*, November 27, 2005; Stevens reviews Jill Watts' *Hattie McDaniel: Black Ambition, White Hollywood* (New York: HarperCollins, 2005) and Mel Watkins' *Stepin Fetchit: The Life and Times of Lincoln Perry* (New York: Knopf Doubleday Publishing Group, 2006).

79. Donald Bogle, *Toms, Coons, Mulattoes, Mammies, and Bucks*, 8.

80. Undated report, *NAACP Collection*.

81. Watts, *Hattie McDaniel*, 154–55.

82. Ibid., 156.

83. Ibid.

84. Watts, *Hattie McDaniel*, 214.

85. Ibid.

86. Ibid., 217.

87. Ibid., 217–18.

88. Watts, *Hattie McDaniel*, 223–25.

89. Janken, *Mr. NAACP*, 271.

90. Watkins, *Stepin Fetchit*, 230; see also Dana Stevens, "Caricature Acting," *New York Times*, November 27, 2005.

91. Letter from Norman O. Houston to Walter White, September 16, 1943, Reel, *NAACP Collection; People's Voice*, September 19, 1942.

92. Dora Apel, *Imagery of Lynching: Black Men, White Men and the Mob* (New Brunswick: Rutgers University Press, 2004), 88.

93. See Amy MacKenzie, "Walter White on Lynching," *The Interracial Review*, September 9, 1936, 134–35.

94. See "Jane White," *Ebony*, February 1978, 122. Walter White had been in love with Poppy Cannon for twenty years. He finally found the courage to marry her in 1949, the same year he divorced his first wife. See Cynthia Stokes Brown, *Refusing Racism: White Allies and the Struggle for Civil Rights* (New York: Teachers College Press, 2002), 69. There were stories of the couple traveling to Europe, and people there assuming that Poppy, a brunette white woman, was the "colored" person.

95. "Walter White: Militant Advocate," *The Crisis*, December 1980, 561.

96. "Walter White," *Encyclopedia Britannica's Guide to Black History*, retrieved June 12, 2011, http://www.britannica.com/blackhistory/article-9076813.

Adam Clayton Powell, Jr.

1. Tony Chapelle, "Adam Clayton Powell, Jr.: Black Power between Heaven and Hell," *The Black Collegian Online*, accessed June 20, 2011, http://www.black-collegian.com/african/adam.shtml.

2. See "Adam Clayton Powell, Jr., 1908–1972," in *Black Americans in Congress, 1870–2007, Office of History and Preservation, Office of the Clerk, U.S. House of Representatives* (Washington, DC: U.S. Government Printing Office, 2008), 300–09.

3. *The Committee on Education and Labor Records, 80th–89th Congress. National Archives and Records Administration* (Washington, DC: Center for Legislative Archives).

4. Thomas A. Johnson, "A Man of Many Roles," *New York Times*, April 5, 1972.

5. Chapelle, "Adam Clayton Powell, Jr; see also F. James Davis, *Who Is Black? One Nation's Definition* (University Park: Pennsylvania State University Press, 1991), 2.

6. Tony Chapelle, "The Black Leader You've Never heard Of," HenryMakow.com Online, accessed June 28, 2011 http://www.henrymakow.com/adam_clayton_powell_sinner_or.html.

7. Wil Haygood, *King of the Cats: The Life and Times of Adam Clayton Powell, Jr.* (New York: Houghton Mifflin, 1993), 78.

8. See Kirkus Review, December 15, 1992, for a review of Wil Haygood's *King of the Cats: The Life and Times of Adam Clayton Powell, Jr.* (New York: Houghton Mifflin, 1993); Peter Daley, "Adam Clayton Powell, Jr.," *The Nation* 254 (January 6, 1992): 24.

9. Richard L. Lyons, "Adam Clayton Powell: Apostle for Blacks," *Washington Post*, April 6, 1972, B5.

10. Adam Clayton Powell, Jr., *Adam by Adam: The Autobiography of Adam Clayton Powell, Jr.* (New York: Kensington Publishing Corp., 1971), 14.

11. Powell, Jr., *Adam by Adam*, 14–17.

12. Ibid., 17.

13. Davis, *Who Is Black?*, 2.

14. Powell, Jr., *Adam by Adam*, 14.

15. Ibid., 27.

16. Ibid., 27–29.

17. Ibid., 30.

18. Charles V. Hamilton, *Adam Clayton Powell, Jr.: The Political Biography of an American Dilemma* (New York: Atheneum, 1991), 47–50.

19. Powell, Jr., *Adam by Adam*, 33; see also Jason Emerson, *Giant in the Shadows: The Life of Robert T. Lincoln* (Carbondale, IL: Southern Illinois University Press, 2012), 368; Emerson maintains that while the racist charge given to Robert Lincoln by Powell was untrue, the charge remained attached to his name.

20. Powell, Jr., *Adam by Adam*, 33.

21. Simon Glickman, "Adam Clayton Powell, Jr.," Contemporary Black Biography (Detroit: Gale Research Inc., 1992).

22. Chapelle, "ACP, Jr.: Black Power."

23. Clyde V. Kiser, "Diminishing Family Income in Harlem, A Possible Cause of the Harlem Riot," Opportunity, *The Journal of Negro Life* 13, No. 6 (National Urban League, June, 1935): 171.

24. Wil Haygood, "The Rise of Adam Clayton Powell, Jr.," (April 11, 2011), accessed August 15, 2012 http://aliciapatterson.org/stories/rise-adam-clayton-powell-jr

25. Kirkus Review, December 15, 1992, review of Wil Haygood's *King of the Cats: The Life and Times of Adam Clayton Powell, Jr.* (New York: Houghton Mifflin, 1993).

26. Peter Wallenstein, "Powell, Adam Clayton, Jr.," *American National Biography* 17 (New York: Oxford University Press, 1999): 771–73; Shirley Washington, *Outstanding African Americans of Congress* (Washington, DC: U.S. Capitol Historical Society, 1998), 71.

27. Powell, Jr., *Adam by Adam*, 72.

28. Haygood, "The Rise of Adam Clayton Powell, Jr."

29. Powell, Jr., *Adam by Adam*, 72.

30. Ibid., 71.

31. Ibid.

32. Chappelle, "ACP, Jr.: Black Power."

33. Wallenstein, "Powell, Adam Clayton, Jr.," 771–773.

34. Powell, Jr., *Adam by Adam*, 71.

35. Thomas J. Craughwell and Edwin Kiester, Jr., *The Bucks Stops Here: The 28 Toughest Presidential Decisions and How They Changed History* (Beverly, MA: Fair Winds Press, 2010), 246; this statement was made in defense of Congressman Marcantonio's protest to Rankin's use of the word "nigger" in describing actor Paul Robeson.

36. Craughwell and Kiester, Jr., *The Buck Stops Here*, 246.

37. Haygood, *King of the Cats*, 221.

38. Hamilton, *Adam Clayton Powell, Jr.*, 178.

39. *Congressional Record*, House, 79th Congress, 1st session (February 13, 1945): 1045.

40. Powell, Jr., *Adam by Adam*, 72.

41. Haygood, *King of the Cats*, 128-129.

42. Craughwell and Kiester, Jr., *The Buck Stops Here*, 246.

43. Morris J. MacGregor, *Integration of the Armed Forces, 1940–1965, Defense Studies* (Washington, DC: U.S. Government Printing Office, 1981), 303.

44. See *Senate Hearings Before the Committee on Armed Services, Universal Military Training, 80th Congress, 2nd Session*, 1948, pp. 645, 688; MacGregor, Integration, 303.

45. *The Philadelphia Inquirer*, April 11, 1948.

46. Chapelle, "ACP, Jr.: Black Power."

47. Haygood, *King of the Cats*, 230.

48. Ibid., 221.

49. Ibid., 220.

50. Ibid.

51. Thomas A. Johnson, "*A Man of Many Roles*," New York Times, April 5, 1972;

memorable response by Powell as to why the House had moved to exclude him from Congress. He later used the phrase as the title for a book of his sermons.

52. Chapelle, "ACP, Jr.: Black Power."

53. Johnson, "A Man of Many Roles."

54. Fred R. Shapiro, ed., *Yale Book of Quotations* (New Haven, CT: Yale University Press, 2006).

55. *Black Americans in Congress*, 371-72.

56. Hamilton, *Adam Clayton Powell, Jr.*, 28.

57. Letter from MLK to Powell, *The Martin Luther King Papers Project* (June 10, 1958), 421.

Robert Purvis

1. "Robert Purvis Dead: Anti-Slavery Leader Expires in Philadelphia, Aged 87—His Work for the Black Race," *New York Times*, April 16, 1898, accessed November 14, 2012 at http://query.nytimes.com/gst/abstract.html?

2. Between June 9 and September 8, 1841, Purvis assisted 117 slaves to freedom; see Margaret Hope Bacon, *But One Race: The Life of Robert Purvis* (Albany, NY: State University of New York, 2007), 81. Robert Purvis was interviewed at the age of eighty-five by Wilbur Siebert, the first historian of the Underground Railroad. Purvis stated that his Vigilant Committee helped approximately one slave a day during this period. Many historians believe Purvis helped approximately 11,000 slaves obtain freedom. The following *New York Times* article says he helped over 9,000 to freedom: See "Robert Purvis Dead," http://query.nytimes.com/gst/abstract.html?

3. Fergus M. Bordewich, *Bound for Canaan: The Underground Railroad and the War for the Soul of America* (New York: HarperCollins, 2005), 236.

4. The words "disfranchisement" and "disenfranchisement" are synonymous; reprinted in Richard Newman, Patrick Rael, and Phillip Lapsansky, eds. *Pamphlets of Protest: An Anthology of Early African-American Protest Literature, 1790–1860* (New York: Rutledge, 2001).

5. Bacon, *But One Race*, 78.

6. William Still, *Still's Underground Rail Road Records: A Life of the Author* (Philadelphia, PA: Porter & Coates, 1886), 711. Available at http://onlinebooks.library.upenn.edu/webbin/book/lookupname?key=Still%2c%20William%2c%201821%2d1902

7. Lisa Vox, "How Did Slaves Resist Slavery?" African-American History, About.com, retrieved November 16, 2011, http://afroamhistory.about.com/od/slavery/a/How-Did-Slaves-Resist-Slavery.htm.

8. U.S. History, *Underground Railroad*, accessed March 30, 2012, http://www.u-s-history.com/pages/h481.html.

9. Moses Grandy, *Life of a Slave* (London: Gilpin, 1843), 9. Available at http://docsouth.unc.edu/fpn/grandy/menu.html

10. Bacon, *But One Race*, 7–8.

11. Ibid., 12.

12. Merton L. Dillon, *The Abolitionists: The Growth of a Dissenting Minority* (Dekalb: Northern Illinois University Press, 1974), 30; Steven E. Woodworth, *Manifest Destinies: America's Westward Expansion and the Road to the Civil War* (New York: Alfred A. Knopf, 2010), 41.

13. Ousmane Kirumu Greene, *Against Wind and Tide: African Americans' Response to Colonization* (Ann Arbor, MI: ProQuest Information and Learning Company, 2007), 256.

14. Ibid.

15. *Bacon, But One Race*, 24.

16. Dorothy Sterling, *We Are Your Sisters: Black Women in the Nineteenth Century* (New York: W. W. Norton and Company, 1997), 121.

17. Ibid.

18. "Part 3: The Forten Women, 1791–1831." *Africans in America: Brotherly Love.* Boston: WGBH, 2000. Video.

19. Joseph Willson and Julia Winch, ed., *The Elite of Our People: Joseph Willson's Sketches of Black Upper-Class Life in Antebellum Philadelphia* (University Park, PA: Pennsylvania State University, 2000), 166, 172.

20. Ibid., 81–82.

21. Ibid., 97–99.

22. "American Libraries: Timeline in Library Development for African Americans." *Old South Leaflets 4*, No. 81 (Boston: Directors of the Old South Work), available at http://www.archive.org/stream/oldsouthleaflet01meadgoog/ oldsouthleaflet01meadgoog_djvu.txt

23. "Robert Purvis Dead: Anti-Slavery Leader Expires in Philadelphia, Aged 87–His Work for the Black Race," *The New York Times*, April 16, 1898, retrieved June 22, 2011, http://query.nytimes.com/mem/archive-free/ pdf?res=9B02EEDF1139E433A25755C1A9629C94699ED7CF

24. Bacon, *But One Race*, 38.

25. "Whittier's Recollection of the Funding of the American Anti-Slavery Society," in *27 Anti-Slavery Convention of 1833, Old South Leaflets* Vol. 4, No. 81 (Boston: Directors of the Old South Work, 1874): 5–11.

26. Bacon, *But One Race*, 38.

27. Samuel Otter, *Philadelphia Stories: America's Literature of Race and Freedom* (New York: Oxford University Press, 2010), 120–121.

28. Edgar W. Knight and Clifton L. Hall, "Up from Slavery: Educational and Other Rights of Negroes," Chapter 10 in *Readings in American Educational History* (New York: Appleton-Century-Crofts, Inc., 1951).

29. Willson and Winch, eds., *The Elite of Our People*, 172.

30. Ibid.

31. Robert Purvis, "On American 'Democracy' and the Negro," a speech made in New York City on May 8, 1860: Aptheker 451-458, on the occasion of the 27th Anniversary of the American Anti-Slavery Society, published in *The Liberator* on May 18, 1860, 78.

32. Ibid.

33. Manning Marable, Nishani Frazier, and John Campbell McMillan, *Freedom on My Mind: The Columbia Documentary History of African Americans* (New York: Columbia University Press, 2003), 511.

34. Altman, "Robert Purvis Was a Dedicated Abolitionist."

35. Willson and Winch, eds., *The Elite of Our People*, 172.

36. Ibid.

37. Altman, "Robert Purvis Was a Dedicated Abolitionist."

Blanche Kelso Bruce

1. Stanley Turkel, *Heroes of the American Reconstruction: Profiles of Sixteen Educators, Politicians, and Activists* (Jefferson, NC: McFarland & Company, 2005), 6.

2. Charles W. Johnson, *Official Report of the Proceedings of the National Republican Conventions of 1868, 1872, 1876, and 1880* (Minneapolis, 1903), 639–40, 644, 658–62, 669.

3. Turkel, *Heroes of the American Reconstruction*, 6.

4. William C. Harris, "Blanche K. Bruce of Mississippi: Conservative Assimilationist," in Howard Rabinowitz, ed., *Southern Black Leaders of the Reconstruction Era* (Urbana: University of Illinois Press, 1982), 30.

5. Nicholas Patler, "A Black Vice President in the Gilded Age? Senator Blanche Kelso Bruce and the National Republican Convention of 1880," *The Journal of Mississippi History Archives* (Summer 2009): 111, accessed July 15, 2011, http://mdah.state.ms.us/pubs/archived_issues.html

6. George F. Hoar, *Autobiography of Seventy Years*, vol. 2 (New York: Charles Scribner's Sons, 1903), 59–60.

7. Patler, "A Black Vice President," 109; Hiram Revels was the first black person to serve in Congress. Revels filled the seat of former Mississippi Senator and Confederate President Jefferson Davis. Revels served for the remainder of the 41st Congress, a partial term, which adjourned in March 1871.

8. Ibid., 110.

9. Ibid., 108.

10. James M. Rosbrow, "Senator from Mississippi," Associated Press, 1927, in "Blanche Kelso Bruce Papers," Manuscript Division, Moorland-Spingarn Research Center, Howard University.

11. *National Republican*, March 6, 1875.

12. Harris, "Blanche K. Bruce of Mississippi," 30.

13. Lawrence Otis Graham, *The Senator and the Socialite: The True Story of America's First Dynasty* (New York: HarperCollins, 2006), 80–81; *Congressional Record, Senate, 44th Congress, 1st Session* (March 31, 1876): 2101–5.

14. David Osher, "Race Relations and War," *The Oxford Companion to American Military History* (New York: Oxford University Press, 1999), 585.

15. *Congressional Record, Senate, 46th Congress, 3rd Session* (February 10, 1881): 1397–8; *Congressional Record, Senate, 46th Congress, 2nd Session* (April 7, 1880): 2195–6; *Congressional Record, Senate, 46th Congress, 3rd Session* (February 10, 1881), 1397–8.

16. Ibid.

17. Graham, *The Senator and the Socialite*, 11.

18. Ibid.

19. "Mrs. Senator Bruce at the President's Reception," *Peoples Advocate*, February 14, 1880.

20. Patler, "A Black Vice President," 106.

21. Johnson, *Official Report of the Proceedings*; "Senator Bruce," *Topeka Kansas Herald*, June 11, 1880.

22. See "Blanche Kelso Bruce (1875–1881)," *Biographical Directory of the United States Congress*.

23. Graham, *The Senator and the Socialite*, 116.

24. Harris, "Blanche K. Bruce of Mississippi," 19.

Charles Wadell Chesnutt

1.   "Charles W. Chesnutt Biographical Information," *The Columbia Encyclopedia*, 6th ed., 2001, Encyclopedia.com, retrieved June 3, 2011, http://library.uncfsu.edu/ Archives/chesnuttCollection/ChaCheBioInfo.htm.

2.   Joseph McElrath, Jr., *Critical Essays on Charles W. Chesnutt* (New York: G.K. Hall & Company, 1999), 139.

3.   Charles W. Chesnutt and Sylvia Lyons Render, ed., *The Short Fiction of Charles W. Chesnutt* (Washington, DC: Howard University Press, 1981), 140.

4.   Henry B. Wonham, *Charles W. Chesnutt, A Study of the Short Fiction* (New York: Twayne Publishers, 1998), 157.

5.   See Charles Waddell Chesnutt, *The Conjure Woman and Other Conjure Tales* (Durham: Duke University Press, 1996). Only seven of the Uncle Julius tales were collected in the *The Conjure Woman*. Chesnutt wrote a total of fourteen Uncle Julius tales, which were later collected in *The Conjure Woman and Other Conjure Tales*.

6.   J. Noel Heermance, *Charles W. Chesnutt: America's First Great Novelist* (Hamden, CT: Archon Books, 1974), 67.

7.   William L. Andrews, *The Literary Career of Charles W. Chesnutt* (Baton Rouge: Louisiana State University Press, 1980), 2–3.

8.   Jae H. Roe, "Keeping an 'Old Wound' Alive: 'The Marrow of Tradition' and the Legacy of Wilmington," *African American Review* Vol. 33, No. 2 (Summer, 1999): 231, accessed June 5, 2011, http://www.jstor.org/stable/2901276.

9.   Andrews, *The Literary Career*, 1.

10.   Charles W. Chesnutt's personal journal, written May 1880.

11.   Paul Lauter, ed., "Charles Waddell Chesnutt (1858–1932)," *The Heath Anthology of American Literature*, 5th ed. (Independence, KY: Cengage, 2005).

12.   Heermance, *Charles W. Chesnutt*, 72. In 1902, Chesnutt applies to the Rowfant Club, a prestigious bibliophile society in Cleveland, Ohio; but he is turned down because of his race.

13.   Lauter, "Charles Waddell Chesnutt (1858–1932)."

14.   DeAnna L. Witter, "The Maturation of Charles Waddell as a Speaker and Writer," accessed November 11, 2011, http://www.eden.rutgers.edu/~c350445/witter1.html.

15.   Ryan Simmons. *Chesnutt and Realism: A Study of the Novels* (Tuscaloosa: University of Alabama Press, 2006), viii, 198.

16.   Joseph McElrath, Jr., ed., *To Be an Author: The Letters of Charles Chesnutt, 1889–1905* (Princeton, NJ: Princeton University Press, 1997), 216–17.

17.   Donald Bogle, *Toms, Coons, Mulattoes, Mammies, and Bucks: An Interpretive History of Blacks in American Films* (New York: Continuum International Publishing Group, 2006), 15–16.

18.   Charles W. Chesnutt, "The Disfranchisement of the Negro," in *Booker T. Washington's The Negro Problem: A Group of Articles by Representative American Negroes* (New York: James Pott and Company, 1903), 79; Sally Ann H. Ferguson, ed., *Charles W. Chesnutt: Selected Writings* (Boston: Houghton Mifflin Company, 2001), 65–81.

19.   Charles W. Chesnutt, "Race Prejudice; Its Causes and Its Cure," in Stephanie P. Browner, ed., *The Charles Chesnutt Digital Archive* website, Berea College, accessed March 24, 2012, http://faculty.berea.edu/browners/chesnutt/Works/Essays/race.html.

20.   Ibid.

21.   Heermance, *Charles W. Chesnutt*, 80–81.

Pinckney Benton Stewart Pinchback

1. Nicholas Lemann, *Redemption: The Last Battle of the Civil War* (New York: Farrar, Straus and Giroux, 2006), 196–98.

2. French Creoles of America, "P. B. S. Pinchback," accessed September 24, 2012, http://www.frenchcreoles.com/CreoleCulture/famouscreoles/Pinchback/pinchback.htm; Louisiana Secretary of State Office, "Pinckney Benton Stewart Pinchback," All about Louisiana: Louisiana Governors, 2012, accessed September 24, 2012, http://www.sos.la.gov/tabid/383/Default.aspx.

3. Kranz, *African-American Business Leaders and Entrepreneurs* (New York: Facts on File, Inc., 2004), 226.

4. James Haskins, *The First Black Governor, Pinckney Benton Stewart Pinchback* (Trenton, NJ: Africa World Press, 1996), 65.

5. George Alexander Sewell, *Mississippi Black History Makers* (Jackson, MS: University Press of Mississippi, 1977), 67–75.

6. Jean Toomer and Darwin T. Turner, eds., *The Wayward and the Seeking: A Collection of Writings* (Washington, DC: Howard University Press, 1982).

7. Ted Tunnell, *Crucible of Reconstruction: War, Radicalism, and Race in Louisiana, 1862–1877* (Baton Rouge, LA: Louisiana State University Press, 1984), 77.

8. Ibid.

9. Cynthia Earl Kerman and Richard Eldridge, *The Lives of Jean Toomer: A Hunger for Wholeness* (Baton Rouge, LA: Louisiana State University Press, 1989), 25.

10. This letter was written by Pinchback's sister in 1863. It remained in the family for years, was passed down to his grandson Jean Toomer, and became the possession of Toomer's second wife and widow, upon his death. See Kerman and Eldridge, *The Lives of Jean Toomer*, 18–19; see also The Marjorie Toomer Collection; see also Kathleen Pfeiffer, Race Passing and American Individualism (Amherst: University of Massachusetts Press, 2002), 82–83.

11. Kranz, *African-American*.

12. Booker T. Washington, Louis R. Harlan, Raymond Smock, eds., *The Booker T. Washington Papers, Volume 13: 1914–1915* (Illinois: University of Illinois Press, 1984), 86.

13. James G. Hollandsworth, *The Louisiana Native Guards: The Black Military Experience During the Civil War* (Baton Rouge: Louisiana State University Press, 1998), 122.

14. Kerman and Elridge, *A Hunger for Wholeness*, 19.

15. Ibid., 19.

16. See U.S. presidential election of 1872.

17. Joseph G. Dawson, III, *Army Generals and Reconstruction: Louisiana, 1862–1877* (Baton Rouge: Louisiana State University Press, 1982), 116–17.

18. Richard Nelson Current, *Those Terrible Carpetbaggers: A Reinterpretation* (Relica Books, 2002); see "Inventory of the Henry Clay Warmoth Papers, 1798–1953," Collection Number 00752, Southern Historical Collection, UNC–Chapel Hill, North Carolina; Joe Gray Taylor, *Louisiana Reconstructed 1863–1877* (Baton Rouge: Louisiana State University Press, 1974).

19. Ella Lonn, *Reconstruction in Louisiana after 1868* (New York: The Knickerbocker Press, 1918), 311.

20. Lemann, *Redemption*, 196–98.

21. French Creoles of America, "P. B. S. Pinchback"; Louisiana Secretary of State Office, "Pinckney Benton Stewart Pinchback."

22. New York Commercial Advertiser correspondent, quoted in William J. Simmons, *Mark of Men: Eminent, Progressive, and Rising* (Cleveland, Ohio: Geo. M. Rewell & Co., 1887), 539–40.

23. See CultureBus.com, "The Life and Time of P. B. S. Pinchback (1837–1921), First Black Governor," accessed September 28, 2012, http://culturebus.com/site/?page=profile&url_id=356&n=Pinchback,_P.B.S; Bruce Grit's name was John Edward Bruce. "Bruce Grit" was the name he most often published under. He was a well-respected black nationalist, historian, journalist, columnist, and bibliophile during the Reconstruction and Jim Crow eras.

Harriet Ann Jacobs

1. See Harriet Ann Jacobs (under pen name "Linda Brent") and Lydia Maria Child, eds., chapter 5: "The Trials of Girlhood," in *Incidents in the Life of a Slave Girl* (Boston: author, 1861). Available at http://xroads.virginia.edu/~HYPER/JACOBS/hj-cover.htm.

2. *Incidents in the Life of a Slave Girl* was published in America and abroad under the name *The Deeper Wrong*, and another condensed version was published in England under the name *A Truer Tale*.

3. See Jacobs and Child, eds., *Incidents*, chapter 4: "The Slave Who Dared to Feel Like a Man."

4. Ibid., vii; see also Jean Fagan Yellin, ed., *The Harriet Jacobs Family Papers* (Chapel Hill: University of North Carolina Press, 2008).

5. Jacobs and Child, eds., *Incidents*, 5.

6. Ibid., 44–45. The names in the book *Incidents in the Life of a Slave Girl* were changed. Dr. Norcom's name was changed in the book to Dr. Flint, her father's name was changed to Daniel, and so forth. Harriet published the book under the pen name Linda Brent.

7. Ibid., 45.

8. See Yellin, ed., *Harriet Jacobs Family Papers*.

9. In a letter from Robert Purvis to Sydney Gay, August 15, 1858 (New York: Columbia University Library); Margaret Hope Bacon, *But One Race: The Life of Robert Purvis* (Albany: State University of New York, 2007), 82.

10. See Yellin, ed., "April 1849–December 1852: Friendship, Fear, Freedom," in the *Harriet Jacobs Family Papers*.

11. Fanny Fern and Joyce W. Warren, ed., *Ruth Hall and Other Writings* (Piscataway, NJ: Rutgers University Press, 1986), xviii.

12. See Jacobs and Child, eds., *Incidents*, chapter 5: "Trials of Girlhood."

13. Kelly Oliver, *Witnessing: Beyond Recognition* (Minneapolis, MN: University of Minneapolis Press, 2001), 103.

14. Margaret Crittenden Douglass, *Educational Laws of Virginia: The Personal Narrative of Mrs. Margaret Douglass, A Southern Woman Who Was Imprisoned for One Month, in the Common Jail of Norfolk, Under the Laws of Virginia, for the Crime of Teaching Free Colored Children to Read* (Boston, MA: Jewett, 1854), 63–64.

15. Jacobs and Child, eds., *Incidents*, 70.

16. Jill Ker Conway, *Written by Herself: Autobiographies of American Women: An Anthology* (New York: Vintage Books, 1992), 10.

Daniel Hale Williams

1. "Williams, Daniel Hale." Adoptions.com. February 9, 2007, retrieved October 17, 2011, http://famous.adoption.com/famous/williams-daniel-hale.html.

2. Harris B. Shumacker, *The Evolution of Cardiac Surgery* (Bloomington: Indiana University Press, 1992), 12.

3. Encyclopedia Britannica, "Reference Room: Daniel Hale Williams," *African American World*, PBS, archived from the original on June 29, 2008.

4. Some biographies place the birth year for Dr. Williams at 1858 and some at 1856. I have placed it at 1856, based on his age in the 1860 U.S. Census records of Hollidaysburg, Pennsylvania, placing his age at 4.

5. Barbara Carlisle Bigelow, ed., *Contemporary Black Biography: Profiles from the International Black Community* Vol. 6 (Detroit: Gale Research Inc., 1994), 254; see also Louise Haber, *Black Pioneers of Science and Invention* (New York: First Odyssey Classics, 1992), 176–77; See *Contemporary Black Biography*, "Daniel Hale Williams" (Detroit: Gale Research Inc., 1992); Haber, *Black Pioneers*, 176.

6. Provident Foundation, "First Open Heart Surgeon," *History: Dr. Daniel Hale Williams*, retrieved September 5, 2011, http://www.providentfoundation.org/history/williams.html.

7. Haber, *Black Pioneers*, 8.

8. Ibid., 179.

9. Ibid., 182.

10. See "Daniel Hale Williams," *Black Inventor Online Museum*, retrieved October 3, 2011, http://www.blackinventor.com/pages/daniel-williams.html.

11. Ibid.

12. Provident Foundation, "Provident Hospital," 2008, accessed November 14, 2011, http://www.providentfoundation.org/.

13. Buckler, *Daniel Hale Williams*, 87.

14. Provident Foundation, "Provident Hospital," 2008.

15. Buckler, *Dale Hale Williams*, "Introduction," x.

16. Booker Taliaferro Washington, Raymond W. Smock, and Louis R. Harlan, *The Booker T. Washington Papers, Volume 9: 1906–1908*, The Open Book ed. (Urbana: University of Illinois Press, 1980), 396.

Jean Toomer

1. See BookRags.com, "Dictionary of Literary Biography on Jean Toomer," accessed November 14, 2012, http://www.bookrags.com/biography/jean-toomer-dlb/

2. Jean Toomer, Robert B. Jones, and Margery Toomer Latimer, eds., *The Collected Poems of Jean Toomer* (Chapel Hill: The University of North Carolina Press, 1988), xiv.

3. Jean Toomer and Mark Whalan, eds., *The Letters of Jean Toomer, 1919–1924* (Knoxville: The University of Tennessee Press, 2006), ii.

4. William Stanley Braithwaite, "The Negro in Literature," *The Crisis* 28 (September, 1924), 209.

5. Toomer and Whalans, eds., *The Letters of Jean Toomer, 1919–1924*, xiv.

6. Ibid.

7. Arna Bontemps, "Introduction to Cane," as appearing in the Harper & Row Perennial Classic edition, 1969.

8. Toomer and Whalan, *The Letters of Jean Toomer, 1919–1924*, 27.

9. See the letter from Jean Toomer (in 1922) to Max Eastman and his assistant, Claude McKay (editors of the Liberator), accessed November 14, 2012, http://aalbc.com/authors/introtocane.htm.

10. Cynthia Earl Kerman and Richard Eldridge, *The Lives of Jean Toomer: A Hunger for Wholeness* (Baton Rouge: Louisiana State University Press, 1989), xiv, 341.

11. See "The Crock of Problems" in Robert B. Jones *Jean Toomer: Selected Essays and Literary Criticisms* (Knoxville: University of Tennessee Press, 1996), 56.

12. Toni Morrison, "Nook Review," *New York Times*, July 13, 1980, review of Darwin Turner's editing of uncollected and autobiographical writings of Jean Toomer in The Wayward and the Seeking.

13. Bontemps, "Introduction to Cane" (1969).

14. Kerman and Eldridge, *The Lives of Jean Toomer*, 72.

15. Scott W. Williams, "Jean Toomer Biography," accessed September 3, 2001, http://www.math.buffalo.edu/~sww/toomer/toomerbio.html.

16. P. D. Ouspensky, *In Search of the Miraculous: The Teachings of G. I. Gurdjieff* (New York: Houghton, Mifflin, Harcourt, 2001), 312–13.

17. Kerman and Eldridge, *The Lives of Jean Toomer*, 340.

18. Williams, "Jean Toomer Biography."

19. Ibid.

20. Kerman and Eldridge, *The Lives of Jean Toomer*, 216.

21. Ibid., 340.

22. Robert A. Bone, *The Negro Novel in America*, rev. ed. (New Haven: Yale University Press, 1965), 81–2.

Victoria Earle Matthews

1. Victoria Earle Matthews was born Victoria Smith. According to birth records, her parents were slaves: Caroline and William Smith, a brown-skinned slave. However, it was common knowledge, and visibly apparent, that her biological father was the white slave master. Some of Caroline's children were by William Smith and some were by the slave owner, due to the circumstance of rape. When Caroline fled at the start of the Civil War, the white master took in his children by Caroline and was raising them as white. The other siblings were left out in the field. Caroline later returned for her children.

2. Ralph E. Luker, "Missions, Institutional Churches, and Settlement Houses: The Black Experience, 1885–1910," *The Journal of Negro History 69*, No. 3/4 (1984): 104.

3. Answers.com, *Oxford Companion to African-American Literature*, accessed November 13, 2012, http://www.answers.com/library/African+American+Literature-letter-1A.

4. See *H. Brown, Homespun Heroines and Other Women of Distinction* (New York: Oxford University Press, Inc., 1988).

5. Pier Gabrielle Foreman, *Activist Sentiments: Reading Black Women in the Nineteenth Century* (Champaign, IL: University of Illinois Press, 2009), 134.

6. Sharifa Rhodes-Pitts, *Harlem Is Nowhere: A Journey to the Mecca of Black America*, (New York: Little, Brown and Company), 2011.

7. Ibid.

8. Ibid.

9. Gerda Lerner, "Early Community Work of Black Club Women," *Journal of Negro History* 59 (April, 1974): 158–62.

10. Rhodes-Pitts, *Harlem Is Nowhere.*

11. See "Black Women's Club Movement" in Tamara L. Brown, Gregory S. Parks, and Clarenda M. Phillips, eds., *African American Fraternities and Sororities: The Legacy and the Vision* (University Press of Kentucky, 2005).

12. Ibid.

13. See Charles H. Wesley, *The History of the National Association of Colored Women's Clubs: A Legacy of Service* (Washington, D.C.: The Association, 1984).

14. Jack Rummel, *African American Social Leaders and Activists* (New York: Facts on File, Inc., 2003).

15. Louis R. Harlan and Raymond Smock, eds., *The Booker T. Washington Papers, Volume 4*, 1895–1898 (Board of Trustees of University of Illinois, 1975); Floris Barnett Cash, "Victoria Earle Matthews," in Darlene Clark Hine, ed., *Black Women in America: Education, Encyclopedia of Black Women in America*, 2nd ed. (New York: Facts on File, Inc., 1997).

16. Steve Kramer, "Matthews, Victoria Earle," *American National Biography Online*, accessed October 11, 2012, http://www.anb.org/articles/15/15-01315.html; *Oxford Companion to African-American Literature*, 2008.

17. Shirley Wilson Logan, *We Are Coming: The Persuasive Discourse of Nineteenth-Century Black Women* (Carbondale: Southern Illinois University Press, 1999), 262.

18. John Cullen Gruesser and Hanna Wallinger (eds.), *Loopholes and Retreats: African American Writers and the Nineteenth Century* (Piscataway, NJ: Transaction Publishers, 2009), 194.

19. Floris Barnett Cash, "Victoria Earle Matthews," in Darlene Clark Hine's, *Black Women.*

20. *Washington Post*, December 13, 1896.

21. Gloria Wade-Gayles, "Black Women Journalist in the South, 1880–1905: An Approach to the Study of Black Women's History," *Callaloo* (February–October, 1981):138–152.

22. S. Kramer, "Uplifting our 'Downtrodden Sisterhood': Victoria Earle Matthews and New York City's White Rose Mission, 1897–1907," *Journal of African American History* 91, No. 3 (2006): 243–266.

23. Hallie Quinn Brown, *Homespun Heroines and Other Women of Distinction* (New York: Oxford University Press, Inc., 1988), 208.

24. Ibid.

25. Henry Louis Gates, ed., *The Schomburg Library of Nineteenth-Century Black Women Writers* (Oxford University Press, 1992).

26. Ibid.

27. See Rhodes-Pitts, *Harlem Is Nowhere.*

28. Mather, Frank Lincoln, *Who's Who of the Colored Race: A General Biographical Dictionary of Men and Women of African Descent*, Vol. 1 (Chicago: Memento Edition, 1915), 222.

29. Rhodes-Pitts, *Harlem Is Nowhere.*

30. Kramer, "Uplifting."

31.   Cheryl D. Hicks, "In Danger of Becoming Morally Depraved: Single Black Women, Working Class Black Families, and New York State's Wayward Minor Laws, 1917–1928," *University of Pennsylvania Law Review* (June 1, 2003), 41–42.

32.   Kramer, "Matthews, Victoria Earle."

33.   Ibid.

Alexander Lucius Twilight

1.   See "African-American Registry, Alexander Twilight, the First Black College Graduate," accessed November 14, 2012, http://aaregistry.org/historic_events/view/alexander-l-twilight-first-african-american-college-graduate; Walter Eugene Howard and Charles E. Prentiss, eds., *Catalogue of Officers and Students of Middlebury College in Middlebury and Others Who Have Received Degrees* (Middlebury, VT: Middlebury College, The Register Co., 1901); Alexander Twilight married Mercy Ladd Merrill on April 20, 1826; he was a representative to the legislature in 1836.

2.   See "Alexander Lucius Twilight" in *Catalogue of Officers and Students of Middlebury College* (Middlebury, VT: Middlebury College, 1901), 74.

3.   Black Past.org, "Alexander Twilight," accessed November 14, 2012, http://www.blackpast.org/?q=aah/twilight-alexander-1795-1857.

4.   Old Stone Home Museum, Orleans County Historical Society, accessed November 14, 2012, http://oldstonehousemuseum.org/.

5.   Howard and Prentiss, *Catalogue*, 74.

Timothy Thomas Fortune

1.   Timothy Thomas Fortune, *Black and White: Land, Labor, and Politics in the South* (New York: Fords, Howard and Hulbert, 1884), 29. Available at http://www.scribd.com/doc/94115833/Timothy-Thomas-Fortune-Black-and-Land-Labor-And-Politics-in-the-South-1884

2.   John Hope Franklin and August Meier, eds., *Black Leaders of the 20th Century* (Champaign, IL: University of Illinois Press, 1982).

3.   See Wikipedia.com, The Free Encyclopedia "Timothy Thomas Fortune," accessed June 22, 2012 http://en.wikipedia.org/wiki/Timothy_Thomas_Fortune.

4.   Fortune, *Black and White*, 61–62.

5.   Newman Ivey White and Walter Clinton Jackson, eds., *Anthology of Verse by American Negroes* (Kessinger Publishing, LLC, 2003), 114.

6.   Booker T. Washington, *The Negro in Business* (Hertel, Jenkins & Company, 1907), 134.

7.   White and Jackson, *Anthology of Verse*, 114.

8.   Emma Lou Thornbrough, *T. Thomas Fortune: Militant Journalist* (Chicago, IL.: The University of Chicago Press, 1972), 4.

9.   Fortune, *Black and White*, 36.

10.   See Shawn Leigh Alexander, *T. Thomas Fortune, The Afro-American Agitator: A Collection of Writings 1880–1928* (University of Florida Press, 2008).

11.   *Freeman* newspaper, Washington, D.C., May 28, 1887.

12.   Fortune, *Black and White*, 121.

13. Waldo E. Martin, Jr., *The Mind of Frederick Douglass* (Durham, NC: University of North Carolina Press, 1986), 90.

14. See Shawn Leigh Alexander, *T. Thomas Fortune, The Afro-American Agitator: A Collection of Writings 1880–1928* (University of Florida Press, 2008), xvii.

15. Martin, *The Mind of Frederick Douglass*, 90.

16. White and Jackson, *Anthology of Verse*, 114.

17. Michael W. Fitzgerald, "T. Thomas Fortune," in William L. Andrews, Frances Smith Foster and Trudier Harris, eds., *The Concise Oxford Companion to African American Literature* (New York: Oxford University Press, 2001), 149.

18. The term "yellow" was often used to describe Negroes who were racially mixed. The term was used by both blacks and whites (as in historical terminology, "yellow niggers").

19. Dave Roediger, "Strange Legacies: The Black International and Black America," *The Lucy Parsons Project*, accessed March 23, 2012, http://flag.blackened.net/lpp/aboutlucy/roediger_strange_legacies.html.

20. See T. Thomas Fortune, *The Filipino: A Social Study in Three Parts, The Voice of the Negro* (May, 1904), 200–1.

21. Karin L. Stanford, *If We Must Die: African American Voices on War and Peace* (Lanham: Rowman and Littlefield Publishers, Inc., 2008), 97.

William Wells Brown

1. Philip Bader, *African-American Writers* (New York: Facts On File, Inc., 2004), 33.

2. William Wells Brown's *Clotel, or, The President's Daughter: A Narrative of Slave Life in the United States* was the first novel written by an African American. It is also the first novel published by an African American, but because it was published in England it was not the first African American novel published in the United States. See the online Civil War Women Blog, "Anna Brown: Wife of American Author William Brown," retrieved March 10, 2012, http://www.civilwarwomenblog.com/2011/09/anna-elizabeth-gray-brown.html.

3. William Wells Brown and Robert Levine, ed., *Clotel, or, The President's Daughter: A Narrative of Slave Life in the United States* (St. Martin's: Bedford Cultural Editions, 2000).

4. William W. Brown, *Narrative of William W. Brown, An American Slave*, Written by Himself (London: Charles Gilpin, Bishopgate-St. Without, 1849), iii; see William L. Andrews, Frances Smith Foster, and Trudier Harris, *The Oxford Companion to African American Literature* (New York: Oxford University Press, 1997), 55.

5. William L. Andrews, "Introduction," *From Fugitive Slave to Free Man: The Autobiographies of William Wells Brown* (New York: Mentor, 1993).

6. Andrews, Foster, and Harris, *The Oxford Companion*, 55.

7. It is commonly accepted that Brown's mother was the mulatto daughter of American frontiersman Daniel Boone. Certainly, some resemblance can be seen between Boone and his grandson William Wells Brown. See Edward W. Farrison, "Phylon Profile XVI: William Wells Brown," Phylon 9, No. 1(1948): 13.

8. William W. Brown, *Narrative*, chapter I.

9. William W. Brown and Ezra Greenspan, ed., *William Wells Brown: Reader* (Athens: University of Georgia Press, 2008), 14–15.

10. Ibid., 15.

11.   Ibid.; see also John M. Vlach, *Back of the Big House: The Architecture of Plantation Slavery* (University of North Carolina Press, 1993), 65.

12.   Brown and Greenspan, *William Wells Brown: A Reader*, 17–19.

13.   Brown, *Narrative*, 57–58.

14.   Brown, *Clotel*, 6–8.

15.   Brown, *Narrative*, 33.

16.   Brown, *Clotel*, 5.

17.   Brown and Greenspan, *William Wells Brown: A Reader*, 70–71.

18.   Ibid., 71.

19.   William Wells Brown and Paul Jefferson, ed., *The Travels of William Wells Brown: Including Narrative of William Wells Brown, a Fugitive Slave and the American Fugitive in Europe* (Princeton, NJ: Markus Wiener Publishers, 1991), 64.

20.   Brown and Greenspan, *William Wells Brown: A Reader*, 55.

21.   Brown and Jefferson, *The Travels of William Wells Brown*, 64.

22.   See William R. Andrews and William L. Andrews, *From Fugitive Slave to Free Man: The Autobiographies of William Wells Brown* (Columbia: University of Missouri, 2003), 76.

23.   Ibid.

24.   Ibid., 77–78.

25.   Brown and Greenspan, *William Wells Brown: A Reader*, 54-55.

26.   Ibid., 79-80.

27.   Ibid., 80.

28.   William Wells Brown, *Black Man, His Antecedents, His Genius, and His Achievements* (Boston: James Redpath Publishers, 1863), 25–26.

29.   Lillian Serece Williams, *Strangers in the Land of Paradise: The Creation of an African American Community, Buffalo, New York, 1900–1940* (Bloomington: Indiana University Press, 1999), 13; Brown, Narrative, 109–111.

30.   Williams, *Strangers*, 13; see also Brown's *Narrative*, 109–11, in which Brown describes how the slave catcher, Mr. Tate, employs a black woman to spy on the family. The family is kidnapped in the middle of the night.

31.   Andrews, *From Fugitive Slave to Free Man*, 80.

32.   See Horace Seldon, "William Wells Brown," *The Liberator Files*, a Boston-based abolitionist newspaper published by William Lloyd Garrison, 1831–1865.

33.   Dorothy Sterling, *Ahead of Her Time: Abby Kelley and the Politics of Antislavery* (New York: W. W. Norton & Company, Inc., 1991), 247.

34.   See "William Wells Brown, 1814–1884," *African American History of Western New York*, accessed November 14, 2012, http://www.math.buffalo.edu/~sww/0history/wwb0.html.

35.   Joe William Trotter and Eric Ledell Smith, eds., *African Americans in Pennsylvania: Shifting Historical Perspectives* (Philadelphia: Pennsylvania State University Press, 1997), 3.

36.   See Civil War Women Blog, "Anna Brown: Wife of American Author William Brown," retrieved March 10, 2012, http://www.civilwarwomenblog.com/2011/09/anna-elizabeth-gray-brown.html.

John Mercer Langston

1. See the back cover of Maurine Christopher's *Black Americans in Congress (1870–2007)* (New York: Thomas Y. Crowell Company, 1976); see also John Mercer Langston, *From the Virginia Plantation to the National Capitol; or The First and Only Negro in Congress from the Old Dominion* (Hartford, CT: American Publishing, 1894)—a 2011 edition is available from Charleston, SC: Nabu Press (Bibliolabs).

2. Leon F. Litwack and August Meier, eds., *Black Leaders of the Nineteenth Century* (Chicago: University of Illinois, 1991) 110–14, 118.

3. Geoffrey Blodgett, "John Mercer Langston and the Case of Edmonia Lewis: Oberlin, 1862" *Journal of Negro History* 53 (July 1968): 201–18. John Mercer Langston was the first known black applicant to a U.S. law school. See John Clay Smith, *Emancipation: The Making of the Black Lawyer, 1814–1944* (Philadelphia: University of Pennsylvania Press, 1993), 34.

4. Christopher, back cover, *Black Americans in Congress* (1870–2007).

5. Ibid.

6. Martin Henry Blatt, Thomas J. Brown, and Donald Yacovone. *Hope and Glory: Essays on the Legacy of the Fifty-Fourth Massachusetts Regiment* (Boston: University of Massachusetts Press, 2001), 22. John Mercer Langston, along with other prominent black leaders (including Frederick Douglass, Henry Highland Garnet, Martin R. Delany, and T. Morris Chester) raised the Fifty-Fourth Regiment in the spring of 1863. They recruited men, signed them up, and put them on trains heading to Boston for training.

7. See Stephen Middleton, ed., *Black Congressmen during Reconstruction: A Documentary Sourcebook* (Greenwood Publishing, January 1, 2002), 125.

8. See William F. Cheek and Aimee Lee Cheek, *John Mercer Langston and the Fight for Black Freedom, 1829–1865* (Urbana: University of Illinois Press, 1989), 105, 117.

9. Stephen Middleton, *The Black Laws: Race and the Legal Process in Early Ohio* (Athens, Ohio: Ohio University Press, 2005), 145.

10. See Cheek and Cheek, *John Mercer Langston.*

11. Litwack and Meier, *Black Leaders of the Nineteenth Century.*

12. See Henry Wreford, "A Negro Sculptress," *The Athenæum*, March 3, 1866.

13. Blodgett, "John Mercer Langston and the Case of Edmonia Lewis," 201–18.

14. Wreford, "A Negro Sculptress."

15. See Voting Rights Act of 1965, available at http://www.ourdocuments.gov/doc.php?flash=old&doc=100.

16. See Cheek and Cheek, *John Mercer Langston.*

Patrick Francis Healy

1. Valerie Jo Bradley, "Black President Runs Michigan State University: Gets Demanding Position," *JET Magazine*, May 21, 1970, 16.

2. Anne Marie Murphy, "Passing Free: Black in the South, Irish in the North, the Healys slipped the Bonds of Race in Civil War America," *Boston College Magazine* (summer, 2003), accessed March 17, 2012. http://bcm.bc.edu/issues/summer_2003/ft_passing.html

3. Ibid.

4. Albert Sidney Foley, *God's Men of Color: The Colored Catholic Priests of the United States, 1854–1954* (New York: Farrar, Straus, 1955), 23–30.

5.   Ibid.

6.   Ibid.

7.   See National Park Service, National Historic Landmark Program at: http://tps. cr.nps.gov/nhl/detail.cfm?ResourceId=1171&ResourceType=Building.

Fredi Washington

1.   Fay M. Jackson, *Pittsburgh Courier*, April 14, 1934.

2.   Sheila Rule, "Obituary of Fredi Washington, 90, Actress: Broke Ground for Black Artists," *New York Times*, June 30, 1994.

3.   "The Papers of Fredi Washington (1925–1979)" and "Biographical Notes: Fredi Washington, 1903–1994," both microfilmed from the holdings of the Amistad Research Center at Tulane University (Woodbridge: Scholarly Resources, Inc., an imprint of Thomson Gale, 2005).

4.   Veronica Chambers, "Lives Well Lived: Fredi Washington; The Tragic Mulatto," *New York Times*, January 1, 1995.

5.   Sheila Rule, "Obituary."

6.   Quintard Taylor and Shirley Ann Wilson Moore, eds., *African American Women Confront the West 1600–2000* (University of Oklahoma Press, 2003), 235.

7.   Ibid, 123.

8.   See "Ina Ray Hutton (birth name 'Odessa Cowen') 1916–1984," at BlackPast.org's U.S. Census 1920, at this Census place: Chicago Ward 3, Cook County (Chicago, Illinois).

9.   Kristin A. McGee, *Some Like It Hot: Jazz Women in Film and Television, 1928–1959* (Middletown, CT: Wesleyan University Press, 2009), 213; Klaus Lansberg, "Eye Appeal and Music Go Hand in Hand on TV," Down Beat, September 7, 8, 1951.

10.   Nadine George-Graves, *The Royalty of Negro Vaudeville: The Whitman Sisters and the Negotiation of Race, Gender, and Class in African American Theater, 1900–1940* (New York: St. Martin's Press, 2000).

11.   See Richard Natale, "Silky Singer Lena Horne Broke Barriers," *Variety* and the *Associated Press*, May 11, 2010.

12.   Chambers, "Lives Well Lived."

13.   Judith Weisenfeld, *Hollywood Be Thy Name: African American Religion in American Film, 1929–1949* (Berkley: University of California Press), 210–11.

14.   David Pilgrim, "The Tragic Mulatto Myth," *Jim Crow Museum of Racist Memorabilia Online*, Ferris State University, November 2000, accessed November 15, 2012, http://www.ferris.edu/jimcrow/mulatto/.

15.   See article "'Part in Imitation is not real me,' says Fredi," *Chicago Defender*, January 19, 1935, national edition, 9.

16.   Taylor and Moore, eds., *African American Women Confront the West*, 235.

17.   Ibid.

18.   Earl Conrad, "Pass or Not to Pass?" *Chicago Defender*, June 16, 1945.

19.   *St. Louis Post-Dispatch*, November 7, 1939.

20.   Chambers, "Lives Well Lived."

21.   Ibid.

22.   See "Square Joe," Turner Classic Film Union.

23.   *Time* Magazine, July 11, 1994, 15.

24. Taylor and Moore, eds., *African American Women Confront the West*, 125.

25. See Wikipedia, "The Hollywood Blacklist," http://en.wikipedia.org/wiki/ Hollywood_blacklist; "The Hollywood Ten," (1950, short documentary), http:// en.wikipedia.org/wiki/The_Hollywood_Ten, both accessed November 14, 2012.

26. Charlene B. Regester, *African American Actresses: The Struggle for Visibility, 1900-1960* (Bloomington: Indiana University Press, 2010), 115.

27. Leslie J. Reagan, Nancy Tomes, and Paula A. Treichler, *Medicines Moving Pictures: Medicine, Health and Bodies in American Film and Television* (University of Rochester Press, Rochester, NY, 2007), 245.

28. Quoted in Fredi Washington to Darr Smith, *Los Angeles Daily News*, August 2, 1949, *Fredi Washington Papers*, Amistad Research Center Microfilm Collection. See also Judith Weisenfeld, *Hollywood Be Thy Name: African American Religion in American Film 1929-1949* (University of California Press: Los Angeles, CA), 216.

29. *Baltimore Afro-American*, July 16, 1949; Weisenfeld, *Hollywood Be Thy Name*, 215.

30. Regester, *African American Actresses*, 129.

31. Weisenfeld, *Hollywood Be Thy Name*, 216.

32. Regester, *African American Actresses*, 127.

33. Ibid.

34. Ibid.

35. Ibid., 129.

36. See "The Papers of Fredi Washington (1925–1979)" and "Biographical Notes: Fredi Washington, 1903–1994," microfilm.

37. Paul Robeson, Jr., *The Undiscovered Paul Robeson: An Artist's Journey, 1898–1939* (New York: John Wiley & Sons, 2001), 100.

38. Chambers, "Lives Well Lived."

39. "The Papers of Fredi Washington (1925–1979)" and "Biographical Notes: Fredi Washington, 1903–1994," microfilm.

Maggie Lena Walker

1. Alan Brinkley, "Reconstruction and the New South," chapter 15 in Emily Barrosse, ed., *American History, A Survey* (Los Angeles: McGraw-Hill), 425.

2. "New research has revealed that Mrs. Walker was actually born in 1864, not in 1867, as she claimed (and most sources have perpetuated). That puts her birth in Richmond, VA during the Civil War and while slavery still existed, not after as she claimed," says Ethan P. Bullard, Museum Curator for the Richmond National Battlefield Park & Maggie L. Walker National Historic Site.

3. Carole Marsh, *Maggie Lena Walker: First Female Bank President* (Peachtree, GA: Gallopade International, September 2002), 1.

4. See Elsa Barkley Brown, "Constructing a Life and a Community: A Partial Story of Maggie Lena Walker," *Magazine of History 7*, No. 4 (summer, 1993), 28.

5. Candice F. Ransom, *Maggie L. Walker: Pioneer Banker and Community Leader* (Minneapolis, MN: Twenty-First Century Books, 2009), 9.

6. Gertrude Woodruff Marlowe, *A Right Worthy Grand Mission: Maggie Lena Walker and the Quest for Black Economic Empowerment* (Washington, DC: Howard University Press, 2003), 1–2.

7. Ransom, *Maggie L. Walker*, 34.

8. Ibid. "The story of Eccles sending Maggie a graduation dress and her mother

intercepting and burning it is a great tale. We know it only through the oral interviews conducted with Walker's grandchildren in the 1980s." (Ethan P. Bullard, Museum Curator for the Richmond National Battlefield Park & Maggie L. Walker National Historic Site).

9.   Ransom, *Maggie L. Walker*, 61.

10. Danuta Bois, "Distinguished Women Past and Present: Maggie Lena Walker (1867–1934)," 1998, accessed August 9, 2011, http://www.distinguishedwomen.com/biographies/walker-ml.html.

11. Ransom, *Maggie L. Walker*, 46.

12. Jeremy Quittner, "Maggie Lena Walker: A Rich Legacy for the Black Woman Entrepreneur," *Money Aisle Bank Browser*, (Bloomberg, 1999), accessed November 14, 2012, http://www.businessweek.com/smallbiz/news/coladvice/reallife/rl990706r.htm.

13. Steven J. Hoffman, *Race, Class, and Power in the Building of Richmond, 1870–1920* (Jefferson: McFarland Publishers, 2004), 161.

14. Ibid.

15. Quittner, "Maggie Lena Walker: A Rich Legacy."

16. Danuta Bois, "Distinguished Women."

17. Quittner, "Maggie Lena Walker: A Rich Legacy."

18. Ibid.

Robert James Harlan

1.   Rayford W. Logan and Michael R. Winston, eds., *Dictionary of American Negro Biography* (New York: W. W. Norton, 1982), 287-88.

2.   Ibid.

3.   There is some discrepancy as to whether Robert James Harlan, a slave, was born in Harrodsburg, Kentucky or Mecklenburg County, Virginia and then brought to the plantation in Kentucky around the age of eight. See Ronald Shannon, *Profiles in Ohio History: A Legacy of African American Achievement* (Bloomington, IN: iUniverse), 33; William J. Simmons and Henry McNeal Turner, in *Men of Mark: Eminent, Progressive, and Rising* (Cleveland, Ohio: Geo M. Rewell & Company, 1887), put Harlan's birthplace as Mecklenburg County; while Logan, in *Dictionary of American Negro Biography*, lists Harlan's birthplace as Harrodsburg, Kentucky.

4.   A biography on John Marshall Harlan states the blood relation between John Harlan and Robert Harlan as an established fact. See Loren P. Beth, *John Marshall Harlan: The Last Whig Justice* (Lexington: The University Press of Kentucky, 1992); see also "Did Robert Harlan Help to Shape John Marshall Harlan's Views on Race?" in Richard Delgado and Jean Stefancic's *Critical Race Theory: The Cutting Edge* (Philadelphia: Temple University Press, 2000), 122–124; see "Brief Biography of Colonel Robert Harlan," *Cincinnati Union*, December 13, 1934.

5.   Simmons and Turner, *Men of Mark*, 420–421.

6.   Delgado and Stefancic, *Critical Race Theory*, 124; see also Logan and Winston, eds., *Dictionary of American Negro Biography*, 287–288.

7.   See "Test Fails to Link Slave, Justice," *The Associated Press*, September 3, 2001, accessed November 14, 2012, http://www.enquirer.com/editions/2001/09/03/loc_test_fails_to_link.html. Despite a test of distant relatives from both clans, the majority of historians speculate that they were half-brothers.

8.   Beth, *John Marshall Harlan*, 13–14.

9. Logan and Winston, eds., *Dictionary of American Negro Biography*, 287–88; see Smithsonian.com, "Past Imperfect: The Great Dissenter and His Half-Brother," December 20, 2012, accessed on November 14, 2012, http://blogs.smithsonianmag.com/history/2011/12/the-great-dissenter-and-his-half-brother/.

10. Shannon, *Profiles in Ohio History*, 34.

11. Ibid.

12. Harlan did not officially purchase his freedom until after the death of his wife, Josephine Floyd. However, at least as early as 1840, Harlan appears in the public records of Lexington, Kentucky with the designation "free man of color" next to his name; see Delgado and Stefancic, *Critical Race Theory*, 122.

13. National Conference of Colored Men of the United States, *Proceedings of the National Conference of Colored Men of the United States, State Capitol building, Nashville, Tennessee, May 6–7, and 9, 1879* (Washington, DC: R.H. Darby, printer, 1879), 30–32.

Richard T. Greener

1. Werner Sollars, Caldwell Titcomb, and Thomas A. Underwood, eds. *Blacks at Harvard: A Documentary History of African-American Experience at Harvard and Radcliffe* (New York: New York University Press, 1993), 2.

2. Michael Robert Mounter, "A Brief Biography of Richard Greener" (Columbia, SC: The Board of Trustees, University of South Carolina, 2001), accessed June 7, 2011, http://www.sc.edu/bicentennial/pages/greenerpages/greenerbio.html.

3. Allison Blakely, *Russia and the Negro: Blacks in Russian History and Thought* (Washington, DC: Howard University Press, 1986), 47.

4. Annetta Louise Gomez-Jefferson, *The Sage of Tawawa: Reverdy Cassius Ransom, 1861-1959* (Kent: Kent State University Press, 2002), 138.

5. W. E. B. Du Bois, "The Talented Tenth," in Booker T. Washington et al., *The Negro Problem* (New York: J. Pott & Company, 1903), 34, 45; Allison Blakely, "Richard T. Greener and The Talented Tenth's Dilemma," *Journal of Negro History* 59 (October, 1974): 305–21.

6. See Harvard University (1780–), Class of 1870, Tenth Report: Fiftieth Anniversary (Riverside Press, 1920), 66.

7. Sollars and Titcomb, *Blacks at Harvard*, 37.

8. Ibid.

9. Ibid., 38.

10. Ibid., 39.

11. Ibid.

12. Mounter, "A Brief Biography of Richard Greener."

13. Sollars and Titcomb, *Blacks at Harvard*, 39.

14. Ibid.

15. J.P. Morgan left her $50,000 in his will (equivalent to approximately $800,000 in modern money).

16. See Jean Strouse, *Morgan: American Financier* (New York: Random House, 1999).

17. The find was made by a man prior to demolition of a house in 2009. Historians apparently confirmed their authenticity in March 2012, as it was released to the press.

18. See Kim Janssen, "It Gives Me Gooseflesh: Remarkable Find in Southside Attic,"

Chicago Sun Times, March 10, 2012, accessed October 11, 2012 http://www. suntimes.com/11149243-417/it-gives-me-gooseflesh-remarkable-find-in-attic. html; Jessica Cumberbatch Anderson, "Richard T. Greener, First Black Harvard Alum, Diploma Discovered in Condemned Chicago House," *The Huffington Post, Black Voices*, March 14, 2012, accessed October 11, 2012 http://www.huffingtonpost. com/2012/03/14/richard-theodore-greener-first-black-harvard-alum_n_1345940. html.

Charles Richard Drew

1. Susan Whitehurst, *Dr. Charles Drew: Medical Pioneer Journey to Freedom* (Mankato, MN: The Child's World, Inc., 2001), 28.

2. See "Charles Drew" Wikipedia, accessed September 28, 2013. http://en.wikipedia. org/wiki/Charles_R._Drew.

3. Laura Purdie Salas, *Charles Drew: Pioneer in Medicine* (Mankato, MN: Capstone Press, 2006), 21.

4. Ibid., 27.

5. Ibid., 6.

6. Ibid., 8.

7. "Who is Charles R. Drew?: Profiles of Dr. Charles Drew, developer of techniques for storing and transfusing blood plasma," accessed October 16, 2012. http://www. essortment.com/dr-charles-r-drew-50409.html.

8. Marshall Cavendish, *Charles Drew Inventor of the Blood Bank 1904-1950 Inventors and Inventions Volume 2* (Tarrytown, NY: MTM Publishing, 2008), 443.

9. "Charles Drew," *The Black Inventor Online Museum*, accessed October 23, 2012 http://www.blackinventor.com/pages/charles-drew.html.

Henry Walton Bibb

1. Henry W. Bibb and Lucius C. Matlack, ed., *Narrative of the Life and Adventures of Henry Bibb, An American Slave, Written by Himself* (New York: MacDonald and Lee Printers, 1849), 15-16.

2. Roger W. Hite, "Henry Bibb and Ante-bellum Black Separatism," *Journal of Black Studies* Volume 4, No. 3 (March 1974), 269–84.

3. Henry Bibb and Charles J. Heglar, *The Life and Adventures of Henry Bibb: An American Slave* (Madison: University of Wisconsin Press, 2001), 220–21.

4. Bibb and Heglar, *The Life and Adventures*, 14.

5. Ibid.

6. Ibid., 13.

7. Ibid., 16.

8. Ibid.

9. Ibid., 43.

10. Ibid. 29.

11. John E. Kleber, *The Kentucky Encyclopedia* (Lexington, The University Press of Kentucky, 1992), 75.

12. William Leake Andrews and Henry Louis Gates, Jr., *Slave Narratives*, (New York, NY: Literary Classics of the United States, 2000), 506.

13. Ibid., 516.

14. Ibid., 527.

15. Ibid., 442.

Henriette Delille

1.   Obituary, Henriette Delille.

2.   Chevel Johnson, "Seeking Beatification for American Black Woman," *The Free Lance Star*, Fredricksburg, VA, April 3, 1999, E6.

3.   Brenna Sanchez, "Delille, Henriette, 1813–1862," *Contemporary Black Biography* (Encyclopedia.com, 2002), retrieved December 18, 2011, http://www.encyclopedia.com; St. Martin de Porres is believed to be the first black saint ever. He was born in Lima, Peru. He was beatified in 1837 and canonized in 1962. Delille would be the first black saint born in North America.

4.   Burial Act for J. Bt. Lille (de Lille) Sarpy, Department of Lot-et-Garonne, St. François Church Register 15, entry 1836:46, Natchitoches, Louisiana.

5.   Bruce Nolan, "Henriette Delille Moves Closer to Sainthood for Work with New Orleans Slaves," *Times-Picayune*, March 29, 2010.

6.   Johnson, "Seeking Beatification for American Black Woman."

7.   Sanchez, "Delille, Henriette, 1813–1862." In 1842, Delille, along with two other black women, Juliette Gaudin and Josephine Charles, established a sisterhood called "Sisters of the Holy Family."

8.   Written by Delille in her 1836 prayer book.

9.   Nolan, "Henriette Delille Moves Closer to Sainthood."

10. The sisterhood was assisted by two French immigrants, Père Etienne Rousselon and Marie Jeanne Aliquot. See Sanchez, "Delille, Henriette, 1813–1862."

11. Renee Tawa, "Order of the Day," *Los Angeles Times*, August 18, 1999.

12. Ibid.

Ellen Craft

1.   Marian Smith Holmes, "The Great Escape from Slavery of Ellen and William Craft," *The Smithsonian*, Smithsonian.com, June 17, 2010, accessed August 8, 2011. http://www.smithsonianmag.com/history-archaeology/The-Great-Escape-From-Slavery-of-Ellen-and-William-Craft.html.

2.   Charles J. Heglar, *Rethinking the Slave Narrative: Slave Marriage and the Narratives of Henry Bibb and William and Ellen Craft* (Westport, CT: Greenwood Press, 2001), 94.

3.   Ann Short Chirhart and Betty Wood, eds., *Georgia Women: Their Lives and Times—Volume I* (Athens, GA: University of Georgia Press, 2009), 83; see also "Escape in Broad Day Light" in Cynthia Jacobs Carter, ed., *Freedom in My Heart: Voices from the United States National Slavery Museum* (National Geographic, 2009), 133.

4.   Chirhart and Wood, *Georgia Women*, 85.

5.   Cathy Moore, *Ellen Craft's Escape from Slavery* (Minneapolis, MN: Millbrook Press, 2011), 8.

6.   Ibid., 2.

7.   Ibid., 10.

8.   Ibid., 11.

9.   Ibid., 12–14.

10.   William Craft and Ellen Craft, *Running a Thousand Miles for Freedom; or The Escape of William and Ellen Craft from Slavery* (North Stratford, NH: Ayer Company Publishers, Inc.), 2.

11.   Chirhart and Wood, *Georgia Women*, 86.

12.   Craft and Craft, *Running a Thousand Miles*, 8.

13.   Ibid.

14.   Ibid., 11–12.

15.   Ibid., 9.

16.   Heglar, *Rethinking the Slave Narrative*, 94.

17.   Georgiana Bruce Kirby, *Years of Experience: An Autobiographical Narrative* (New York: G. P. Putnam's Sons, 1887), 304–5.

18.   Craft and Craft, *Running a Thousand Miles*, 32.

19.   Ibid., 32–33.

20.   Ibid., 34.

21.   Ibid., 34-35.

22.   Ibid., 69.

23.   Ibid.

24.   Michael A. Chaney, *Fugitive Vision: Slave Image and Black Identity in Antebellum Narrative* (Bloomington: Indiana University Press, 2008), 94.

25.   Ibid., 78.

26.   Ibid., 80.

27.   See *Baltimore Bulletin of Education*, Volumes 41–46, 1963.

28.   Craft and Craft, *Running a Thousand Miles*, 85.

29.   Cathy Moore, *The Daring Escape of Ellen Craft* (Minneapolis, MN: Millbrook Press, 2002), 48.

30.   Judith Bloom Fradin and Dennis Brindell Fradin, *5000 Miles to Freedom: Ellen and William Craft's Flight from Slavery* (Washington, DC: National Geographic Society, 2006), 92.

31.   Edward T. James, Janet Wilson James, and Paul Boyer, eds., *Notable American Women, 1607–1950: A Biographical Dictionary* Vol. 2 (Cambridge, MA: Radcliffe College, 1971), 397.

32.   Ibid.

William Cooper Nell

1.   Dorothy Porter Wesley, and Constance Porter Uzelac, eds., *William Cooper Nell: Nineteenth-Century African American Abolitionist, Historian, Integrationist; Selected Writings, 1832-1874* (Baltimore, MD: Black Classic Press, 2002), 46–47; see *Boston City Directory of 1863*, which listed the post office as Nell's address.

2.   Marion Kilson, "Black History Month, Honoring a First in African American History, William Cooper Nell and The Colored Patriots of the American Revolution," *The Black Commentator*, February 28, 2008, No. 266.

3.   Donald M. Jacobs, ed., *Courage and Conscience: Black and White Abolitionists in Boston* (Indianapolis: Indiana University Press, 1993), 216.

4.   Joan Potter, *African American Firsts* (New York: Kensington Publishing Corp., 2002), 134.

5.   Wesley and Uzelac, *William Cooper Nell*, 6.

6. Robert P. Smith, "William Cooper Nell: Crusading Black Abolitionist," *The Journal of Negro History* 55 (July, 1970): 182–99.

7. Wesley and Uzelac, *William Cooper Nell*, 286.

8. General Colored Association [of Massachusetts] I, No. 22 (May 28, 1831): 3, 87.

9. Henry Louis Gates and Evelyn Brooks Higginbotham, *African American Lives* (New York: Oxford University Press, 2004), 624.

10. James Oliver Horton, *Free People of Color: Inside the African American Community* (Washington, D.C.: Smithsonian Institution Press, 1993), 46.

11. *The Liberator*, December 28, 1855, 206–7.

12. Oliver Johnson, *William Lloyd Garrison and His Times; or Sketches of the Anti-Slavery Movement in America* (Boston: Houghton, Mifflin, and Company, 1881), 101.

13. Gates and Higginbotham, *African American Lives*, 624.

14. Porter, *African American Firsts*, 134.

15. Kilson, "Black History Month."

16. Gates and Higginbotham, *African American Lives*, 624.

17. Ibid.

18. Patrick T. J. Browne, "To Defend Mr. Garrison: William Cooper Nell and the Personal Politics of Anti-Slavery," *New England Quarterly* 70 (1997), 415.

19. *The North Star*, August 12, 1853; *The Liberator*, September 2, 1853, December 16, 1853.

20. See "The Taney Hunt against Colored Americans," *The Liberator Files*, August 28, 1857, filed under "Dred Scott Decision, Nell, William Cooper, 1857."

21. Gates and Higginbotham, *African American Lives*, 624.

22. Ibid.

23. Wesley and Uzelac, *William Cooper Nell*, 515.

24. Smith, "William Cooper Nell: Crusading Black Abolitionist," 182–99.

25. Ibid.

26. New Hampshire Marriage Records 1637-1947 and New Hampshire Deaths and Burials 1784-1949, on file at the New England Genealogical and Historical Society, Boston, Mass.

Mordecai Wyatt Johnson

1. George L. Hutchinson, *The Harlem Renaissance in Black and White* (The President and Fellows of Harvard College, 1995), 219.

2. Richard Ishmael McKinney, *Mordecai: The Man and His Message: The Story of Mordecai Wyatt Johnson* (Washington, DC: Howard University Press, 1997), 60. Although Dr. Johnson was voted president unanimously on January 26, 1926, he assumed the post on September 1, 1926.

3. Ibid.; "1929: Mordecai Wyatt Johnson," Naacp.org Spingarn Medal Winners: 1915 to Today, retrieved March 2, 2012, http://www.naacp.org/pages/spingarn-medal-winners.

4. McKinney, *Mordecai: The Man and His Message*, 42.

5. Mohandas Karamchand Gandhi, interview with Howard Thurman in Harijan, March 14, 1936, quoted in Mary King, *Mahatma Gandhi and Martin Luther King, Jr.: The Power of Nonviolent Action* (Paris: UNESCO Publishing, 1999), 211; King, "His Influence Speaks to World Conscience," *Hindustan Times*, January 30, 1958, in

Papers 4:354–355.

6.   Thomas John Edge, "The Social Responsibility of the Administrator: Mordecai Wyatt Johnson and the Dilemma of Black Leadership, 1890–1976," Electronic Doctoral Dissertations for the University of Massachusetts, Amherst, Paper AAI3325148, January 1, 2008.

7.   McKinney, *Mordecai: The Man and the Message*, 1.

8.   Jessie Carney Smith and Linda T. Wynn, *Freedom Facts and Firsts: 400 Years of African American Civil Rights Experience* (Visible Ink Press, 2009), 313.

9.   McKinney, *Mordecai: The Man and His Message*, 60.

10.   See Zachery R. Williams, *In Search of the Talented Tenth: Howard University Public Intellectuals and the Dilemmas of Race, 1926–1970* (Columbia, MO: University of Missouri Press, 2009), 51.

11.   Ibid., 60.

12.   Ibid., 55–56. Charles Hamilton Houston would later become the chief counsel for the NAACP.

13.   Ibid.

14.   Ibid.

15.   Ibid.

16.   The actual date of Johnson's birth is uncertain. Several dates are recorded in history, including January 4th, January 12th, and December 12th of 1890. What appears consistent is the year (1890); See Columbus Salley, *The Black 100: A Ranking of the Most Influential African Americans Past and Present* (New York: Kensington Publishing Corp, 1996), 100.

17.   McKinney, Mordecai: *The Man and His Message*, 4.

18.   Ibid.

19.   Ta-Nehisi Coates, The Atlantic "Our First Black President," September 11, 2011 accessed November 12, 2012 http://www.theatlantic.com/national/archive/2011/09/our-first-black-president/244942/#bio

20.   Faustine Childress Jones-Wilson, *Encyclopedia of African American Education* (Greenwood Publishing Group, 1996), 234.

21.   Salley, *The Black 100*, 45.

22.   "Johnson, Mordecai Wyatt (1890–1976)," *Remembered and Reclaimed: An Online Reference Guide to African American History*, BlackPast.org, accessed November 14, 2012, http://www.blackpast.com/?q=aah/johnson-mordecai-wyatt-1890-1976.

23.   Salley, *The Black 100*, 150.

24.   "Johnson, Mordecai Wyatt," *Encyclopedia of World Biography* (Encyclopedia. com, 2005), accessed September 14, 2012, http://www.encyclopedia.com/doc/1G2-3435000097.html.

25.   McKinney, *Mordecai: The Man and His Message*, 100.

26.   Jones-Wilson, *Encyclopedia of African American Education*, 235.

27.   "Johnson, Mordecai Wyatt," *Encyclopedia of World Biography*.

28.   Larry S. Gibson, *Young Thurgood: The Making of a Supreme Court Justice* (Amherst: Prometheus Books, 2012), See chapter 5: "Educating a Social Engineer."

29.   Jones-Wilson, *Encyclopedia of African American Education*, 235.

30.   McKinney, *Mordecai: The Man and His Message*, 1.

31.   Ibid.

32.   See Susan Altman, *The Encyclopedia of African American Heritage* (New York: Facts on File, 1997).

33.   Avondale Patillo United Methodist Church, "Black Religious Leaders: Rev. Dr.

Mordecai Johnson 1890-1976," retrieved March 7, 2012, http://apmethodist.org/
resources/black-religious-leaders.htm#johnson.

BIBLIOGRAPHY

"1929: Mordecai Wyatt Johnson." *Naacp.org Spingarn Medal Winners: 1915 to Today.* Accessed March 2, 2012. http://www.naacp.org/pages/spingarn-medal-winners.

"Adam Clayton Powell, Jr., 1908–1972." *Black Americans in Congress, 1870–2007.* Office of History and Preservation, Office of the Clerk, U.S. House of Representatives. Washington, DC: US Government Printing Office, 2008.

African–American Registry. "Alexander Twilight, the First Black College Graduate." Accessed November 14, 2012. http://aaregistry.org/historic_events/view/alexander-l-twilight-first-african-american-college-graduate.

"Alexander Twilight." Black Past.org. Accessed November 14, 2012. http://www.blackpast.org/?q=aah/twilight-alexander-1795-1857.

Alexander, Shawn Leigh. *T. Thomas Fortune, The Afro-American Agitator: A Collection of Writings, 1880–1928.* Gainesville, FL: University of Florida Press, 2008.

Altman, Susan. *The Encyclopedia of African–American Heritage.* New York, NY: Facts on File, Inc., 1997.

"American Libraries: Timeline in Library Development for African Americans." *Old South Leaflets* 4, No. 81. Boston, IL: Directors of the Old South Work, 1901.

Anderson, Jessica Cumberbatch. "Richard T. Greener, First Black Harvard Alum, Diploma Discovered in Condemned Chicago House." *The Huffington Post, Black Voices,* March 14, 2012. Accessed October 11, 2012. http://www.huffingtonpost.com/2012/03/14/richard-theodore-greener-first-black-harvard-alum_n_1345940.html.

Andrews, William L. *The Literary Career of Charles W. Chesnutt.* Baton Rouge, LA: Louisiana State University Press, 1980.

_____, and Frances Smith Foster, and Trudier Harris. *The Oxford Companion to African American Literature.* New York, NY: Oxford University Press, 1997.

_____, and William R. Andrews. *From Fugitive Slave to Free Man: The Autobiographies of William Wells Brown.* Columbia, MO: University of Missouri, 2003. New York, NY: Mentor Books, 1993.

"Anna Brown: Wife of American Author William Brown." *Civil War Women Blog.com.* Accessed March 10, 2012. http://www.civilwarwomenblog.com/2011/09/anna-elizabeth-gray-brown.html.

Apel, Dora. *Imagery of Lynching: Black Men, White Women, and the Mob.* New Brunswick, NJ: Rutgers University Press, 2004.

Aptheker, Herbert. *A Documentary History of the Negro People in the United States.* New York, NY: 1951.

"Austin Beating Sends Shillady on North Trail." *New York Times,* AP story, Austin American, August 23, 1919.

Bacon, Margaret Hope. *But One Race: The Life of Robert Purvis.* Albany, NY: State University of New York, 2007.

Bader, Philip. *African-American Writers.* New York, NY: Facts On File, Inc., 2004.

Baltimore Bulletin of Education, Vol. 41–46. University Park: Pennsylvania State University Press, 1963.

Barthelemy, Anthony G. *Collected Black Women's Narratives.* New York: Oxford University Press, 1988.

Bauerlein, Mark. *Negrophobia: A Race Riot in Atlanta, 1906.* San Francisco, CA: Encounter Books, 2001.

Bennett, Lerone, Jr., *Before the Mayflower: A History of the Negro in America, 1619-1962.* Chicago, IL: Johnson Publishing Co., 1969.

_____, *Confrontation: Black and White.* Chicago, IL: Johnson Publishing Co., 1965.

Beth, Loren P. *John Marshall Harlan: The Last Whig Justice.* Lexington, KY: The University Press of Kentucky, 1992.

Bibb, Henry and Charles J. Heglar. *The Life and Adventures of Henry Bibb: An American Slave.* Madison, WI: University of Wisconsin Press, 2001.

_____, and Lucius C. Matlack, ed. *Narrative of the Life and Adventures of Henry Bibb, An American Slave Written by Himself.* New York, NY: MacDonald and Lee Printers, 1849.

Bigelow, Barbara Carlisle, ed. *Contemporary Black Biography: Profiles from the International Black Community.* Detroit, MI: Gale Research Inc., 1992.

Black Americans in Congress, 1870–2007. Office of History and Preservation, Office of the Clerk, US House of Representatives. Washington, DC: US Government Printing Office, 2008.

Blakely, Allison. "Richard T. Greener and the Talented Tenth's Dilemma." *Journal of Negro History,* vol. 59, no. 4, October, 1974.

_____. *Russia and the Negro: Blacks in Russian History and Thought.* Washington, DC: Howard University Press, 1986.

Blatt, Martin Henry, Thomas J. Brown, and Donald Yacovone. *Hope and Glory: Essays on the Legacy of the Fifty-Fourth Massachusetts Regiment.* Boston, MA: University of Massachusetts Press, 2001.

Blodgett, Geoffrey. "John Mercer Langston and the Case of Edmonia Lewis: Oberlin, 1862." *Journal of Negro History,* vol.53, no. 3, July, 1968.

"Bodies of Dead Negroes Taken out of the City." *The Atlanta Journal and Constitution*, September 23, 1906: 2.

Bogle, Donald. *Heat Wave: The Life and Career of Ethel Waters*. New York: HarperCollins, 2011.

_____. *Toms, Coons, Mulattoes, Mammies, and Bucks: An Interpretive History of Blacks in American Films*. New York: Continuum International Publishing Group, 2006.

Bois, Danuta. "Distinguished Women Past and Present: Maggie Lena Walker (1867–1934)." Accessed August 9, 2011. http://www.distinguishedwomen.com/biographies/walker-ml.html.

Bontemps, Arna. "Introduction to Cane," as appearing in the Harper & Row Perennial Classic edition, 1969.

Bordewich, Fergus M. *Bound for Canaan: The Underground Railroad and the War for the Soul of America*. New York, NY: HarperCollins, 2005.

Boromé, Joseph A. "Robert Purvis and His Early Challenge to American Racism." *Negro History Bulletin* 30 (1967): 8–10.

Boulware, Marcus H. *The Oratory of Negro Leaders: 1900–1968*. Westport, CT: Greenwood Publishing Group, 1969.

Bradley, David. "Anatomy of a Murder." *The Nation*, June 12, 2006.

Bradley, Valerie Jo. "Black President Runs Michigan State University: Gets Demanding Position," *JET Magazine*, May 21, 1970: 16.

Bradt, Steve. "One-drop Rule Persists: Bi-racials Viewed as Members of Their Lower-status Parent Group." *Harvard Gazette* online, December 9, 2010. Accessed March 3, 2011. http://news.harvard.edu/gazette/story/2010/12/%E2%80%98one-drop-rule%E2%80%99-persists/.

Brandt, Nat. *Harlem at War: The Black Experience in WWII*. New York, NY: Syracuse Press, 1997.

Brawley, Benjamin Griffith. *The Negro in Literature and Art in the United States*. Chapel Hill, NC: University of North Carolina Press, 1937.

"Brief Biography of Colonel Robert Harlan." *Cincinnati Union*, December 13, 1934.

Brinkley, Alan. "Chapter 15: Reconstruction and the New South." Edited by Barrosse, Emily. *American History: A Survey*, Los Angeles, CA: McGraw-Hill.

Brissot de Warville, J.P., Durand Echevarria, and Mara Socenau Vamons, eds. *New Travels in the United States of America*, 1788. Cambridge, MA: Belknap Press of Harvard University Press, 1964.

Brodhead, Richard H. *The Journals of Charles W. Chesnutt*. Durham, NC: Duke University Press, 1993.

Brown, Cynthia Stokes. *Refusing Racism: White Allies and the Struggle for Civil Rights*. New York, NY: Teachers College Press, 2002.

Brown, Elsa Barkley. "Constructing a Life and a Community: A Partial Story of Maggie Lena Walker." *Magazine of History* 7, No. 4 (Summer, 1993).

Brown, Hallie Q. *Homespun Heroines and Other Women of Distinction*. Xenia, Ohio: Aldine Printing Company, 1926.

Brown, Josephine. *Biography of an American Bondman, by His Daughter, Documenting the American South*. Boston, MA: R. F. Wallcut, 1856. Retrieved March 15, 2012, http://docsouth.unc.edu/neh/brownj/summary.html.

Brown, Tamara L., Gregory S. Parks, Clarenda M. Phillips, eds. *African American Fraternities and Sororities: The Legacy and the Vision*. Lexington, KY: The University Press of Kentucky, 2005.

Brown, William Wells. *Black Man, His Antecedents, His Genius, and His Achievements*. Boston, MA: James Redpath Publishers, 1863. Available at http://docsouth.unc.edu/neh/brownww/brown.html.

_____, and Ezra Greenspan, eds. *William Wells Brown: Reader*. Athens, GA: University of Georgia Press, 2008.

_____, and Paul Jefferson, eds. *The Travels of William Wells Brown: Including Narrative of William Wells Brown, a Fugitive Slave and the American Fugitive in Europe*. Princeton, NJ: Markus Wiener Publishers, 1991.

_____, and Robert Levine, eds. *Clotel, or, The President's Daughter: A Narrative of Slave Life in the United States*. Bedford, St. Martins: Bedford Cultural Editions, 2000.

_____. *Three Years in Europe: Or Places I Have Seen and People I Have Met*. London, UK: Gilpin, 1852.

Brown, William Wells. *Narrative of William W. Brown, A Fugitive Slave, Written by Himself*. Boston, MA: Anti-Slavery Office, 1847. Available at http://docsouth.unc.edu/neh/brown47/brown47.html.

_____. *Narrative of William W. Brown, An American Slave, Written by Himself*. London, UK: Charles Gilpin, 5 Bishopgate-St. Without, 1849.

Browne, Patrick T. J. "'To Defend Mr. Garrison': William Cooper Nell and the Personal Politics of Anti-Slavery." *New England Quarterly* 70, no. 3 (1997): 415–42.

Browner, Stephanie P. "Biography of Charles W. Chesnutt." *The Charles Chesnutt Digital Archive*, Berea College.

Buckler, Helen. *Daniel Hale Williams: Negro Surgeon*. New York, NY: Pitman Publishing Company, 1954.

Burial Act for J. Bt. Lille (de Lille) Sarpy, Department of Lot-et-Garonne, St. François Church Register 15, entry 1836:46, Natchitoches, Louisiana.

Butts, J. W., and Dorothy James. "The Underlying Causes of the Elaine Riot of 1919." *Arkansas Historical Quarterly* 20, No.1 (Spring, 1961): 95–104.

Cameron, James. *A Time of Terror*. Baltimore, MD: Black Classic Press, 1994.

Carter, Cynthia Jacobs, ed. *Freedom in My Heart: Voices from the United States National Slavery Museum.* National Geographic, 2009.

Cash, Floris Barnett. *African American Women and Social Action: The Clubwomen and Volunteerism from Jim Crow to the New Deal, 1896–1936.* Westport, CT: Greenwood Press, 2001.

_____. "Victoria Earle Matthews." *Notable Black American Women.* Detroit, MI: Gale Research, 1992.

Catterall, Helen Tunnicliff and James J. Hyden. *Judicial Cases Concerning American Slavery and the Negro.* New York, NY: Octagon Books, 1968.

Cavendish, Marshall. *Charles Drew Inventor of the Blood Bank 1904-1950 Inventors and Inventions* Volume 2. Tarrytown, NY: MTM Publishing, 2008.

Chambers, Veronica. "Lives Well Lived: Fredi Washington, The Tragic Mulatto." *New York Times,* January 1, 1995.

Chaney, Michael A. *Fugitive Vision: Slave Image and Black Identity in Antebellum Narrative.* Bloomington, IN: Indiana University Press, 2008.

Chapelle, Tony. "Adam Clayton Powell, Jr.: Black Power between Heaven and Hell." *The Black Collegian Online.* Accessed June 20, 2011. http://www.black-collegian.com/african/adam.shtml.

"Charles W. Chesnutt Biographical Information." *The Columbia Encyclopedia, 6th ed.; Encyclopedia.com,* 2001. Accessed June 3, 2011. http://library.uncfsu.edu/Archives/chesnuttCollection/ChaCheBioInfo.htm.

"Charles W. Chesnutt Library Archives and Special Collections." Fayetteville State University's history, historical sketch, 2012. Accessed November 14, 2012. http://library.uncfsu.edu/Archives/archivesspecialcollectionsdept.htm.

"Chased Negroes All Night." *The Atlanta Journal and Constitution,* September 23, 1906.

Cheek, William, and Aimee Lee Cheek. *John Mercer Langston and the Fight for Black Freedom, 1829–1865.* Urbana: University of Illinois Press, 1989.

Chesnutt, Charles Waddell, and Joseph McElrath, Jr, and Robert C. Leitz, III., eds. *To Be an Author: The Letters of Charles Chesnutt, 1889–1905.* Princeton, NJ: Princeton University Press, 1997.

_____, and Sylvia Lyons Render, eds. *The Short Fiction of Charles W. Chesnutt.* Washington, DC: Howard University Press, 1981.

_____. "Race Prejudice: Its Causes and Its Cure." *Alexander's Magazine,* July 15, 1905.

_____. *The Conjure Woman.* Durham, NC: Duke University Press, 1996.

Chirhart, Ann Short, and Betty Wood, eds. *Georgia Women: Their Lives and Times,* Vol. I. Athens, GA: University of Georgia Press, 2009.

Christopher, Maurine. *Black Americans in Congress.* New York, NY: Thomas Y. Crowell Company, 1976.

Clarke, Lewis Garrard, and Milton Clarke. *Narrative of the Sufferings of Lewis and Milton Clarke: Sons of a Soldier of the Revolution, During a Captivity of More Than Twenty Years Among the Slaveholders of Kentucky, One of the So Called Christian States of North America.* Boston, MA: Bela Marsh, 1845.

Coates, Ta-Nehisi. "Our First Black President." *The Atlantic*, September 11, 2011. Accessed November 12, 2012. http://www.theatlantic.com/national/archive/2011/09/our-first-black-president/244942/#bio.

Congressional Record, Senate, 44th Congress, 1st Session. March 31, 1876: 2101–5; *46th Congress, 2nd Session.* April 7, 1880: 2195–6; *46th Congress, 3rd Session.* February 10, 1881: 1397–8.

Conrad, Earl. "Pass Or Not to Pass?" *Chicago Defender*, June 16, 1945.

Conway, Jill Ker. *Written by Herself: Autobiographies of American Women: An Anthology.* New York: Vintage Books, 1992.

Cooney, Charles F. "Walter White and the Harlem Renaissance." *Journal of Negro History* 57 (July, 1972): 231–40.

Craft, William, and Ellen Craft. *Running a Thousand Miles for Freedom; Or the Escape of William and Ellen Craft from Slavery.* North Stratford: Ayer Company Publishers, Inc., 1848.

Craughwell, Thomas J., and Edwin Kiester, Jr. *The Bucks Stops Here: The 28 Toughest Presidential Decisions and How They Changed History.* Minneapolis, MN: Fair Winds Press, 2010.

Cripps, Thomas. *Slow Fade to Black: The Negro in American Film, 1900–1942.* New York, NY: Oxford University Press, 1977.

"Crisis in the Making: U.S. Negroes Tussle with the Issue." *Newsweek*, June 7, 1948: 28–29.

"Critical Period Faces Negro, Walter White Tells Meeting." *NAACP Papers.* Press Release, Annual Mass Meeting, Part I, Reel 14, January 5, 1931.

Crowe, Charles. "Racial Massacre in Atlanta." *Journal of Negro History* 54, No. 2 (1969): 650–73.

Current, Richard Nelson. *Those Terrible Carpetbaggers.* Relica Books, 2002.

Cutter, Martha. *Unruly Tongue: Identity and Voice in American Women's Writing, 1850–1930.* Jackson, MS: University Press of Mississippi, 1999.

Daley, Peter. "Adam Clayton Powell, Jr." *The Nation*, vol. 254 (January 6, 1992).

"Daniel Hale Williams." Black Inventor Online Museum. Accessed October 3, 2011, http://www.blackinventor.com/pages/daniel-williams.html.

Davis, Floyd James. *Who is Black?: One Nation's Definition of Race.* University Park, PA: Penn State University Press, 2001.

Davis, Kimberly. "Multiracial Identity Points to Racial Struggle in U.S." News 21 UMD Staff, Aug. 7, 2009. Accessed July 27, 2012. http://thenewvoters.news21.com/mixedrace/multiracial-identity-racial-struggle.

Dawson, Joseph G., III. *Army Generals and Reconstruction: Louisiana, 1862–1877.* Baton Rouge, LA: Louisiana State University Press, 1982.

Delgado, Richard, and Jean Stefancic. *Critical Race Theory: The Cutting Edge.* Philadelphia, PA: Temple University Press, 2000.

Dillon, Merton L. *The Abolitionists: The Growth of a Dissenting Minority.* Dekalb, IL: Northern Illinois University Press, 1974.

Douglass, Margaret Crittenden. *Educational Laws of Virginia: The Personal Narrative of Mrs. Margaret Douglass, A Southern Woman Who Was Imprisoned for One Month in the Common Jail of Norfolk, Under the Laws of Virginia, for the Crime of Teaching Free Colored Children to Read.* Boston, MA: Jewett, 1854. Available at http://archive.org/details/personalnarrativ00doug.

Edge, Thomas John. "The Social Responsibility of the Administrator: Mordecai Wyatt Johnson and the Dilemma of Black Leadership, 1890–1976." *Electronic Doctoral Dissertations for the University of Massachusetts, Amherst.* Paper AAI3325148, January 1, 2008.

Eigen Quote. "P.B.S. Pinchback." *Eigen's Political and Historical Quotations.* http://politicalquotes.org.

Emerson, Jason. *Giant in the Shadows: The Life of Robert T. Lincoln.* Carbondale, IL: Southern Illinois University Press, 2012.

Encyclopedia Britannica, "Reference Room: Daniel Hale Williams." *African American World*, PBS, archived from the original on June 29, 2008.

"The Equality of Rights in the Territories: Speech of Harrison G. Blake: Made in the House of Representatives, in committee of the whole, June 12, 1860." (1860).

"Facts of Last Night's Reign of Terror." *The Atlanta Constitution*, September 23, 1906.

Farrison, W. Edward. "Phylon Profile XVI: William Wells Brown." *Phylon 9*, No. 1 (1st Quarter, 1948): 13. Clark Atlanta University. Accessed January 5, 2012, http://www.jstor.org/stable/271339.

Ferguson, Sally Ann H., ed. *Charles W. Chesnutt: Selected Writings.* Boston, MA: Houghton Mifflin Company, 2001.

Fern, Fanny, and Joyce W. Warren, eds. *Ruth Hall and Other Writings.* Piscataway, NJ: Rutgers University Press, 1986.

"Fillmore Signs Fugitive Slave Act—September 18, 1850." *American President: A Reference Resource.* Miller Center, University of Virginia, 2012. Accessed January 30, 2012. http://millercenter.org/president/events/09_18.

Fleming, Robert. *The Wisdom of the Elders* (New York: NY, 1996).

Foley, Albert Sidney. *Bishop Healy, Beloved Outcaste: The Story of a Great Priest Whose Life Has Become a Legend.* New York, NY: Farrar Straus and Young, 1954.

_____. *God's Men of Color: The Colored Catholic Priests of the United States, 1854–1954.* New York, NY: Farrar Straus and Young, 1955.

Foner, Eric. *Freedom's Lawmakers: A Directory of Black Officeholders during Reconstruction.* New York, NY: Oxford University Press, 1993.

Foner, Philip Sheldon, and Robert J. Branham, eds. *Lift Every Voice: African American Oratory, 1787–1900.* Tuscaloosa, AL: University of Alabama Press, 1998.

Ford, Lynn. "A Survey of Indiana's African American History." *The Indianapolis Star,* February, 2002. Originally published as "White Hoosier Mob Beat, Hanged 2 Blacks." *The Indianapolis Star,* February, 1990. Accessed June 25, 2011. http://www2.indystar.com/library/factfiles/history/black_history/.

Foreman, Pier Gabrielle. *Activist Sentiments: Reading Black Women in the Nineteenth Century.* Champaign, IL: University of Illinois Press, 2009.

Fortune, Timothy Thomas. *Black and White: Land, Labor, and Politics in the South.* New York, NY: Fords, Howard, and Hulbert, 1884.

_____. Freeman, May 28, 1887.

_____. "The Filipino: A Social Study in Three Parts." *The Voice of the Negro* 1 (February 1904): 93–109; (May 1904): 197–203; (June 1904): 240–246.

Fradin, Judith Bloom, and Dennis Brindell Fradin. *5,000 Miles to Freedom: Ellen and William Craft's Flight from Slavery.* Washington, DC: National Geographic Society, 2006.

Franklin, John Hope and August Meier, eds. *Black Leaders of the 20th Century.* Champaign, IL: University of Illinois Press, 1982.

Frazier, E. Franklin. *Black Bourgeoisie.* New York, NY: Simon and Schuster, 1997.

French Creoles of America. "P. B. S. Pinchback." *Creole Culture: Famous Creoles.* http://www.frenchcreoles.com/CreoleCulture/famouscreoles/Pinchback/pinchback.htm.

Furnas, J.C. *Goodbye to Uncle Tom.* New York, NY: Apollo Editions, 1956.

Gates, Henry Louis, Jr., ed. *The Schomburg Library of Nineteenth Century Black Women Writers.* New York, NY: Oxford University Press, 1987.

_____, and Evelyn Brooks Higginbotham. *African American Lives.* New York, NY: Oxford University Press, 2004.

General Colored Association [of Massachusetts] Vol. I, No. 22, May 28, 1831: 87.

Genovese, Eugene. *Roll, Jordan, Roll: The World the Slaves Made.* New York, NY: First Vintage Books Edition, 1976.

George-Graves, Nadine. *The Royalty of Negro Vaudeville: The Whitman Sisters and the Negotiation of Race, Gender, and Class in African American Theater,1900–1940.* New York, NY: St. Martin's Press, 2000.

Getchell, Mary. "Studies in American Fiction" Vol. 34, No. 2 (Autumn 2006). Accessed November 11, 2011. http://research.uvu.edu/simmons/reviews.html.

Gibson, John W., and William H. Crogman. *The Colored American from Slavery to Honorable Citizenship.* Naperville, IL: J. L. Nichols & Co., 1903.

Gibson, Larry S. *Young Thurgood: The Making of a Supreme Court Justice*. Amherst, MA: Prometheus Books, 2012.

Ginzburg, Ralph. *100 Years of Lynchings*. Baltimore, MD: Black Classic Press, 1988.

Glass, Andrew. "Freed Slave Presides Over Senate: February 14, 1879." *The Politico*, February 14, 2008. Accessed July 23, 2011. http://www.politico.com/news/stories/0208/8508.html.

Glickman, Simon. "Adam Clayton Powell, Jr." *Contemporary Black Biography*. Detroit, MI: Gale Research Inc., 1992.

Gomez-Jefferson, Annetta Louise. *The Sage of Tawawa: Reverdy Cassius Ransom, 1861-1959*. Kent, Ohio: Kent State University Press, 2002.

"Governor Calls Shillady Offender," *New York Age*, August 30, 1919.

Graham, Lawrence Otis. *The Senator and the Socialite: The True Story of America's First Dynasty*. New York, NY: HarperCollins, 2006.

Grandy, Moses. *Life of a Slave*. London: Gilpin, 1843. Available at http://docsouth.unc.edu/fpn/grandy/menu.html.

Greene, Ousmane Kirumu. *Against Wind and Tide: African Americans' Response to Colonization*. Ann Arbor, IL: ProQuest Information and Learning Company, 2007.

Greenhouse, Linda. "Thurgood Marshall, Civil Rights Hero, Dies at 84." *New York Times*, January 25, 1993.

Grosz, Agnes Smith. *The Political Career of Pinckney Stewart Pinchback*. Louisiana Historical Quarterly 27, (1944): 527–612.

Gruesser, John Cullen, and Hanna Wallinger, eds. *Loopholes and Retreats: African American Writers and the Nineteenth Century*. Piscataway, NJ: Transaction Publishers, 2009.

Haber, Louise. *Black Pioneers of Science and Invention*. New York, NY: First Odyssey Classics, 1992.

Hales, Douglas. *A Southern Family in White and Black: The Cuneys of Texas*. College Station, Texas: Texas A&M University Press, 2003.

Hamilton, Charles V. Adam Clayton Powell, Jr.: *The Political Biography of an American Dilemma*. New York, NY: Atheneum Books, 1991.

"Harvard University (1780–), Class of 1870." *Tenth Report: Fiftieth Anniversary*. Boston, MA: Riverside Press, 1920.

Hawkins, Walter. *From Slavery to Bishopric* (1891).

Haygood, Wil. *King of the Cats: The Life and Times of Adam Clayton Powell, Jr.* New York, NY: Harper Collins Publishers, 2006.

_____. "The Rise of Adam Clayton Powell, Jr." (1988). Accessed November 14, 2012. http://aliciapatterson.org/stories/rise-adam-clayton-powell-jr.

Heglar, Charles J. *Rethinking the Slave Narrative: Slave Marriage and the Narratives of Henry Bibb and William and Ellen Craft*. Westport, CT: Greenwood Press, 2001.

Hening, William Walter ed. *The Statutes at Large: Being a Collection of all the Laws of Virginia from the First Session of the Legislature in the year 1619*. Richmond: Printed by and for Samuel Pleasants, Junior printer to the Commonwealth, 1809, 2:170

Hicks, Cheryl D. "In Danger of Becoming Morally Deprived: Single Black Women, Working Class Black Families, and New York State's Wayward Minor Laws, 1917–1928." *University of Pennsylvania Law Review*, June 1, 2003.

Hite, Roger W. "Henry Bibb and Ante-bellum Black Separatism." *Journal of Black Studies* 4, No. 3 (March, 1974).

Hoar, George F. *Autobiography of Seventy Years*. Vol. 2. New York, NY: Charles Scribner's Sons, 1903.

Hochschild, Jennifer L. "The Skin Color Paradox and the American Racial Order." Chapel Hill, NC: *The University of North Carolina Press*. Social Forces, Volume 86, Number 2 (December, 2007).

Hoffman, Steven J. *Race, Class, and Power in the Building of Richmond, 1870–1920*. Jefferson, NC: McFarland Publishing Company, 2004.

Holmes, Marian Smith. "The Great Escape from Slavery of Ellen and William Craft." Smithsonian.com, June 17, 2010. Accessed August 8, 2011. http://www.smithsonianmag.com/history-archaeology/The-Great-Escape-From-Slavery-of-Ellen-and-William-Craft.html.

"Honorable Robert Harlan." *Cincinnati Gazette*, May 1, 1886.

Horton, James Oliver. *Free People of Color: Inside the African American Community*. Washington, DC: Smithsonian Institution Press, 1993.

Howard, Walter Eugene, and Charles E. Prentiss, eds. "Catalogue of Officers and Students of Middlebury College in Middlebury and Others Who Have Received Degrees." Middlebury, VT: Middlebury College, The Register Co., 1901.

Hrabowski, Freeman A., III. "Liberal Education, Leadership for a New Age: Higher Education's Role for Producing Minority Leaders." Association of American Colleges and Universities Online, Summer, 2004. Accessed July 30, 2011. http://www.aacu.org/liberaleducation/le-sp04/le-sp04feature2.cfm.

Hutchinson, George. *The Harlem Renaissance in Black and White*. Cambridge, MA: Harvard University Press, 1995.

Hutson, Jean Blackwell. "Victoria Earle Matthews." In Edward T. James, Janet Wilson James, and Paul S. Boyer, eds., *Notable American Women, 1607–1950*, vol. 2 of 4 vols. Cambridge, MA: Harvard University Press, 1971: 510–11.

Inscoe, John C. *Writing the South through the Self: Explorations in Southern Autobiography*. Athens, GA: The University of Georgia Press, 2011.

"Inventory of the Henry Clay Warmoth Papers, 1798–1953," Collection Number 00752. Southern Historical Collection, UNC–Chapel Hill, North Carolina.

Jackson, Carlton. *Hattie: The Life of Hattie McDaniel.* Landham, MD: Madison Books, 1990.

Jackson, Fay M. *The Pittsburgh Courier.* Pittsburgh, PA, April 14, 1934.

Jackson, Kenneth T. *The Ku Klux Klan in the City 1915-1930.* New York: Oxford Press, 1973.

Jacobs, Donald M. *Courage and Conscience: Black and White Abolitionists in Boston.* Indianapolis, IN: Indiana University Press, 1993.

Jacobs, Harriet Ann (under pen name "Linda Brent"), and Lydia Maria Child, eds. *Incidents in the Life of a Slave Girl.* Boston, MA, 1861. Available at http://xroads.virginia.edu/~HYPER/JACOBS/hj-cover.htm.

James, Edward T., Janet Wilson James, Paul Boyer, eds. *Notable American Women, 1607–1950: A Biographical Dictionary*, Vol. 2. Cambridge, MA: Radcliffe College, 1971.

"Jane White," *Ebony*, February, 1978: 122.

"Jane White Papers, 1924–2001," Northampton, MA: Sophia Smith Collection, Smith College.

Janken, Kenneth Robert. *White: The Biography of Walter White, Mr. NAACP.* New York, NY: The New Press, 2003.

_____. *Walter White: Mr. NAACP.* Chapel Hill, NC: University of North Carolina Press, 2006.

Janssen, Kim. "It Gives Me Gooseflesh: Remarkable Find in Southside Attic." *Chicago Sun Times*, March 10, 2012. Accessed October 11, 2012. http://www.suntimes.com/11149243-417/it-gives-me-gooseflesh-remarkable-find-in-attic.html.

Johnson, Charles W. *Official Report of the Proceedings of the National Republican Conventions of 1868, 1872, 1876, and 1880.* Minneapolis, MN, 1903.

Johnson, Chevel. "Seeking Beatification for American Black Woman." *The Free Lance Star*, April 3, 1999: E6.

Johnson, Kevin R., ed. *Mixed Race America and the Law: A Reader.* New York, NY: New York University Press, 2003.

"Johnson, Mordecai Wyatt (1890–1976)." *Remembered and Reclaimed: An Online Reference Guide to African American History.* BlackPast.org, 2007–2011. Accessed November 14, 2012. http://www.blackpast.com/?q=aah/johnson-mordecai-wyatt-1890-1976 .

"Johnson, Mordecai Wyatt." *Encyclopedia of World Biography.* Encyclopedia.com, 2005. Accessed September 14, 2012. http://www.encyclopedia.com/doc/1G2-3435000097.html.

Johnson, Oliver. *William Lloyd Garrison and His Times; Or Sketches of the Anti-Slavery Movement in America.* Boston, MA: Houghton Mifflin, and Company, 1881.

Johnson, Thomas A. "A Man of Many Roles." *New York Times*, April 5, 1972.

Jones, Robert B. *Jean Toomer: Selected Essays and Literary Criticisms.* Knoxville, TN: University of Tennessee Press, 1996.

Jones, Suzanne W., ed. *Crossing the Color Line: Readings in Black and White*. Columbia: University of South Carolina Press, 2000.

Jones-Cornwell, Ilene. "Adam Clayton Powell, Jr." In Jessie Carney Smith, ed., *Notable Black American Men*. Farmington Hills, MI: Gale Research, Inc., 1999.

Jones-Wilson, Faustine Childress. *Encyclopedia of African American Education*. Westport, CT: Greenwood Publishing Group, 1996.

Kerman, Cynthia Earl, and Richard Eldridge. *The Lives of Jean Toomer: A Hunger for Wholeness*. Baton Rouge, LA: Louisiana State University Press, 1989.

Kilson, Marion. "Black History Month, Honoring a First in African American History: William Cooper Nell and the Colored Patriots of the American Revolution." *Black Commentator*, No. 266, February 28, 2008.

King's statement of December 5, 1955 as quoted in Mary King, *Mahatma Gandhi and Martin Luther King, Jr.: The Power of Nonviolent Action*. Paris, France: UNESCO Publishing, 1999: 133, 211.

King, Martin Luther, Jr. "His Influence Speaks to World Conscience," *Hindustan Times*, January 30, 1958, in Papers 4:354–355.

Kirby, Georgiana Bruce. *Years of Experience: An Autobiographical Narrative*. New York: G. P. Putnam's Sons, 1887. Available at http://faculty.etsu.edu/LLOYDT/English%204087_5087/Readings/georgiana_bruce_kirby.htm.

Kiser, Clyde V. "Diminishing Family Income in Harlem, A Survey by Milbank Minority Fund in 1933: A Possible Cause of the Harlem Riot." *The Journal of Negro Life* 13, No. 6. National Urban League, June, 1935.

Knight, Edgar W., and Clifton L. Hall. *Readings in American Educational History*. New York, NY: Appleton-Century-Crofts, Inc., 1951.

Kramer, Steve. "Matthews, Victoria Earle." *American National Biography Online*. Accessed October 11, 2012. http://www.anb.org/articles/15/15-01315.html; *Oxford Companion to African-American Literature*, 2008.

_____. "Uplifting Our 'Downtrodden Sisterhood': Victoria Earle Matthews and New York City's White Rose Mission, 1897–1907." *The Journal of African American History* 91 (Summer 2006).

Kranz, Rachel. *African–American Business Leaders and Entrepreneurs*. New York, NY: Facts on File, Inc., 2004.

Lamb, Yvonne Shinhoster. "James Cameron: Survived Lynching, Found Museum." *Washington Post*, June 13, 2006. Accessed November 14, 2012. http://www.washingtonpost.com/wp-dyn/content/article/2006/06/12/AR2006061201594.html.

Langston, John Mercer. *From the Virginia Plantation to the National Capitol; or The First and Only Negro in Congress from the Old Dominion*. Hartford, CT: American Publishing, 1894.

Lansberg, Klaus. "Eye Appeal and Music Go Hand in Hand on TV." *Down Beat*. September 7 and 8, 1951.

Lau, Peter F. *Democracy Rising: South Carolina and the Fight for Black Equality Since 1865*. Lexington, KY: The University Press of Kentucky, 2006.

Lauter, Paul, ed. "Charles Waddell Chesnutt (1858–1932)." *The Heath Anthology of American Literature*, 5th ed. Independence, KY: Cengage, 2005.

Leab, Daniel. *From Sambo to Superspade: The Black Experience in Motion Pictures*. Boston, MA: Houghton Mifflin, 1975.

Lemann, Nicholas. *Redemption: The Last Battle of the Civil War*. New York, NY: Farrar, Straus, and Giroux, 2006.

Lerner, Gerda. "Early Community Work of Black Club Women." *Journal of Negro History* 59 (April, 1974): 158–62.

Letter from Jean Toomer in 1922 to Max Eastman and his assistant, Claude McKay (editors of *The Liberator*). Accessed November 14, 2012. http://aalbc.com/authors/introtocane.htm.

Letter from MLK to Powell. *The Martin Luther King Papers Project*. June 10, 1958: 421.

Letter from Robert Purvis to Sydney Gay, dated August 15, 1858. New York, NY: Columbia University Library.

Litwack, Leon F., and August Meier, eds. *Black Leaders of the Nineteenth Century*. Chicago, IL: University of Illinois Press, 1991.

Locke, Alain LeRoy. *The New Negro: An Interpretation*. New York, NY: Arno Press, 1925.

Logan, Rayford W. *Howard University: The First Hundred Years, 1867–1967*. New York, NY: New York University Press, 1969.

_____, and Michael R. Winston, eds. *Dictionary of American Negro Biography*. New York, NY: W. W. Norton, 1982.

Logan, Shirley Wilson. *"We Are Coming": The Persuasive Discourse of Nineteenth-Century Black Women*. Carbondale, IL: Southern Illinois University Press, 1999.

Lonesome, Robyn, and Nathan Huggins. *Charles Drew*. New York, NY: Chelsea House Publishers, 1990.

Lonn, Ella. *Reconstruction in Louisiana after 1868*. New York, NY: The Knickerbocker Press, 1918.

Love, Spencie, and John Hope Franklin. *One Blood: The Death and Resurrection of Charles R. Drew*. Chapel Hill, NC: University of North Carolina Press, 1997.

Luker, Ralph E. "Missions, Institutional Churches, and Settlement Houses: The Black Experience, 1885–1910." *The Journal of Negro History* 69, No. 3/4 (1984): 101–13.

Lyons, Richard L. "Adam Clayton Powell: Apostle for Blacks." *Washington Post*, April 6, 1972: B5.

MacGregor, Morris J. *Integration of the Armed Forces 1940–1965*. Defense Studies Series. Washington, DC: US Government Printing Office, 1981.

MacKenzie, Amy. "Walter White on Lynching." *The Interracial Review*, September 9, 1936: 134–35.

Madison, James. *A Lynching in the Heartland: Race and Memory in America*. New York, NY: Palgrave Macmillan, 2003.

"Mahone Makes a Dicker." *New York Times*, September 16, 1889.

Marable, Manning, Nishani Frazier, and John Campbell McMillan. *Freedom on My Mind: The Columbia Documentary History of African Americans*. New York NY: Columbia University Press, 2003.

Marchant, Frances R. "Richard Theodore Greener: A Story of a Busy Man." Columbia, SC: University of South Carolina, South Caroliniana Library, Manuscripts Collections, 1882.

Marlowe, Gertrude Woodruff. *A Right Worthy Grand Mission: Maggie Lena Walker and the Quest for Black Economic Empowerment*. Washington, DC: Howard University Press, 2003.

Marryat, Frederick. *A Diary in America*. Paris, 1839.

Marsh, Carole. *Maggie Lena Walker: First Female Bank President*. Peachtree City, GA: Gallopade International, September, 2002.

Martin, Liam. *A Brief History of Social Identity: From Kinship to Multirace*. Lincoln, NE: iUniverse, 2005.

Martin, Waldo E., Jr. *The Mind of Frederick Douglass*. Chapel Hill, NC: University of North Carolina Press, 1986.

Mather, Frank Lincoln. *Who's Who of the Colored Race: A General Biographical Dictionary of Men and Women of African Descent*. Vol.1. Chicago, IL: Memento Edition, 1915: 222.

Matthews, Victoria Earle. *Aunt Lindy*, 1893. Available at http://www.facstaff.bucknell.edu/gcarr/19cUSWW/VEM/AL.html.

_____. "Dangers Confronting Southern Girls in the North." *Southern Woman* 27, September, 1898.

McCloy, Donald R., and Richard Ruetten. *Quest and Response: Minority Rights and the Truman Administration*. Lawrence, KS: University Press of Kansas, 1973.

McGee, Kristin A. *Some Like It Hot: Jazz Women in Film and Television, 1928–1959*. Middletown, CT: Wesleyan University Press, 2009.

McHenry, Robert. *Her Heritage: A Biographical Encyclopedia of Famous American Women*. Cambridge, MA: Pilgrim New Media, Inc., 1994. To obtain, try Amazon.com. CD-ROM available from http://www.PLGRM.com.

McKinney, Richard Ishmael. *Mordecai, The Man and His Message: The Story of Mordecai Wyatt Johnson*. Washington, DC: Howard University Press, 1997.

Middleton, Stephen, ed. *Black Congressmen During Reconstruction: A Documentary Sourcebook*. Westport, CT: Praeger, 2002.

_____. *The Black Laws: Race and the Legal Process in Early Ohio*. Athens, OH: Ohio University Press, 2005.

Miletsky, Zebulon. "Race on Trial: Passing and the Van Houten Case in Boston." Paper presented at the annual meeting of the 94th Annual Convention. Hilton Cincinnati Netherland Plaza, Cincinnati, Ohio, Sep 30, 2009.

Mjagkij, Nina, ed. *Organizing Black America: An Encyclopedia of African American Associations.* New York, NY: Garland Publishing, 2001.

Moore, Cathy. *Ellen Craft's Escape from Slavery.* Minneapolis, MN: Millbrook Press, 2011.

_____. *The Daring Escape of Ellen Craft.* Minneapolis, MN: Millbrook Press, 2002.

Morrison, Toni. Review of Darwin Turner's editing of uncollected and autobiographical writings of Jean Toomer in *The Wayward and the Seeking, New York Times* Nook Review, July 13, 1980.

Mounter, Michael Robert. "A Brief Biography of Richard Greener." Columbia, SC: The Board of Trustees, University of South Carolina, 2001. Accessed June 7, 2011. http://www.sc.edu/bicentennial/pages/greenerpages/greenerbio.html.

"Mrs. Senator Bruce at the President's Reception." *Peoples' Advocate,* February 14, 1880.

Murphy, Anne Marie. "Passing Free: Black in the South, Irish in the North, the Healys slipped the Bonds of Race in Civil War America." *Boston College Magazine,* 2003. Accessed March 17, 2012. http://bcm.bc.edu/issues/summer_2003/ ft_passing.html.

Murray, Pauli, ed. *States' Laws on Race and Color.* Athens, GA: University of Georgia, 1997.

NAACP Collection, Letter from Walter White to Norman Houston, September 10, 1943.

Nash, Gary B. *Red White and Black: The Peoples of Early America.* Upper Saddle River, NJ: Prentice-Hall, 1974.

Natale, Richard. "Silky Singer Lena Horne Broke Barriers." *Variety* and the Associated Press, May 11, 2010.

National Conference of Colored Men of the United States, *Proceedings of the National Conference of Colored Men of the United States, State Capitol Building, Nashville, Tennessee, May 6-7, and 9, 1879.* Washington, DC: R.H. Darby, printer, 1879.

National Republican, March 6, 1875.

Newkirk, Vann R. *Lynching in North Carolina: A History, 1865–1941.* Jefferson, NC: McFarland and Company, 2009.

Newman, Richard. "Patrick Francis Healy." *American National Biography Online.* February, 2000. http://www.anb.org/login.html?url=%2Farticles%2Fhome.html&ip=216.255.60.9& nocookie=0.

_____, and Patrick Rael, and Phillip Lapsansky, eds. *Pamphlets of Protest: An Anthology of Early African-American Protest Literature, 1790–1860.* New York, NY: Routledge, 2000.

Nolan, Bruce. "Henriette Delille Moves Closer to Sainthood for Work with New Orleans Slaves." *Times-Picayune,* March 29, 2010.

"Alexander Twilight." Old Stone Home Museum, Orleans County Historical Society. Accessed November 14, 2012, http://oldstonehousemuseum.org/.

Oliver, Kelly. *Witnessing: Beyond Recognition*. Minneapolis, MN: University of Minneapolis Press, 2001.

Osher, David. "Race Relations and War." *The Oxford Companion to American Military History*. New York, NY: Oxford University Press, 1999.

O'Toole, James M. *Passing for White: Race, Religion, and the Healy Family, 1820–1920*. Amherst, MA: University of Massachusetts Press, 2003.

Otter, Samuel. *Philadelphia Stories: America's Literature of Race and Freedom*. New York, NY: Oxford University Press, 2010.

Ouspensky, P. D. *In Search of the Miraculous: The Teachings of G. I. Gurdjieff*. New York NY: Houghton Mifflin–Harcourt, 2001.

Ovington, Mary White. *Portraits in Color*. New York, NY: The Viking Press, 1927.

"Part in Imitation is not real me,' says Fredi." *Chicago Defender*, January 19, 1935, national edition.

"Past Imperfect: The Great Dissenter and His Half-Brother." Smithsonian.com. December 20, 2011. Accessed November 14, 2012. http://blogs.smithsonianmag.com/history/2011/12/the-great-dissenter-and-his-half-brother/.

Patler, Nicholas. "A Black Vice President in the Gilded Age? Senator Blanche Kelso Bruce and the National Republican Convention of 1880." *The Journal of Mississippi History Archives* (Summer, 2009): 111. Accessed July 15, 2011. http://mdah.state.ms.us/pubs/archived_issues.html.

People's Voice, September 19, 1942.

Pilgrim, David. "The Tragic Mulatto Myth," *Jim Crow Museum of Racist Memorabilia*, Ferris State University, November, 2000. Accessed November 15, 2012. http://www.ferris.edu/jimcrow/mulatto/.

Potter, Joan. *African American Firsts*. New York, NY: Kensington Publishing Corp., 2002.

Powell, Adam Clayton, Jr. *Adam by Adam: The Autobiography of Adam Clayton Powell, Jr.* New York, NY: Kensington Publishing Corp., 1971.

"President's Papers." Virginia State University Archives.

Proceedings of the National Conference of Colored Men of the United States. State Capitol Building, Nashville, Tennessee, May 6–7, and 9, 1879. Washington, DC: National Conference of Colored Men of the United States, 1879: 30–32.

Provident Foundation. "First Open Heart Surgeon, Dr. Daniel Hale Williams." Accessed September 5, 2011. http://www.providentfoundation.org/history/williams.html.

Purvis, Robert. "On American 'Democracy' and the Negro." Speech, May 18, 1860.

Quittner, Jeremy, and L. L. Bloomberg. "Maggie Lena Walker: A Rich Legacy for the Black Woman Entrepreneur." Money Aisle Bank Browser, 1999. Accessed November 14, 2012. http://www.businessweek.com/smallbiz/news/coladvice/reallife/rl990706r.htm.

Rabinowitz, Howard, ed. *Southern Black Leaders of the Reconstruction Era*. Urbana, IL: University of Illinois Press, 1982.

"Racial Violence and Terror." *Section 6, Plantation to Ghetto. Amistad Digital Resources for Teaching*. August 28, 2009.

Rainey, Glen W. "The Race Riot in Atlanta." Master's thesis, Emory University, 1929.

Ransom, Candice F. *Maggie L. Walker: Pioneer Banker and Community Leader*. Minneapolis, MN: Twenty-First Century Books, 2009.

Reagan, Leslie J., Nancy Tomes, and Paula A. Treichler. *Medicines Moving Pictures: Medicine, Health and Bodies in American Film and Television*. Rochester, NY: University of Rochester Press, 2007.

Regester, Charlene B. *African American Actresses: The Struggle for Visibility, 1900-1960*. Bloomington, IN: Indiana University Press, 2010.

Rhodes-Pitts, Sharifa. *Harlem Is Nowhere: A Journey to the Mecca of Black America*. New York, NY: Little, Brown and Company, 2011.

"Robert Purvis Dead: Anti-Slavery Leader Expires in Philadelphia, Aged 87—His Work for the Black Race." *New York Times*, April 16, 1898. Accessed November 14, 2012. http://query. nytimes.com/gst/abstract.html?res=9B02EEDF1139E433A25755C1A9629C94699ED7CF.

Robeson, Paul, Jr. *The Undiscovered Paul Robeson: An Artist's Journey, 1898–1939*. John Wiley & Sons, New York: NY, 2001.

Roe, Jae H. "Keeping an 'Old Wound' Alive: 'The Marrow of Tradition' and the Legacy of Wilmington." *African American Review* 33, Issue 2 (Summer, 1999): 231. Accessed June 5, 2011. http://www.questia.com/library/1G1-55577117/keeping-an-old-wound-alive-the-marrow-of-tradition.

Roediger, Dave, and Franklin Rosemont, eds. *Haymarket Scrapbook*. Chicago, IL: Charles H. Kerr Publishing Co., 1986.

Rosbrow, James M. Rosbrow. "Blanche K. Bruce Led one of the Most Remarkable Careers in American History." Bruce Kelso Bruce Papers, Manuscript Division, Moorland-Spingarn Research Center, Howard University, September 9, 1945.

Rule, Sheila. "Obituary of Fredi Washington, 90, Actress: Broke Ground for Black Artists." *New York Times*, June 30, 1994.

Rummel, Jack. *African American Social Leaders and Activists*. New York, NY: Facts on File, Inc., 2003.

Russell, Kathy, Midge Wilson, and Ronald E. Hall. *The Color Complex: The Politics of Skin Color Among African Americans*. New York, NY: Harcourt Brace Jovanovich, 1992.

Salas, Laura Purdie. *Charles Drew: Pioneer in Medicine*. Mankato, MN: Capstone Press, 2006.

Salley, Columbus. *The Black 100: A Ranking of the Most Influential African Americans Past and Present*. New York, NY: Kensington Publishing Corp., 1996.

Sanchez, Brenna. "Delille, Henriette, 1813–1862." *Contemporary Black Biography.* Encyclopedia.com, 2002. Accessed December 18, 2011. http://www.encyclopedia.com.

Schraff, Anne E. *Dr. Charles Drew: Blood Bank Innovator.* Berkeley Heights, NJ: Enslow Publishers, June, 2003.

Schuyler, George S. *Pittsburgh Courier*, September 5, 1942.

Scruggs, Charles. "Modern American Poetry: Newly Discovered Articles by Jean Toomer." *Arizona Quarterly* 51, No. 2, Summer, 1995. Available at http://www.english.illinois.edu/maps/poets/s_z/toomer/essays.htm.

Seldon, Horace. "William Wells Brown." *The Liberator Files, A Boston-Based Abolitionist Newspaper Published by William Lloyd Garrison, 1831–1865.* www.liberator.com.

Senate Hearings Before the Committee on Armed Services, Universal Military Training, 80th Congress, 2nd Session, 1948.

"Senator Bruce." *Topeka Kansas Herald*, June 11, 1880.

Sewell, George Alexander. *Mississippi Black History Makers.* Jackson, MS: University Press of Mississippi, 1977.

Shannon, Ronald. *Profiles in Ohio History: A Legacy of African American Achievement.* Bloomington: iUniverse, 2008.

Shapiro, Fred R., ed. *Yale Book of Quotations.* New Haven, CT: Yale University Press, 2006.

Sherrard-Johnson, Cherene, and Shirley Samuels, eds. *A Companion to American Fiction, 1780–1865.* Malden, MA: Blackwell Publishing, 2004.

Shumacker, Harris B., Jr. *The Evolution of Cardiac Surgery.* Bloomington, IN: Indiana University Press, 1992.

Simmons, Ryan. *Chesnutt and Realism: A Study of the Novels.* Tuscaloosa, AL: University of Alabama Press, 2006.

Simmons, William J., and Henry McNeal Turner. *Men of Mark: Eminent, Progressive, and Rising.* Cleveland, OH: Geo M. Rewell & Company, 1887.

Singh, M.P. *Quote Unquote: A Handbook of Quotations.* New Delhi, India: Lotus Press, 2006.

Smith, Jessie Carney, ed. *Notable Black American Men.* Farmington Hills, MI: Gale Research, 1999.

_____, and Linda T. Wynn. *Freedom Facts and Firsts: 400 Years of African American Civil Rights Experience.* Canton, MI: Visible Ink Press, 2009.

Smith, John Clay. *Emancipation: The Making of the Black Lawyer, 1814–1944.* Philadelphia, PA: University of Pennsylvania Press, 1993.

Smith, Norman R. *Footprints of Black Louisiana.* Bloomington, IN: Xlibris Corporation, 2010.

Smith, Robert P. "William Cooper Nell: Crusading Black Abolitionist." *The Journal of Negro History* 55, No. 3 (July, 1970): 182–199. http://www.jstor.org/stable/2716420.

Smyth, John Ferdinand Dalziel. *A Tour in the United States of America.* (1784; reprint, NY, 1968).

Sollars, Werner, Caldwell Titcomb, and Thomas A. Underwood, eds. *Blacks at Harvard: A Documentary History of African–American Experience at Harvard and Radcliffe.* New York, NY: New York University Press, 1993.

Stallworth, Paul M. "Robert James Harlan." In Rayford W. Logan and Michael R. Winston, eds. *Dictionary of American Negro Biography.* NY: Norton, 1983.

Stanford, Jeff. Turner Classic Movies (TCM) Online. Turner Entertainment Networks, A Time Warner Company. Accessed November 11, 2012. http://www.tcm.com/tcmdb/title/561387/Square-Joe/.

Stanford, Karin L. *If We Must Die: African American Voices on War and Peace.* Lanham, MD: Rowman and Littlefield Publishers, Inc., 2008.

Sterling, Dorothy. *Ahead of Her Time: Abby Kelley and the Politics of Antislavery.* New York, NY: W.W. Norton & Company, Inc., 1991.

_____. *We Are Your Sisters: Black Women in the Nineteenth Century.* New York, NY: W.W. Norton and Company, 1997.

Stevens, Dana. "Caricature Acting." *New York Times*, November 27, 2005.

Still, William. *Still's Underground Rail Road Records: A Life of the Author.* Philadelphia, PA: Porter & Coates, 1886.

Strouse, Jean. *Morgan: American Financier.* New York, NY: Random House, 1999.

Swain, Carol. 1993. *Black Faces, Black Interests: The Representation of African Americans in Congress.* Cambridge, MA: Harvard University Press.

Sweet, Frank W., *Legal History of the Color Line: The Rise and Triumph of the One-Drop Rule.* Palm Coast, FL: Backintyme Publishing, 2005.

Tate, Katherine. *Black Faces in the Mirror: African Americans and Their Representatives in the U.S. Congress.* Princeton, NJ: Princeton University Press, 2003.

Tawa, Renee. "Order of the Day." *Los Angeles Times*, August 18, 1999.

Taylor, Joe Gray. *Louisiana Reconstructed, 1863–1877.* Baton Rouge, LA: Louisiana State University Press, 1974.

Taylor, Quintard, and Shirley Ann Wilson Moore, eds. *African American Women Confront the West, 1600–2000.* Norman, OK: University of Oklahoma Press, 2003.

Taylor, Yuval, ed. *I Was Born a Slave: An Anthology of Classic Slave Narratives.* Chicago, IL: Lawrence Hill Books, 1999.

Tenzer, Lawrence Raymond. *The Forgotten Cause of the Civil War: A New Look at the Slavery Issue.* Manahawkin, NJ: Scholars' Pub. House, 1997.

"Test Fails to Link Slave, Justice." Associated Press, September 3, 2001. Accessed November 14, 2012. http://www.enquirer.com/editions/2001/09/03/loc_test_fails_to_link.html.

"Two Riot Calls were Rung for First Time." *The Atlanta Journal and Constitution*, September 23, 1906: 1.

"The Aftermath of the Atlanta Riots." *The Voice*, January 1907.

The Boston Journal, Oct. 5, 1894.

The Committee on Education and Labor Records, 80th–89th Congress. National Archives and Records Administration. Washington, DC: Center for Legislative Archives.

"The Eleanor Roosevelt Papers." George Washington University.

"The Jane White Papers, 1924–2001." Sophia Smith Collection, Smith College, Northampton, Massachusetts.

The Liberator, September 2, 1853; December 16, 1853; *The Liberator*, December 28, 1855.

"The Life and Time of P. B. S. Pinchback (1837–1921), First Black Governor." *CultureBus. com*. Accessed September 28, 2012. http://culturebus.com/site/?page=profile&url_id=356&n=Pinchback,_P.B.S.

The North Star, August 12, 1853.

The Philadelphia Inquirer, April 11, 1948.

The St. Louis Post-Dispatch, November 7, 1939.

"The Papers of Fredi Washington (1925–1979)," See V: "Biographical Notes: Fredi Washington, 1903–1994." Filmed from the holdings of the Amistad Research Center at Tulane University. Scholarly Resources, Inc., an imprint of Thomas Gale. Woodbridge, CT: 2005. Microfilm. http://microformguides.gale.com/Data/Download/8389000C.pdf.

"The Taney Hunt Against Colored Americans." *The Liberator Files*, August 28, 1857. Filed under "Dred Scott Decision: Nell, William Cooper, 1857."

"They Had A Dream: Blanche Bruce, The Silent Senator." *Washington Evening Star*, January 9, 1971.

Thornbrough, Emma Lou. *T. Thomas Fortune: Militant Journalist*. Chicago, IL: The University of Chicago Press, 1972.

"Timothy Thomas Fortune." *Dictionary of Literary Biography*. Farmington Hills, MI: Thomson Gale Publishing, 2005–2006.

Toomer, Jean. *Cane* (with an "Afterword" by Rudolph P. Byrd and Henry Louis Gates). New York, NY: W. W. Norton & Company, 2011.

_____, and Darwin T. Turner. *Cane*. New York, NY: Liveright Publishing Corporation, 1975.

_____, and Darwin T. Turner, eds. *The Wayward and the Seeking: A Collection of Writings by Jean Toomer*. Washington, DC: Howard University Press, 1983.

_____, and Mark Whalan, eds. *The Letters of Jean Toomer, 1919–1924*. Knoxville, TN: The University of Tennessee Press, 2006.

_____, and Robert B. Jones, and Margery Toomer Latimer, eds. *The Collected Poems of Jean Toomer*. Chapel Hill, NC: The University of North Carolina Press, 1988.

Toppin, Edgar A. *Loyal Sons and Daughters: Virginia State University, 1882 to 1992*. Norfolk, VA: Pictorial Heritage Publishing Company, 1992.

_____. "Walter White and the Atlanta NAACP's Fight for Equal Schools, 1916–1917." *History of Education Quarterly* (Spring 1967): 3–21.

Torrey, Jesse. *American Slave Trade*. London, UK: Reprinted by C. Clement and published by J.M. Cobbett, 1822.

Trotter, Joe William, and Eric Ledell Smith, eds. *African Americans in Pennsylvania: Shifting Historical Perspectives*. Philadelphia, PA: Pennsylvania State University Press, 1997.

Tunnell, Ted. *Crucible of Reconstruction: War, Radicalism, and Race in Louisiana, 1862–1877*. Baton Rouge, LA: Louisiana State University Press, 1984.

Turkel, Stanley. *Heroes of the American Reconstruction: Profiles of Sixteen Educators, Politicians, and Activists*. Jefferson, NC: McFarland & Company, 2005.

US History: Underground Railroad. Accessed March 30, 2012. http://www.u-s-history.com/pages/h481.html.

Van Houten v. Morse 162 Mass. 414 (1894), Anna D. Van Houten vs. Asa P. Morse, Suffolk. January 19, 1894 - November 30, 1894. http://chnm.gmu.edu/aq/photos/texts/162mass414.htm.

Vitoria-Zworykin. "Walter Francis White." *Encyclopedia of World Biography*, 2nd ed. Gale Research, 1998: 238.

Vlach, John Michael. *Back of the Big House: The Architecture of Plantation Slavery*. Chapel Hill, NC: University of North Carolina Press, 1993.

Voting Rights Act of 1965. http://www.ourdocuments.gov/doc.php?flash=old&doc=100.

Vox, Lisa. "How Did Slaves Resist Slavery?" African–American History, About.com. Accessed November 16, 2011. http://afroamhistory.about.com/od/slavery/a/How-Did-Slaves-Resist-Slavery.htm.

Wade-Gayles, Gloria. "Black Women Journalist in the South, 1880–1905: An Approach to the Study of Black Women's History." *Callaloo* (February–October, 1981): 138–152.

Waldrep, Christopher. *African Americans Confront Lynching: Strategies of Resistance from the Civil War to the Civil Rights Era*. Lanham, MD: Rowman and Littlefield Publishers, Inc., 2009.

Waldron, Edward E. *Walter White and the Harlem Renaissance*. Port Washington, NY: Kennikat Press, 1978.

Wallenstein, Peter. "Powell, Adam Clayton, Jr." *American National Biography*. New York, NY: Oxford University Press, 1999.

"Walter White." *Encyclopedia Britannica's Guide to Black History*. Accessed June 12, 2011. http://www.britannica.com/blackhistory/article-9076813.

"Walter White: Militant Advocate." *The Crisis* 87, No. 10 (December, 1980): 561.

"Walter White (1893–1955)," *New Georgia Encyclopedia: History and Archaeology.* Accessed October 11, 2011. http://www.georgiaencyclopedia.org/nge/Article.jsp?id=h-747.

Washington, Booker T. *The Negro in Business.* Boston, MA: Hertel, Jenkins, & Company, 1907.

_____. *The Negro Problem: A Series of Articles by Representative American Negroes of Today.* New York, NY: James Pott & Company, 1903.

_____, and Louis R. Harlan, and Raymond Smock, eds. *The Booker T. Washington Papers. Vol. 13: 1914–1915.* Urbana, IL: University of Illinois Press, 1984.

Washington, Shirley. *Outstanding African Americans of Congress.* Washington, DC: US Capitol Historical Society, 1998.

Watkins, Mel. *Stepin Fetchit: The Life and Times of Lincoln Perry.* New York, NY: Knopf Doubleday Publishing Group, 2006.

Watts, Jill. *Hattie McDaniel: Black Ambition, White Hollywood.* New York, NY: HarperCollins, 2005.

Weiner, Marli F. *Mistresses and Slaves: Plantation Women in South Carolina: 1830-80.* Champaign, IL: Board of Trustees of University of Illinois, 1998.

Weisenfeld, Judith. *Hollywood Be Thy Name: African American Religion in American Film, 1929–1949.* Berkley, CA: University of California Press, 2007.

Weld, Theodore Dwight. *American Slavery As It Is: Testimony of a Thousand Witnesses.* New York, NY: American Anti-Slavery Society, 1839.

Wesley, Charles H. *The History of the National Association of Colored Women's Clubs: A Legacy of Service.* Washington, DC: The Association, 1984.

Wesley, Dorothy Porter, and Constance Porter Uzelac, eds. *William Cooper Nell: Nineteenth-Century African American Abolitionist, Historian, Integrationist; Selected Writings, 1832–1874.* Baltimore, MD: Black Classic Press, 2002.

Whitaker, Robert. *On the Laps of Gods: The Red Summer of 1919 and the Struggle for Justice that Remade a Nation.* New York, NY: Crown Publishing Group, 2008.

White, Newman Ivey, and Walter Clinton Jackson, eds. *Anthology of Verse by American Negroes.* Whitefish, MT: Kessinger Publishing, LLC, 2003.

White, Walter. *A Man Called White: The Autobiography of Walter White.* Athens, GA: University of Georgia Press, 1995.

_____. "Arkansas Race Riots Laid to Bad System," *Chicago Daily News,* October 18, 1919.

_____. "I Investigate Lynchings." *American Mercury,* January, 1929. Accessed January 17, 2012. http://nationalhumanitiescenter.org/pds/maai3/segregation/text2/investigatelynchings.pdf.

_____. "The Eruption of Tulsa." *The Nation*, June 29, 1921: 909–910.

_____, and Kenneth Robert Janken, eds. *Rope and Faggot: A Biography of Judge Lynch*. Notre Dame, IN: University of Notre Dame Press, 2002.

Whitehurst, Susan. *Dr. Charles Drew: Medical Pioneer Journey to Freedom*. Mankato, MN: The Child's World, Inc., 2001.

"Whittier's Recollection of the Funding of the American Anti-Slavery Society." *In The Anti-Slavery Convention of 1833*. Old South Leaflets 4, No. 81. Boston: Directors of the Old South Work, 1874: 5–11. Wikipedia.com. "The Hollywood Blacklist." Accessed November 14, 2012. http://en.wikipedia.org/wiki/Hollywood_blacklist.

"William Wells Brown, 1814–1884." *African American History of Western New York*. Accessed November 14, 2012. http://www.math.buffalo.edu/~sww/0history/wwb0.html.

"Williams, Daniel Hale." Adoptions.com. Accessed October 17, 2011. http://famous.adoption.com/famous/williams-daniel-hale.html.

Williams, Lillian Serece. *Strangers in the Land of Paradise: The Creation of an African American Community in Buffalo, New York, 1900-1940* (Blacks in the Diaspora). Bloomington, IN: Indiana University Press, 2000.

Williams, Scott W. "Jean Toomer Biography." *The Jean Toomer Pages*. May, 1996. Accessed September 24, 2012. http://www.math.buffalo.edu/~sww/toomer/toomerbio.html.

Williams, Zachery R. *In Search of the Talented Tenth: Howard University Public Intellectuals and the Dilemmas of Race, 1926–1970*. Columbia, MO: University of Missouri Press, 2009.

Williamson, Joel. *New People: Miscegenation and Mulattoes in the United States*. New York, NY: The Free Press, 1980.

Willson, Joseph, and Julia Winch, eds. *The Elite of Our People: Joseph Willson's Sketches of Black Upper-Class Life in Antebellum Philadelphia*. University Park, PA: Pennsylvania State University, 2000.

Wilson, Sondra Kathryn. *In Search of Democracy: The NAACP Writings of James Weldon Johnson, Walter White, and Roy Wilkins (1920–1977)*. New York, NY: Oxford University Press, 1999.

_____. *The Selected Writings of James Weldon Johnson. Volume I: New York Age*. New York, NY: Oxford University Press, 1995.

Witter, DeAnn L. "The Maturation of Charles Waddell as a Speaker and Writer." Accessed November 11, 2011. http://www.eden.rutgers.edu/~c350445/witter1.html.

Woll, Allen L. *Black Musical Theatre: From Coontown to Dreamgirls*. Cambridge, MA: Da Capo Press, 1991.

Wonham, Henry B. *Charles W. Chesnutt: A Study of the Short Fiction*. New York, NY: Twayne, 1998.

Woodworth, Steven E. *Manifest Destinies: America's Westward Expansion and the Road to the Civil War*. New York, NY: Alfred A. Knopf, 2010.

Wreford, Henry. "A Negro Sculptress." *Athenæum* 39, March 3, 1866: 302.

Yellin, Jean Fagan, ed. "September 1810–November 1843: Slavery and Resistance." *Harriet Jacobs Family Papers*. Chapel Hill, NC: University of North Carolina Press, 2008.

INDEX

ABOUT THE AUTHOR

Michelle Gordon Jackson is an author, columnist, and screenwriter. She is a graduate of Howard University and the former daughter-in-law of Maynard H. Jackson, Jr., the first Black mayor of Atlanta, Georgia. Ms. Jackson, a native of Atlanta, currently resides in her hometown.

For inquiries, to schedule a booking, or to contact the author, send an email to: jacksonscribe@gmail.com

JACKSONSCRIBE PUBLISHING COMPANY
········· ATLANTA, GEORGIA ·········

Made in the USA
Middletown, DE
22 March 2024

51925457R00232